Inside Yahoo!

Inside Yahoo!

Reinvention and the Road Ahead

KAREN ANGEL

John Wiley & Sons, Inc.

ISBN 0-471-00793-5

Printed in the United States of America.

10 9 8 7 6 5 4 3 2 1

Preface

"*F*aced with the prospect of showing up every day at a small desk and laboriously manufacturing a lengthy document with hundreds of footnotes, the human spirit seems to gravitate toward other distractions."[1] That's how Jerry Yang and David Filo explain the origins of the "distraction" from finishing their electrical engineering Ph.D.s that turned into a $130 billion company at its height and a wildly popular Web directory right from the start. "Part of their success was due to the intensity with which they tracked down Web pages, and part of it was due to their timing,"[2] they admit in *Yahoo! Unplugged* (IDG Books, 1995), coyly referring to themselves in the third person.

Like Yang and Filo, I know all about laborious manufacturing and lengthy documents, but for me there was no escape hatch. My book is the story of the Internet symbol that sprang from a trailer on Stanford University's campus and the brains of two tech talents, an extrovert from Taiwan and an introvert from Moss Bluff, Louisiana. But it's the story of Yahoo with one big difference: Unlike other such accounts, mine is informed by key players who have rarely or never been heard from before—among them, the interim-management team that got Yahoo up and running and was later relegated to invisibility by the company's principals, the Reuters exec whose investment gave him a plum vantage point on Yahoo's board of directors, a manager who headed e-commerce and Yahoo Finance business development for the company, and Yahoo's own M&A specialist, who orchestrated all its acquisitions, including the controversial GeoCities and Broadcast.com buys.

Yahoo itself declined my request for participation—not surprising for a company that has gone from basking in the overblown praise of Wall Street and the media to squirming under the harsh spotlight cast by unhappy investors and critical journalists. "Once again Yahoo! knocked the ball out of the park," gushed Credit Suisse First Boston analyst Lise Buyer in October 1998. "We are raising our estimates (yet again)."[3] In June 1999, *Fortune* magazine beamed, "The company's execution so far has been picture perfect."[4]

Fast-forward to March 2001, when the *Wall Street Journal* trumpeted, "Yahoo! Inc. has seen the enemy—and it is them."[5] *BusinessWeek*, which had dubbed Yahoo "the lord of the Web"[6] back in September 1998, came out with "Inside Yahoo!: The Untold Story of How Arrogance, Infighting, and Management Missteps Derailed One of the Hottest Companies on the Web."[7]

Today, Yahoo is struggling to win back its pampered-pet status and reverse that trajectory of all-important indicators— stock price, revenues, reputation. The last thing it needs is a reporter putting a period, an exclamation point, or any other full-stop punctuation on its story while the ending is so ambivalent. (Speaking of punctuation, for the sake of simplicity and to take it easy on my readers' eyes, I've dropped the exclamation point after the company's name.) But again, like Yang and Filo, I believe in my timing, and that the crossroads where Yahoo now finds itself is a good place to stop and take stock.

KAREN ANGEL

New York, New York
March 2002

Acknowledgments

I'd like to thank former *Fortune* staff writer Jodi Mardesich and former *Industry Standard* senior writer Laura Rich, my unofficial coauthors—and eyes and ears in San Jose and Los Angeles, respectively—for all their help.

Thanks to Ethan Schwartz for elucidating the finer points of cash burn.

And thanks to my mother for all her weather reports, without which I surely would have frozen years ago.

K. A.

Contents

Inside Yahoo!

Chapter **1**

Stanford, 1994

Key Events

- April: Jim Clark and Marc Andreessen form Mosaic Communications to market the Mosaic browser, which was released by the National Center for Supercomputing Applications in 1993 and sparked the Internet revolution.
- October: Mosaic changes its name to Netscape Communications.
- October: The first version of Netscape Navigator is launched.

*L*ooking back on Internet mania, one company stands out: Yahoo. It's as potent a symbol as any of the late 1990s phenomenon that swept popular culture, the stock market, the entrepreneurial set, and the economy at large. This is the story of two procrastinating graduate students who turned what was a part-time project into a major media company, its starry rise in fortunes, and its equally stunning fall from grace. Yahoo's guide to the World Wide Web, a directory that simply catalogues Web sites and makes them easier to find, is the most used of its kind. More than 200 million people a month reportedly were clicking on it in late 2001, to find everything from current stock quotes and news to chat rooms about biochemical warfare and infertility—and that audience gave Yahoo a reach greater than that of most major media networks.

It was this reach—and the notion that in the future, everyone would be using the Internet for everything for which they had turned to television, radio, newspapers, and movies—that propelled Yahoo's stock to such incredible heights that at its peak, Yahoo was worth more than traditional media companies like the Walt Disney Company and News Corporation—combined. Yahoo held the promise of becoming *the* major media company of the twenty-first century.

In 1996, when Yahoo went public, investors went crazy for its stock. The stock continued to climb throughout the late 1990s and 2000, hitting a split-adjusted high of $237.50. But in March 2000, the inflated Internet bubble began to lose air. The stock market crashed in April and continued to decline throughout the rest of the year. And with that decline came the demise of many well-known dot-coms, including Pets.com, Living.com, and Value America. As the dot-coms began to fail, they stopped advertising. At one point, 47 percent of Yahoo's advertisers were dot-coms that themselves were flying high,

3

flush with venture capital dollars to spend on marketing and gaining the greatest mind share, because at the time, the conventional wisdom said whichever company could grow the fastest, and attract the most "eyeballs," would be the one that would succeed.

Reality hit. Investors no longer were salved by talk of future profits at the expense of current growth. Investors wanted to see these companies show profits. Now.

Ironically, the demise of hundreds of dot-coms also hurt Yahoo, one of the few dot-coms that seemed to have everything going for it. And in January 2001, Yahoo lowered its future outlook for the first time and began the second of what would be five consecutive unprofitable quarters. Revenues were slipping. And someone had to accept the blame.

Yahoo's chief executive officer, 51-year-old Tim Koogle, took the fall. He resigned, and in his place as CEO, Yahoo's board hired a Hollywood veteran, Terry Semel. He, with partner Bob Daly, had headed the venerable Warner Brothers entertainment conglomerate for seven years. But was he the leader Yahoo needed to steer the ship from treacherous dot-com waters toward safer, profitable shores?

Sure, after he had left Warner and started his own investment firm, Windsor Media, he became a venture capitalist of sorts, plowing millions of dollars into Internet entertainment start-ups like the Digital Entertainment Network (DEN) and Nibblebox. But his bets don't make him look like a seer. DEN burned through more than $60 million building television-style shows that would be "netcast"—broadcast over the Net—to an audience that never materialized. A good idea, but one before its time, and a costly lesson learned.

As a vote of faith in the company, and in himself, Semel bought 1 million shares of Yahoo stock in a private placement.

When he joined Yahoo, its shares were worth $17.62. Eight months later, he had lost $6.5 million of his investment on paper.

Yahoo is struggling to transform its business to one where its users, who are accustomed to getting everything for free, are willing to pay for some services, like online personals, real-time stock quotes, and Web storage space for e-mail and photos. At Yahoo's peak, more than 90 percent of its sales came from advertisers. In November, it still was deriving 80 percent of its revenues from that stagnating source.

Sales continued to decline, and though Yahoo's cost-cutting measures were lauded by analysts, they weren't enough to bring the company back to profitability. In October, Yahoo reported its fourth consecutive quarterly loss and its lowest revenues since the third quarter of 1999.

When Semel announced the distressing news in October 2001, he did it against the backdrop of the September 2001 terrorist attacks against the United States. Though the attacks weakened an already anemic economy, Semel pointed out that in the midst of the fear and uncertainty, one thing was clear: The Internet was an invaluable tool in the time of crisis. While telephone networks around New York City and Washington, D.C., failed, millions of users communicated with friends and loved ones via Yahoo Mail and Yahoo's Internet telephony. Within three hours of the attacks, Yahoo had posted three buttons: one for the American Red Cross, one for the New York Firefighters 9-11 Disaster Relief Fund, and another for the Salvation Army. Within two weeks, Yahoo users had donated more than $30 million to the relief funds. "That's when you know you're part of something big," Semel said during the company's October 10 conference call, in his marked Brooklyn accent.

The Internet most certainly is something big. But will Yahoo remain something big, on its own?

$\backsim$

*T*he hobby that would become Yahoo coalesced in spring 1994. Just months away from completing their dissertations in computer-assisted design, with their Ph.D. adviser conveniently off on sabbatical for the year, Jerry Yang and David Filo were obsessively compiling a list of their favorite Web sites, among them such choice samples as Brian's Lava Lamp, Nerf: Foam Weapons Arsenal, and Quadralay's Armadillo Home Page. Soon they were spending almost all their time on the index—up to 40 hours a week—and very little on their dissertations.

The browser Mosaic, precursor to Netscape, had just been developed by Marc Andreessen and his team at the University of Illinois' National Center for Supercomputing Applications, meaning millions would soon be flocking to the Web. In 1990, the number of Web sites was all of about 12, and they belonged to universities and government. But by 1993, after Mosaic ushered in point-and-click navigation by replacing the complicated text interfaces that ruled the Web with a simple graphical browser, the number of sites rose into the thousands and was poised to leap into the millions. And Yang and Filo were ready to provide a contextual framework for this jumbled mass of content. "Two years earlier, nobody needed a Web index; two years later, someone else would have been forced to make some sort of comparable index," they write in *Yahoo! Unplugged*.[1]

Or as Yang told *Red Herring* in an interview in 1995, "We jumped on Mosaic at the beginning of 1994. We really didn't think much of it at first. Nobody did. Maybe Andreessen or somebody. I kept bugging Dave to show me the sites he had found. So he made his hot-list, and I made my hot-list, and he wrote some software to combine both our lists. It started out as a collection of computer-related sites that we were interested in—very much in the vein of what the Web was designed for: to share documents with many people. There was really no altruism involved—we were doing the work, and there was no cost to distribute it, so why not distribute it? I think the inspiration to start listing other sites came from David one day. Maybe he was bored with his thesis. Initially we collected some of the friskier, weirder sites on the Web, and it took off by word of mouth. We were in a unique situation in the summer of 1994 to be able to experience that kind of grass-roots growth, fueled by a lot of interest that was not our doing, and then just sitting back to watch the access logs go up. I don't think that could happen today."[2]

The two developed their own Web-searching software to help them find and index sites. Their grand scheme involved conquering the Web by visiting and categorizing as many sites as they could, creating subcategories when the categories grew too unwieldy, and then subcategories for the subcategories. Stanford donated a trailer to house their operation, legendarily littered with overheating terminals, pizza boxes, dirty clothing, and golf clubs. The index itself inhabited Yang's student workstation, Akebono (http://akebono.stanford.edu), named after a formidable Hawaiian sumo wrestler, while the search software was stored on Filo's workstation, Konishiki, also a sumo great. They christened the index Jerry's Guide to the World Wide Web.

"How often do you guys browse the Web, and for how long?" a questioner asked them during a BusinessWeek Online chat in July 1995.

"We live, breathe, sleep on the Web . . . just kidding," Yahoos612 (Yang) replied.

"No, he's not," corrected Yahoo df (Filo).[3]

Despite their mutual appreciation for sumo wrestling, the pairing of Yang, then 25, and Filo, 27, was hardly intuitive. In fact, it would be difficult to find two partners with such different backgrounds and personalities, but they did share an unconventional childhood. At the age of eight, the outgoing Yang, Yahoo's goodwill ambassador-to-be, had emigrated from Taiwan with his mother, a widowed English professor, and younger brother. They settled in San Jose, California, where Yang morphed into a tennis-playing academic ace. His leadership skills surfaced early as senior class president and valedictorian at Piedmont Hills High, and he won a full undergrad scholarship to nearby Stanford University—and every other college he applied to, including Berkeley and Cal Tech. Within four years, Yang had bagged a B.S. and an M.A. in electrical engineering. Among the part-time jobs he held to help make ends meet, he worked as a book shelver and sorter in the university library, a stint he told *Fortune* taught him how to store information systematically. One of Yang's strengths is his ability to apply what he learns in daily life, according to Stanford professor John Hennessy. "Like all the best students, Jerry has channeled his everyday experiences well," Hennessy said in *Fortune*.[4]

While Yang was struggling to learn English, which he mastered well enough to move from remedial to advanced classes by his third year in San Jose, Yahoo's future head technologist was growing up in a commune in Moss Bluff, Louisiana, sharing a garden and kitchen with six other families and learning to pitch in. "I remember looking at the Erector Set catalogue and wanting the fancy pieces—the three-speed motor versus the little one we had," Filo told *Wired* in January 1999. "But we had a really big set. We could build cranes; we could build bridges. When I was in the fifth grade, my family built a house. My brother and I helped with the roofing, nailing shingles down; we held things. We put up sheet rock and did electrical stuff. I was always fascinated with tools—table saws, routers, lathes.

There are eight of us in the family, and the house originally was only about 1,400 square feet. Our bedrooms were seven by eight feet, but we each had our own. Engineering in general is about building things, solving problems. To this day there are so many problems with what we're doing at Yahoo—things still need fixing. What motivated Jerry and me all along was really simple: You try to come up with nice solutions."[5]

The commune experience, however, didn't improve his social skills. When friends and acquaintances describe Filo, the words that crop up again and again are "quiet," "reserved," and even "withdrawn." In fact, "some of Filo's friends affectionately nicknamed him the Unabomber because he was so introspective," writes David A. Kaplan in *The Silicon Boys and Their Valley of Dreams* (William Morrow, 1999).[6] But if Filo didn't often wow people on an interpersonal level, he did excel academically, landing at Tulane for college before entering Stanford, where he and Yang met in 1989.

Their friendship solidified three years later on a six-month teaching-assistant program in Japan. Another relationship Yang formed there also would play a central role in his life: He met a Stanford student named Akiko Yamazaki, a Costa Rican of Japanese parentage who would later become his wife. And in Japan, Yang's and Filo's paths crossed with that of another Stanford student, Srinija Srinivasan ("Ninj"), who was studying artificial intelligence and information organization and would later join Yahoo as Chief Ontologist. Japan itself would be home to Yahoo's first international outpost, the No. 1 site in that country.

When Yang and Filo returned to Palo Alto and Stanford, everyone was buzzing about Mosaic. In 1993, when Filo's overgrown list of Web-site bookmarks numbered 200, making it useless, they began work on their database.

Trying to pressure Filo into helping come up with a snappier name for the site, Yang briefly changed its name to David and Jerry's Guide to the World Wide Web. "I got sick of taking all the credit," Yang explained in an interview in June 1999 on "Big Thinkers," a program aired on the cable station TechTV. "David hated it. He hates to have his name associated with it. One night we locked ourselves in a room and said, 'We need to come up with something easy to remember.' We wanted to call it 'yet another something,' looked up all the words that started with y-a. Yahoo stuck out. In *Gulliver's Travels*, it means somebody who is rude, a subhuman species who were rude and uncivilized. That's us."[7] In another sign of the self-deprecating humor friends and cohorts say is typical of Yang and Filo, they decided to make Yahoo an acronym for Yet Another Hierarchical Officious Oracle.

In any case, that playful, irreverent name change provided Yahoo with the ammunition to become a top Internet brand. As early as 1998, market-research firm IntelliQuest reported that 44 percent of Internet users were familiar with Yahoo, and only America Online (AOL) and Netscape had greater name-brand recognition. "The Yahoo brand contains the promise of the product: that the Internet will be a liberating and exhilarating experience," says Owen Shapiro, senior analyst at market and brand-research firm Leo J. Shapiro & Associates.

"When we started the business, our VCs [venture capitalists] said we absolutely need to keep the name," Yang told "Big Thinkers." "I'd be lying to say we knew what branding meant in 1994. David and I were tech people, but we knew how creating something that's easy to remember, that's easy to use—that's the key ingredient to a brand."[8]

Yang and Filo organized Yahoo into a hierarchy of 19 categories (later pared down to 14), such as Art, Business, Computers, Economy, Education—but emphatically not Erotica, an area they would later add and then restrict—generating cries of censorship—after some users complained. Every click on a heading gave way to a pageful of links, and clicking on those yielded still more. The user could click through several levels before hitting bottom—an impossibility today, given the millions of sites Yahoo has indexed. To narrow the field and produce more targeted results, Yang and Filo created a search engine that returned a list of Web sites based on keywords entered by the user.

The ability to track where on Yahoo their users went, and where on the Web they had come from, was "built into the bones of the system," Tim Koogle told Charles S. Sigismund, author of *Champions of Silicon Valley* (John Wiley & Sons, 2000). The goal: "We can use that as a true, real-time measure of what is most popular and most needed—and use it as a road sign to guide us toward deeper and deeper levels of content that we ought to aggregate around."[9] And of course, they could use it to sell targeted advertising.

The index was, and still is, assembled by humans, in contrast to the mechanical Web-searching "spider" technology, or 'bots, Yahoo's competitors used. And Yahoo never claimed to be comprehensive, like the other indexes: Its goal was to offer the best of the Web and to reflect the Zeitgeist. "One of the reasons Yahoo is successful today is it's pretty human—it's more of a social-engineering product than software," Yang said. "We're a reflection of the community, and the more socially aware we are, the better the community we'll build. I don't think that technology-driven companies are going to be able to do this as well as we can, although it will take more time and resources on our part. The way we gather information lets us stay close to what's on the Web—we have a good sense of what people are putting up, and can stay with the trends. Over time, we'll build nifty features and will stay on top of the technology."[10]

On top of other people's technology, that is, since Yahoo lacked proprietary search technology. So Yahoo's strength was also one of its biggest weaknesses—that its prime capital was human, and the fruits of those humans' labor were eminently reproducible.

Yang was well aware of that vulnerability but also had an answer to it. "We can't protect the links we list, and there are people out there copying it," he said. "There are a lot of Yahoo-like things out there. We don't go after them because it's not worth our time and money. Someday that may be an issue, but we're not really worried now because we have a critical mass."[11]

As Yahoo grew, so did the number of people accessing it, from a trickle to a stream to a deluge in a matter of months. In April 1994, Yang and Filo had compiled a hundred sites and were getting a thousand hits a week. Five months later, in September, the numbers had grown to 2,000 sites and 50,000 hits a day. Netscape introduced its beta browser the next month and decided to link the directory button on its corporate Web site to Yahoo (the search button linked to a competing site, Infoseek). "We simply wanted to make the browser easy for people to use, and Yahoo was the best directory available at the time," explains Mike Homer, then Netscape's vice president of marketing.

The Netscape link sent Yahoo's user numbers through the roof, giving Yang and Filo strong evidence they had the makings of a business. By January, they had 10,000 sites and 1 million hits a day (at least according to their own promotional materials) and were stressing Stanford's limited hardware capacity to the max. Since the university couldn't afford to buy more servers, it asked Yang and Filo to find another host. Meanwhile, as word about Yahoo spread, venture capitalists and execs from companies like MCI and AOL came knocking on their trailer door.

"We didn't think about turning commercial until late summer of last year, when we realized that the site was using too many resources to remain at Stanford as a grad-student project," Yang said in 1995. "So we had to find somewhere off campus to host it. Though we didn't realize it then, that was fundamentally a decision to turn it commercial."[12]

Marc Andreessen finally rode to the rescue with an e-mail inviting Yang and Filo to avail themselves of Netscape's resources. "Marc contacted me and said, 'These guys are good guys—would you be willing to help them out?' " Homer recounts. "We went out and bought an SGI [Silicon Graphics Inc.] server for several thousand dollars, and that was what we used to run the Yahoo directory."

Now Yang and Filo had solved one problem, but like other Internet entrepreneurs of the time, they still had no idea how to cash in on their creation. "We all knew the Internet was going to change things," says Larry Augustin, a classmate of theirs at Stanford and the founder of VA Linux, which makes computers that run on the operating system Linux and set a record in 1999 for the biggest first-day gain ever, 708 percent, for an initial public offering (IPO). "We'd all been using the Internet for 10 years, and it was nothing special to us. Nobody outside of this academic community was able to access it or understand it. Then the browser made it easy for people to use. We could see the user base growing at a huge rate, but none of us knew how we'd end up having businesses or making money."

Yang admitted as much to *Fortune*: "David had it in his gut very early on that Yahoo could ultimately be a consumer interface to the Web rather than simply a search engine or piece of technology. We weren't really sure you could make a business out of it though."[13] In fact, Yang wasn't even sure he *wanted* to make a business out of it, according to Dave Zinman, founder of Focalink, one of the first online-ad servers, who heard Yang speak to his Stanford M.B.A. class in 1994. At the time, Zinman was in the process of writing a business plan for Focalink based on the assumption that sites would make money selling ads. Zinman says, "I wanted to know, 'Are you going to place advertising on the site?' He said, 'No, we don't want to commercialize Yahoo. We want to keep it a grass-roots site.' " Yang didn't stick to that position for long, though.

While at Stanford, Yang, Filo, and Augustin had written a business plan for a giant online shopping mall they called The Galleria, thinking it would offer a more explicit route to revenues. "They had Yahoo going and I had VA Linux going, but neither of us had funding," Augustin says. "We decided to set aside what we were doing and come up with a business plan that made sense, but none of us was really excited about dropping what we were doing."

Instead of dropping Yahoo, Yang and Filo enlisted their future head of production, Tim Brady, then a second-year M.B.A. student at Harvard and Yang's former roommate as an undergrad at Stanford, to write a business plan for them. Gil Margalit, a Stanford M.B.A. who was looking to wring opportunity out of the Internet in 1994, heard about Yahoo while networking and called Yang and Filo. The three met at Cafe Verona on Hamilton Street in Palo Alto, where Jim Clark and Marc Andreessen had met a year earlier to hatch Netscape.

"Their eyes were really red from sleep deprivation, especially David Filo, who was almost falling asleep every few minutes," remembers Margalit, who founded Rainfinity, an

Internet-infrastructure builder, in 1998. "They questioned me to see if I knew what the Internet was all about, do we share the same views."

The pair had just fielded a $2 million buyout offer from Steve Case of AOL, who had informed them that if they declined, AOL would create its own Yahoo. "At the time of funding, we figured we had a three-month lead over our competitors," Yang said the next fall. "As of today, there is no one out there competing with us directly, but there are a lot of people working on it. We talked to AOL in March. They tried to buy us, and we said no, and they said, 'We'll crush you in two months.' They haven't yet, but they certainly own the browsers and you have to be aware of that. I'm certainly aware of what the competition can do. There's very little resting on any laurels. We're a zero-revenue company right now, so I don't think we're in a position to be comfortable about anything."[14]

Margalit, who thought the quiet Filo and charismatic Yang made an odd couple, remembers them asking, " 'Should we sell or not?' These guys were very smart—when they ask a question, it's not because they don't have a strong indication of what their answer is. They could tell if it's worth at least $2 million to AOL, they could get at least as much later selling to someone else."

Though Yang and Filo were palpably bright, neither one had held a real day job before, meaning they were also extremely green. They hadn't set out to create a business, Margalit notes, but rather were driven to it "by all this buzz around them." The buzz only intensified, with more VCs coming around and a feature story in *Newsweek* in March singling out Yahoo as the one to watch—and coining the expression "did a Yahoo," later reconstituted for the company's famous slogan, "Do you Yahoo!?"

In March 1995, Yang and Filo, with the help of Tim Brady, had their business plan, and they asked Margalit to critique it. The business plan set forth Yahoo's ambition to become the *TV Guide* of the Internet. The plan clearly called for an advertising-based model that, in some ways, was remarkably similar to Yahoo as it exists today. To attract advertisers and build market share, Yahoo would add content such as "newsfeeds" and create a sense of community through bulletin boards and chat groups. Personalization, as it would later appear in My Yahoo, was already part of the package, and one the company's founders were considering a potential source of subscription revenue.

The business plan also emphasized the benefits of Yahoo's "first mover advantage"—and put the number of its "daily accesses" at 2 million, though in the *Newsweek* article the same month, the figure cited, and attributed to Yang, was 200,000. In *Yahoo! Unplugged*, Yang and Filo peg the number of daily hits at 10,000 to 15,000 just a couple of months earlier. These discrepancies highlight the difficulty in getting accurate online-user figures and the slipperiness of the results, both then and now.

The plan stressed the importance of Yahoo's independence, editorial impartiality, and brand equity—all major themes for Yahoo later. And the plan maintained that the service would be free to the end user, a pledge Yahoo has largely kept, perhaps to its detriment.

There were, of course, also major differences. In a passage consistent with the Net's staunchly anticommercial mind-set in its early history, the company stated it would "sell advertising space on the five most frequently accessed Yahoo index pages"—only. The founders envisioned a poll of eight advertisers rotated "through the five pages over a 3-month period." The truth, of course, is today there's no part of Yahoo that isn't for sale—even its once-sacrosanct search listings.

Yahoo listed its second-biggest source of income as licensing deals, a revenue stream that thus far hasn't materialized for the company. And the company wildly underestimated its revenues for 1996 by 380 percent, predicting $4.15 million while the real figure would approach $20 million.

Ironically, the business plan lists the unprepossessing Filo as president and CEO while Yang appears as chairman and chief financial officer (CFO), but, Margalit says, that was just a stroke of convention. "Right from the beginning, they were very modest and expected to hire someone to run the company." And of course, the fuzzy title they both eventually assumed, Chief Yahoo, supports the notion that they wanted to remain in the background. In another interesting note, the founders apparently foresaw that porn would be a controversial area for them, since they stated that they planned to create a "censored version of Yahoo" that was "free from pornographic listings" for licensees.

On March 5, Yahoo was incorporated, and in April, it landed $1 million in venture funding from Sequoia Capital, in its first investment in a dot-com. Yahoo got Sequoia's attention because Randy Adams, founder of the Internet Shopping Network (ISN), which he claims is the first online retailer, owed Sequoia General Partner Mike Moritz a favor. Prior to ISN, Adams had started four software companies in Silicon Valley, built them up, and sold them. Of those, only one, AppSoft, developed for Steve Jobs' NeXT computer platform and funded by Sequoia, was a failure. When Jobs stopped producing NeXT machines, Adams had to shut AppSoft down. "I felt I had a debt to pay off to Moritz," Adams says. "AppSoft was the only one of my companies that didn't pay off for investors, and it was the only company that had been funded by Sequoia and Moritz."

Marc Andreessen—with whom Adams had "a close e-mail correspondence"—had told him about Yahoo. Adams checked out the site, was impressed, and invited Yang and Filo to lunch. "They wanted to buy, and they couldn't afford much, so we ate at Fresh Choice salad bar in Menlo Park," Adams recalls. "They'd had an offer from AOL, but they were more interested in building the business. I thought if I could put them in touch with the right people and they could get some money, they could build it. Coincidentally, Mike Moritz called about the same week Jerry had said they were looking for some venture money, so it clicked I owed Mike, and I gave him their name."

Moritz visited Yang and Filo in their infamous trailer, talked to them for about an hour, and was treated to a demo of Yahoo. "So, how much are you going to charge subscribers?" Moritz asked.[15]

"Dave and I looked at each other and said, 'Well, it's going to be a long conversation,' " Yang recalled—because of course, the two were planning to keep their service free. "But two hours later, we convinced them that Yahoo should be free, and I think we're the only company Sequoia's funding that has a free product."[16]

While Yahoo's proposed business model may have been uncharted territory, it had a few things—*millions* of things, actually—going for it. "We have a successful product with millions of users, which is pretty rare for a company seeking venture financing," Tim Brady pointed out.[17]

The discussions continued for about six weeks afterward, while Yang and Filo were fielding offers from AOL and other companies. "We finally decided in April on VC funding over corporate funding because we wanted to be an independent voice, and I think going with a corporate sponsorship would have tainted the site," Yang explained to *Red Herring*. "We had an ideal start as part of an educational institution, being a non-commercial, free service. We thought that VC money would buy us time for the environment to work itself out and for our business model to get clearer. In retrospect, I think we got a late start, getting funding in April."[18]

Yang and Filo had talked to about a dozen VCs—many of whom had never even seen an e-mail—but decided on Moritz, Yang told *Fortune*, "because he seemed to have more soul, and he shared our values. Like us he's cheap, and he's not a big believer that technology solves everything. But he does believe in the human element and in the art of what we were doing as well as the science."[19] In turn, Moritz said, "Jerry would be considered an unusual entrepreneur today because he actually wanted to build a company that is really lasting. He's not yet another grotesque Doonesbury caricature of an entrepreneur."[20]

In April, Sequoia—which had funded Apple Computer, Cisco Systems, and Oracle Corporation—handed $1 million over to Yahoo in return for a quarter share in the company, thus valuing the company at $4 million. "It would prove to be the best $1 million ever invested in Silicon Valley," Kaplan trumpets in *The Silicon Boys and Their Valley of Dreams*.[21] In early 1999, the value of that initial investment rose to $8 billion; in January 2000, at Yahoo's apex, it shot to more than $30 billion. Ironically, Yang and Filo, who also each received 25 percent stakes in the company, ended up with the same value they would have had they accepted Steve Case's $2 million.

Contrary to published reports, Mike Homer says, Netscape never made Yang and Filo an offer: Many of Netscape's software clients were competitors of Yahoo's, so teaming up would have created a conflict of interest. Nor, Homer says, did Netscape kick Yahoo's server out of its offices after the company accepted Sequoia's money, as some accounts have held. Instead, the decision to relocate the server was made by Yahoo, "on their own," he maintains.

"I give Mike [Moritz] credit for his good sense of smell and his willingness to jump into the water and buy a seat for the Internet play at a time when most other VCs were watching from the sidelines, waiting for someone else to show them how you can make money from an Internet service company," Margalit says. "It was a service, and the service was free, and that didn't make sense to a lot of these people." Of course, that still doesn't make sense to a lot of people, including Yahoo itself, which is trying to charge for more and more services. Giving services away free may have worked during the Net's early boom years, when dot-coms were plentiful and flush with cash to spend on advertising, but in today's harsh climate, it's no longer an option.

Chapter

Pioneer Way, 1995

Key Events

- August: Netscape's IPO gains 108 percent in a record-setting first day.
- August: Microsoft releases the first version of its Internet Explorer browser and launches the Microsoft Network, precursor to MSN.
- September: eBay launches its online-auction site.
- October: AOL introduces GNN Direct Internet service.
- December: Microsoft reshifts its strategy to focus on the Internet.

As soon as Sequoia became involved, Yahoo shifted into moneymaking mode. "The first thing they did was bring in an interim-management company to figure out what to do with Yahoo," Gil Margalit says.

And to head that team, says Randy Adams, who sat on Yahoo's board of directors for the first year, until it went public, "we hired a guy named Phil Monego, a rent-a-CEO."

Philip Monego ran an outfit called Technology Perspectives that was well-known in the Valley. Since 1987, he and his team had gotten a half-dozen companies up and running, including Viacom Online and Playboy Online. Yang called him just before accepting Sequoia's $1 million, and Yang, Filo, and Monego met at the Blue Chalk billiard parlor and restaurant in Palo Alto—with entrées up to $17, a big step up from the Fresh Choice salad bar. Monego, who used Yahoo and thought it a great tool, was excited about the possibility of working with its creators. The three talked about Yang and Filo's various options, including Steve Case's "offer to buy the boys," as Monego puts it, a similar offer they'd received from Microsoft, their thoughts about commercializing Yahoo, and their meetings with various VCs. In addition to Sequoia's offer, they'd gotten a bite from Kleiner Perkins, but KP's offer was contingent on Yahoo merging with another fledgling service, Architext (later Excite), that the VC had already funded. And from the start, Yang and Filo were dead set against losing their independence.

"I was expecting a couple of bright college kids who were Internet junkies," says Monego, now CEO of San Mateo–based Voquette Media Service, which creates and delivers rich media for corporate customers. "What I discovered were two of the brightest, most visionary people I'd ever met at any age, who were committed to an ideal, which was to make the Internet more usable for everyone. Jerry, in particular, had a vision for how the Internet could change our lives. He was extraordinary in his ability to grasp the size of the Internet and how it could be complete. None of us got that large in our vision."

In fact, many who crossed paths with Yang and Filo in the early stages agree it was this sense of mission—not a hunger for success or money—that drove them and their disciples. "We all worked hard, but it didn't matter," says Eric Hall, who Monego brought in as CFO and who, like many in Silicon Valley who hoped to participate in the bubble's upside, is now a VC, with McKenna Venture Accelerator in Mountain View. "We all loved what we did and believed in the company. Sounds corny, but the attitude changed in later start-ups I worked with. Many employees in later ventures would get wide-eyed and upset if you asked them to work more than eight hours or on weekends. It just wasn't that way in the early days of the Internet at Yahoo or Netscape."

Later that same week, Monego met with Moritz at Sequoia's spare Menlo Park offices, an accurate reflection of its partners' penny-pinching philosophy. "Mike was committed to put a million dollars into Yahoo and no more," Monego says. "It was either going to prove itself or fail on that million. He also said he was looking for some adult supervision to come in and build an organization around David and Jerry. Mike would have liked me to step right up to the full-time CEO role, but I had other commitments." (Monego isn't the only one who contends he was offered the opportunity to lead Yahoo but declined. Similarly, Randy Adams says, "Just before the IPO, Jerry tried to talk me into being CEO, but I said, 'Nah, nah, I'm trying to run this Internet Shopping Network.' ")

The same day they deposited Sequoia's check—April 10, just a little over a year to the day before Yahoo would go public—Monego and Hall went hunting for office space and signed a lease at 110 Pioneer Way, an almost laughably appropriate address for their new roles. Monego had met Hall in 1991 at ImagiNation Network, a spin-off of the first games site, Sierra Online. Monego and the third member of his interim team, Randy Haykin, who came in as vice president of sales and marketing, had met the year before through consulting gigs at Paramount Technology Group. In 1999, Haykin's San Francisco VC shop, iMinds, would invest $500,000 in Monego's company, Voquette. To complete the incestuous circle, it was Hall who had brought Monego to Paramount.

In Mountain View, just a mile and a half from Netscape, Yahoo's first digs occupied the back corner of a boxy one-story building where semiconductors had once been manufactured. With a mere 1,500 square feet, the staff, small as it was, had to double up in offices. "Philip and I shared an office," Hall says. "We couldn't get out of our chairs at the same time without hitting each other." The furniture was used or bargain-basement: desks from an auction house, whiteboards from a going-out-of-business sale, folding tables and chairs. Yang, Filo, Monego, Hall, and Haykin spackled and painted the walls themselves. Total capital expenditures for the first month of business: $25,000.

Frugality was the name of the game. "One of [Moritz's] questions to me during the interview process with Philip and Randy was, 'Paper clips or staples—do you need both?' " Hall remembers. "The right answer, which I gave him, was, 'No. You could save money by only using one.' I later found out that Mike was put off by my T. Anthony briefcase, which was a gift from my wife for Christmas. He thought it was a bit too ostentatious for a CFO. Philip informed him that I had been driving the same car for 16 years and that he could personally vouch that I would be tight with the money."

Filo, who changed his title from Chief Yahoo to Cheap Yahoo, was the cheapest of all. Hall found a good deal on PCs, he recalls, "but Dave found a local PC clone builder that would beat the price by $200 per CPU [central processing unit]. They were great machines, too, and built to his specifications." Both Filo and Yang drove old, disreputable cars—a Toyota Tercel and an Oldsmobile Cutlass, respectively—but Filo's "was the ugliest car you've ever seen," Hall says. "It had more Bondo on the roof than metal." Filo had taken the car to a state-prison body shop near his home in Louisiana to get the roof patched. But it was so rusty that one of Yahoo's new hires had no trouble poking his fist through it during a staff photo session in August 1995. (See Figure 2.1.)

Yang and Filo also had a logo cheaply designed by tapping the talents of yet another one of their Stanford classmates. Just days before the Internet World show in San Jose that April, David Shen—later hired as Gooey Yahoo, responsible for making the site warm and fuzzy—came up with the whimsical uneven lettering and squinty O's that resemble eyes. In return, Shen got $500 and some stock. Despite proposals by Web-site design boutiques CKS and Poppe Tyson to outdo Shen, his logo still stands virtually untouched more than six years later. ("The only time I've seen Jerry angry was when he stormed out of a meeting with CKS," Hall says. "CKS was being a bit critical of Yahoo's efforts and also being a bit pompous.")

The ability to inspire others to contribute to your cause for little or no personal gain is a hallmark of successful entrepreneurs, and one Yang and Filo had in spades. The goodwill of their friends and of the Internet community—embodied in the free computing resources they received from Stanford, the business plan written by Tim Brady, the server and directory-button link provided by Netscape, and the logo—helped Yahoo get off the ground. "The fact that they were two students doing this for free was their allure," Margalit comments. "People felt more compelled to support these guys." That dynamic, of course, would soon change in a big way, as Yahoo's market cap ballooned and the company morphed into an outsized symbol of great expectations.

Yahoo's frugality extended to its tech systems as well. In 1998, when Margalit was about to form Rainfinity, he met with Filo and Chief Technical Officer (CTO) Farzad Nazem, nicknamed Zod, to see whether he could do business with Yahoo. He was stunned by Yahoo's lack of investment in systems security—an oversight that would haunt the site in 2000 when hackers bombarded it with requests and brought it down for several hours, revealing its vulnerability. Yahoo's entire operation seemed to depend on a hundred servers run by two Silicon Valley hosting companies, a bad idea in the event of a regional power failure. "Very little architectural thought was given to assuring high availability and noninterrupted service," Margalit says. "They had only two data centers, both on the West Coast, without disaster recovery. When we proposed what we wanted to do with the architecture, which would have required them to put a second network-interface card in each one of their servers [clustering the servers and the load-balancing devices in such a way that if any of them were to go down or experience a bottleneck, the other surviving members of the cluster would take over], David said, 'Well, that's expensive.' A network-interface card was about $50, so there was $5,000 involved for the company. When you consider the trade-off—the company is sitting on hundreds of millions of dollars of investors' money—being concerned about $5,000, that's a reflection of the frugal view." (So was Yahoo's Spartan lobby, whose bright yellow and purple colors reminded Margalit of a Mexican restaurant.)

Margalit also was struck by the fact that Yahoo had developed most of its information technology (IT) infrastructure in-house, "more than you would expect from a company in the line of business of Yahoo," he says. "The general feeling I had is that given the techie background of the founders, they took great pride in developing their own IT, even though a lot of it was commercially available in the marketplace." He also interpreted this as a reluctance to pay outsiders for software the company thought it could develop less expensively itself. It was a sign that Yahoo had learned from the critics who called it poor in proprietary technology. And Yahoo would draw on its developers' skills again and again rather than fork out huge sums to acquire technology.

Yahoo also made some smart decisions regarding architecture—rapidly Filo's province, while Yang focused on strategy and PR—that enabled the site to scale up with nary a hiccup. "Yahoo seemed to do a much better job of taking advantage of the natural partitioning the Web allows" than its competitors, says Eric Ver Ploeg, a VC at VantagePoint Venture Partners and former classmate of Yang and Filo's in Stanford's electrical engineering Ph.D. program, which he completed. Ver Ploeg says that by segregating areas of Yahoo on separate computers—putting finance.yahoo.com on one machine and personals.yahoo.com on another, for example—Yahoo created a simple yet extremely scalable system. Each area could be split into infinite chunks, each chunk assigned to a computer, and more computers added to handle the ever-increasing load of traffic. And the company could save money by spreading the same URL across a bunch of computers. Since processing power usually carries a price premium, it can cost less to use a hundred computers with less processing power than 50 with more.

The first person Yang and Filo hired was Srinija Srinivasan ("Ninj"), their former cohort in Japan. As Chief Ontologist, she oversaw Web-site review and categorization. They also hired a half-dozen local college students to work with Ninj as professional surfers, checking links, ensuring each site offered some basic value, and selecting and highlighting the best ones. "We'd get hundreds and then thousands, then tens of thousands of requests per day" from sites that wanted to be included in the hierarchy, Monego says. The surfers—with the help of the entire staff, each of whom was expected to click through a daily regimen of 100 to 300 sites—added hundreds of new URLs a week, sometimes as many as a thousand a day.

Yahoo exercised at least limited editorial oversight, nixing sites that dealt in mass destruction as well as those that misrepresented their intent. "We won't list things like how to build an atomic bomb or how to blow up New York City buildings," Yang said. "We're definitely free-speechers, but we also understand that we have a responsibility: Kids are on the Web. Another issue is something that came up the other day. Some high school kid submitted something and said that it was the official site for Rochester High School—but actually Rochester High School didn't have an official site. He then started putting sex stuff up there. It's back to the issue of trust. Where do you draw the line; what kind of claims can you make in terms of calling things official sites?"[1] It's a question that to this day, Yahoo continually confronts.

Tim Brady, author of Yahoo's first business plan, graduated early from Harvard and signed on as director of marketing. Another friend of Yang and Filo's from Stanford, Donald Ajit Lobo, joined as a systems engineer. According to an internal payroll document dated April 1995, Yang (listed as Chih-Yuan Yang, his given name) and Filo received salaries of $40,000 each, while

Brady grossed a princely $60,000. Monego, Hall, and Haykin got about 50 percent of their pay in stock, a deal that turned out to be very lucrative for them.

But other than their compensation, attractive as it was, the interim-management team received very little credit from Yahoo for its contributions. "Yahoo's DNA was set in the first six months of its life," Haykin says. "The DNA was set by positioning, it was set by PR, sales efforts that the company rode to greatest heights on, and the Web site—the way Jerry and I shaped the product in its early days. The team also brought a process to a young company that it would have lacked without the help it received from a more experienced group of mentors and leaders.

"I felt very comfortable leaving knowing the company was in capable hands, but I was surprised in recapping the story, they always left us out," continues Haykin, who received a full-time offer from Yahoo but turned it down in order to keep his fingers in multiple pies. "I was disappointed by that, but I really liked the guys a lot and respect them, and for some reason, that's the choice they made. Maybe it's difficult to say you started a company with a group of consultants."

⤙

*H*aykin was working at Paramount when an intern called him over and said, "You've got to see this thing Akebono." Duly impressed, Haykin was happy to come aboard when Monego called him several months later. He put together a marketing team composed of four reps, one in the Bay Area, two in Los Angeles, and one in New York. The head of the team, Andy Batkin, had started a firm called Interactive Marketing that helped companies promote themselves via the Web. In 1996, Batkin sold his company to Softbank, Yahoo's biggest investor, but Interactive Marketing continued to handle Yahoo's ad sales throughout that year.

Though it was clear advertising would play a key role, Yahoo was still hashing out its business model, using bits and pieces of Tim Brady's plan. Licensing its directory or search capability, competitor AltaVista's model, also seemed to hold potential, but the search field was already crowded. "We were experimenting," Monego says. "Nothing was clear at the time." The business plan eventually was finished in November by CEO Tim Koogle and Chief Operating Officer (COO) Jeff Mallett.

Haykin had little precedent to follow. In October 1994, the first banner ads had appeared on HotWired, *Wired* magazine's Web site. Sites such as Time Warner's Pathfinder service and CNET had followed suit, but certainly no one had yet proven Web advertising could support a business. The big challenge was creating banner ads that wouldn't slow the system down by taking too long to load. "We're putting a lot of time into making the ads unobtrusive and interesting, and trying to intelligently integrate them," Yang said.[2]

Like Monego and Hall, Haykin had agreed to devote only three or four days a week to Yahoo so he could leave himself free for other commitments, one of which was working to build AOL's Greenhouse, an incubator for Net start-ups. "Both groups knew that I was working in an interim position at the other," Haykin says. "Word of Yahoo started spreading at AOL—they became nervous. As Yahoo grew, I had more and more VPs at AOL come up to me and try to figure out what they were doing. We all finally realized it was competitive."

Just how competitive became clear that summer, when Monego, Yang, and Filo met Steve Case at Il Fornaio, yet another rung up in the restaurant food chain, to talk about possible collaborations. Case was no more amenable than he'd been the previous March—and just as determined to quash Yahoo. "The discussion was about how we could work closely with AOL given that Steve had been rebuffed in his earlier overture," recalls Monego, who at 48 called himself the Gray-Haired Yahoo. "I offered to sell AOL 10 percent of Yahoo for $4 million, and Steve told me that he didn't think that was a reasonable value, that his plans were to build their own search and categorizing capability, and somewhat confidently, he told us that he expected to put Yahoo out of business."

Ironically, given that AOL and Time Warner (TW) later joined forces, Moritz also reportedly offered Yahoo to TW for less than $10 million but was rejected. "They were actively shopping to Time Warner," says Manish Shah, publisher of *IPO Maven* newsletter and president of the investment-news site 123jump.com. "Time Warner was saying, 'Come on—it's not even worth $2 million.' So negotiations fell apart. Obviously, the value dramatically changed after that. At one point, they could have bought Time Warner."

There were already signs that both AOL and Time Warner were off the mark. In June the tech-media company International Data Group, Inc. (IDG) held its first Internet Conference at the Radisson Miyako Hotel in San Francisco. Val Landi, executive VP for IDG, remembers hearing Yang speak there. "It was his first presentation in public," Landi says. "He was wonderful—he was so articulate and charismatic about Yahoo as a brand. Bob Metcalfe [then VP of technology for IDG, founder of 3Com, and coinventor of Ethernet], leaned over and said to me, 'This is going to be the first great Internet brand'—and that's what happened, of course."

Another sign of Yahoo's potential staying power was the

distribution and revenue-sharing deal it had struck with Reuters. John Taysom, then a marketing VP for Reuters, had transferred to Palo Alto from London to help ease a new acquisition, Teknekron Software Systems, now Tibco, into the fold. He'd been using Yahoo but didn't know Yang and Filo were based at Stanford until he read about them in a local paper. "So, I rang them and said, 'How about we put some news on your index, and then people will come back daily to get breaking news, and then they'll come back and do searches on things that are relevant,' " Taysom says. Yang's response: "If you hadn't called me, I would have called you."

Yang, Filo, and Taysom had "a momentous meeting," according to Taysom, at his house in Palo Alto. The two Stanford students clearly already saw Yahoo as a media company, not just a directory, and agreed with Taysom that breaking news was the sort of content they needed to retain and attract users. The notion of being an independent news agency, like Reuters, intrigued them. "When we wrote the contract, we had to stipulate that because of our independence, they wouldn't put our content next to advertising that might be politically biased or had to do with alcohol," Taysom says. "They quickly came back with a set of rules for the independence of Yahoo. They wanted to be the Switzerland of information on the Web. They saw Reuters as a model for independence. What we saw when we looked at Yahoo, especially a bit later on when they'd received venture money, was a company that had a bunch of off-the-shelf PCs running open-source code and receiving database hit rates that were incredibly impressive."

Like Hall and Monego, Taysom was swept up by Yang and Filo's infectious sense of mission. "Making money wasn't much on their minds," Taysom says. "It was a great meeting because they realized we were trying to do more than make money. We had a mission. What they had was an index to data that didn't change very often but was huge in scope, potentially covering every known activity, and what we had was a light, a torch, that was the news that illuminated sections of that data. We were using our light to light up parts of their content, to draw your attention to it. We recognized we could help each other."

Yahoo also provided a wake-up call for Reuters. Taysom saw the directory as the sort of "disruptive technology" that could prove a significant threat to the news agency in the future. He wanted a piece of the opportunity Yahoo represented, but in 1994, when the first meeting took place, there was no company to invest in yet. In exchange for content, Yang and Filo initially agreed to supply Reuters with consumer data provided by I/PRO, an online-advertising auditor founded by Stanford M.B.A. Ariel Poler; a year earlier, Yang and Filo had written code for Poler for $25 an hour. "The idea was that Reuters supplied the news information that made people visit Yahoo daily, the news items would pique their interest to 'to tell me more,' starting a Web search, the activity would be recorded by I/PRO and provided to Yahoo, which would provide it to Reuters, which would publish it and hence stimulate advertising to pay for the news items," Taysom explains. But in the end, Yahoo opted for an ad-revenue-sharing deal over providing consumer data, because, Taysom says, "they were too smart to give it to us."

Yang and Filo had already realized that protecting consumer privacy was critical to the success of an Internet business. "There was always an uneasiness about collecting information on people," Haykin says. "Jerry felt very strongly about privacy very early on. He was a thought leader in that area."

In August 1995, Reuters began feeding Yahoo 10 headlines a day on five topics: top stories, politics, business, sports, and oddball stories. "We had a formula that Jerry and I hacked out whereby if the headline was on view with other index data from Yahoo, the presumption was that they got the bigger share of the revenue because the user would have found the headline through use of the index," Taysom explains. "But for the full story on display, the reverse logic applied. It was very successful for both of us."

In fact, according to Haykin, "the revenue from this deal, from day one, has been at the center of Yahoo's growth." Meanwhile, the deal transformed Reuters from a company few in the United States had ever heard of into a brand-name source for news.

Building on that prestigious contract, Haykin and his ad reps assembled a pilot program of six advertisers, including General Motors and Visa, which each paid $20,000 a month. Tim Brady had said the home page wouldn't be sold, "just as you don't see any ads on the cover of a magazine,"[3] but that resolution quickly fell by the wayside. The site's commercial launch was set for early August. In the BusinessWeek Online chat in July, Yang had expressed his views on advertising: "We are trying to have a handful of sponsors to sponsor various categories of Yahoo, but we don't envision tons of advertising/yellow page stuff on Yahoo. The goal is to maintain a clear separation between the 'directory' part, which is objective and is consistent with our editorial tone, and the 'commercial' part, which is clearly sponsored content."[4]

Yang and Filo's motto was, "If we don't like it, we figure you won't like it."[5]

Haykin remembers the depth of Yang's concern about breaching Internet etiquette and turning users off by introducing advertising. "We debated for months what to do about the business model," Haykin says. "I remember driving with Jerry in a car. We'd gone to visit John Taysom. We had a long debate back and forth about what was the right business model for Yahoo. Would we scare away users if we put advertising on the site? He was very nervous about that, cautious, and smart. He had some really good arguments as to how that could hurt the company. Me, being the Harvard M.B.A., I was pushing for revenue. He felt that the users of Yahoo would feel we'd commercialized Yahoo if we weren't careful how we did it and would stop coming because we'd violated the Internet culture."

But Yahoo's research revealed alienating its devoted users wasn't as big a risk as Yang feared. The company had placed a survey on its home page asking whether people would be open to seeing ads and new features and promotions, and to registering personal information on the site. Instead of the 5,000 to 10,000 responses Yahoo expected based on the response rate for surveys done by other sites that Haykin had heard about through the grapevine, it received 90,000 responses—with more than half indicating a willingness to register. The highest prediction in the office pool was 10,000 responses. "This not only gave us strong input as to what we were doing right and wrong, but also gave us conviction," Haykin says. "We could tell we had a very strong and loyal early base of people."

In preparation for its commercial launch, Yahoo trimmed its top-level categories from 19 to 14, debuted news from Reuters, and of course, added advertising. It introduced a section with thumbnail reproductions of 18 Web sites that had paid between $5,000 and $10,000 a month to be included. And it created a weekly e-mail featuring hot sites for users who signed up for it.

The launch date was set for a Monday. That Friday, it looked like calamity had struck. Moritz, Monego, Haykin, and other members of Yahoo's staff were waiting for Yang in a conference room to discuss the launch. Melody Kean Haller, Yahoo's account rep from its newly hired PR firm, Niehaus Ryan Haller (now Niehaus Ryan Wong), remembers Yang entering the room and announcing, "We can't launch."

Everyone wanted to know what the problem was. "Jerry said, 'I don't know. It's up to David,' " Haller says. "He gave us a complete, absolute stonewall. There was no question. David is the tech genius. Jerry had no doubt about what David was saying. Trusted him completely. The advertising people were aghast. They thought, will the advertisers ever trust us again? We told them this would run, and now it's not." Haller asked Yang to bring Filo to the conference room to explain the problem. "David stood in the doorway—he wouldn't even come in the room," she recalls. "I asked him, 'What is the danger?' I tried to get him to walk us through the problem. He said, 'I don't know if it will work on this scale.' He was afraid if they opened up the doors to customers all at once, what if it didn't work?"

Haller suggested they run a beta test over the weekend, e-mailing a thousand or so steady users, whose addresses Filo had because they'd e-mailed Yahoo at one time or another, and asking them to preview the redesigned site. If the new features and software to host the ads stood up under the traffic, they'd know it was safe to launch. Filo agreed. The redesign performed well and debuted on schedule that Monday.

The appearance of ads on Yahoo triggered "a lot of e-mail saying, 'You sold out. I can't believe you're doing this,' "[6] Tim Brady said in *Architects of the Web*, by Robert H. Reid (John

Wiley & Sons, 1997). But the protests died down after a few days. The advertising program, however, "grew like wildfire," Haykin says. The next quarter, Yahoo gained 20 new advertisers, and the quarter after that, 50. While the average price of an ad was $20 per thousand page views, the most desirable advertisers got a break, with three to six months often thrown in free, Hall says. Yahoo also kicked off its promotions program with a sign-up for Visa cards through Citicorp on its home page.

Right after Yahoo's commercial launch, Netscape shot out of the gate with a record-setting IPO. Its shares surged 108 percent to $71, giving it a $2.2 billion market cap. Clearly, the timing for Net plays was right. "We were all there that morning at Yahoo when the news came through about the IPO," Haykin remembers. "We were in shock. Jerry has a relationship with Netscape, plus we'd been talking to Netscape about all kinds of partnerships and advertising relationships. It was like an air of disbelief. We wandered around for half an hour looking at each other and saying, 'Do you believe this?' It kind of dawned on everyone how successful Yahoo could be. But I still don't think anyone had any idea where Yahoo would get from a market-cap standpoint. It was kind of like, 'This could be a good-sized company.'"

Meanwhile, Haller was busy positioning Yang and Filo as the poster children for the Web. "The challenge was all about taking them from a noncommercial cult thing into a business without alienating their fan base," says Haller, who was Yahoo's account exec until she left Niehaus in October to form Antenna Group. "It was all about the greater good. I thought it was the ultimate counter to Microsoft's monopolistic practices.

"Every story we were telling about Yahoo had two agendas: One was to evangelize the Internet, with Jerry and David being represented as the quintessential expression of the Internet. If you want to know anything about the Internet, you use Yahoo. The other, which was very important initially, was the issue of how not to lose those initial users, how to launch a commercial, slick site with ads without alienating their largely college-age users."

In the fledgling business of promoting the Internet, Niehaus was a top firm, with clients that included future AOL acquisitions O'Reilly & Associates and Global Network Navigator as well as SPRY, for which CompuServe paid a whopping $100 million. The PR agency was one of only a handful that had chosen the Internet as a specialty, and it regularly invited journalists to its South San Francisco offices to surf the Web. Yahoo paid the agency one-third of its fee in stock, or 25,000 shares split among its three partners, by far the best part of the deal, according to Haller. "I thought, if I'm going to share your risk, I'm going to share your upside," Haller says. But in fact, Yahoo couldn't have afforded Niehaus if it hadn't accepted stock as payment.

In the six months she handled the Yahoo account, Haller's team generated 600 articles, not just in business and trade magazines but also in mainstream publications like *People* and *Rolling Stone*, an impressive feat. The publicity brought countless overtures from companies looking to partner with Yahoo, including offers from Times Mirror, Interactive Data Corporation, and Ziff Davis, which ended up investing in Yahoo and collaborating with it on Yahoo Europe, Yahoo Computing, and *Yahoo! Internet Life* magazine.

The publicity was great, but Yahoo's ability to make money was still the burning question. Even Moritz thought it was "very unclear what the business was"[7] and was at a loss to cite any other instance where a VC had funded a company that gave away its product for free. "Mike had taken a flier on this company, and he was very anxious to understand how he was going to get his million dollars back," Monego says.

Yahoo's board of directors—Yang, Filo, Moritz, Monego, Hall (who was corporate secretary and a nonvoting member), and Randy Adams—spent most of their monthly meeting brainstorming about business models. They chewed over advertising, licensing, and subscription versions—as well as a fusion of the three. How to maintain Yahoo's high level of service while undergoing the transformation to commerce was Yang's chief preoccupation in the meetings. Hall raised the idea of charging for higher placement in the search listings—now standard operating procedure for portals—but Yang shot it down. "One of the ideas we had was if you wanted to be at the top of the camera section and you were at cameraworld.com, you'd have to pay for it," Hall says. "But that was never accepted as being a viable revenue model—it went against David and Jerry's view of what the site should be. Jerry's belief was that the search had to be fast and free for everyone."

Yang and Filo were determined not to abandon their ideals. "There was a great deal of discussion and debate about the open democracy of the Web and the need to give back as well as take," Monego says. Yang and Filo insisted on including search links to competitors such as Lycos, Infoseek, and AltaVista on the home page so users who weren't satisfied with Yahoo's results would know where else to look. "We will let the users decide what's best for them," Yang told BusinessWeek Online. "As we always say, Yahoo also stands for 'you always have other options.' "[8]

While Yahoo was gathering commercial steam, Moritz had been shopping for a CEO. Tim Koogle agreed to meet with Moritz's headhunter, Alan Sabourin—but only as a favor because Sabourin had found him his previous job, president of Intermec, a Seattle maker of bar-code scanners. During his three-year tenure, Koogle had taken Intermec from $150 million to $300 million in sales. Yahoo piqued Koogle's interest, and on a Sunday in June, he met Yang and Filo at the Tied House brewpub in Mountain View.

"Here were a couple of very smart guys who were genuinely passionate about what they were doing and not in it for the money or the ego or the fame," Koogle told *Fortune*. "They also struck me as being well aware of what they didn't know. Then there was this thing they'd built called Yahoo. And in spite of the fact that they had spent no money on promotion or branding, it was getting what we call strong organic takeup— people were finding it and using it, and telling their friends about it. Whenever you see something like that, it usually indicates that it's something people really, really want."[9]

Yang and Filo were drawn to Koogle, then 43, because he seemed "willing to put up with a lot of change,"[10] Yang said. With Koogle's nine years in operations and corporate venture capital at Motorola, they felt he had the goods to shepherd Yahoo through many stages of growth. And best of all, the demanding Moritz—who had interviewed a half-dozen candidates for the job before okaying Koogle—was satisfied, too. "He's very decisive and very focused," Moritz said of Koogle.[11]

Besides, Koogle belonged to the Stanford club, with an M.S. and a Ph.D. in engineering. And he, too, had an entrepreneurial streak: rebuilding wealthier students' car engines—a skill he learned from his mechanic father—to help put himself through Stanford and later cofounding a number of tech start-ups. Like Yang and Filo, he gave off casual, nonmaterialistic vibes. He lived in a one-bedroom apartment for three years after he moved to the Valley and then replaced it with a modest house. The folksy turns of phrase he'd picked up as a kid growing up in Alexandria, Virginia—among them, "possum syndrome"[12] for indecisive people and "rowboat syndrome"[13] for those stuck in the past—reinforced the low-key impression. "There are lots of people in Silicon Valley who start and end with 'How do I make lots of money?' " Koogle said. "I'm not about that."[14] In August, he came aboard as president and CEO.

From the unique vantage point granted to Taysom as an observer on Yahoo's board until its IPO, he saw Koogle in action. Among Koogle's finest early accomplishments, he quickly established metrics—unique visitors, repeat visitors, page views, amount of inventory sold—to help advertisers and analysts gauge Yahoo's progress. "Moritz's choice of Koogle was inspired," Taysom says. "Koogle was very strong on performance-measurement targets and allowing the Chief Yahoos to be the Yahoos whilst he was the steady but never indulgent management guy. He was very impressive. It's hard to put across just how well the whole phase was handled."

Other hires swiftly followed. Thirty-year-old Jeff Mallett left his job as vice president and general manager of Novell's worldwide consumer division to sign on as COO. Gary Valenzuela, a former CFO for software company TGV, joined as CFO, and Anil Singh, who had spent 13 years in sales for high-tech start-ups, as a sales executive and then senior VP of sales. Karen Edwards, a BBDO refugee, became VP for brand marketing.

The personalities of top management meshed remarkably well. Consensus-happy Koogle ("T.K.")—considered a detriment after the bursting of the bubble called for more authoritarian leadership—fit Yahoo's informal culture and wasn't fazed by ceding center stage to Yang, a natural with a mic. Together they focused on strategy. The wired, scrappy Mallett, nicknamed Sparky and called "one of the best managers I've ever run across" by Hall, owned day-to-day operations. Filo was happy to retreat to his cubicle, where he could play tech guru in peace, hiding behind a mass of papers or grabbing some shuteye under his desk. Filo's girlfriend at the time was in New York. He'd call her at night from his cubicle, work until he fell asleep to make up for the lost time, go home in the morning to shower, and return to the office around noon.

Monego left Yahoo in September. By the time Haykin and Hall left in November, Yahoo's staff numbered 25.

$\backsim$

*N*ow the company was established enough to round up new investors. It had dozens of paying advertisers, 20,000 Web pages, and millions of daily hits. As a parting gift, Monego had begun negotiating with the giant Japanese software publisher and distributor Softbank, the computer-magazine publisher Ziff Davis, and Reuters—all companies that fit Yang's forward-looking goal: "to leverage strategic relationships for future financing, rather than raising money." In other words, all three companies had content and clout Yahoo could put to work for it.

"Primarily, we're a brand," Yang said, explaining Yahoo's choice of partners. "We're trying to promote the brand and build the product so that it has reliability, pizzazz, and credibility. The focus of all the business deals we are doing right now is not on revenues but on our brand."[15]

That November, the second round of financing closed, with Reuters contributing $1 million for a 2.5 percent stake (which it sold later for a total of $80 million, 80 times its initial investment), and Softbank and Ziff Davis each $2 million for 5 percent stakes. (To hedge its bet, Reuters developed a search-engine project internally named Rahoo, and spent tens of millions of dollars on search and retrieval database hardware and software. Reuters later scrapped Rahoo, no doubt due to all the competition it faced.) In a dazzling coup, Yahoo's management had asked for, and received with no fight, a $40 million valuation just eight months after Sequoia had valued Yahoo at $4 million.

"OK, you guys had a million bucks and you've burnt about a half of it already," Koogle told his troops, according to *Champions of Silicon Valley*. "We're going to start some revenue and we're going to keep the head count really tight. We're going to make this thing profitable. But this is going to be a big game. One thing I've learned in the past is, go raise money when you don't need it. Capitalize the hell out of your business. Even to the extent that you give up a little in dilution. And get ready. Because if you want to play big, play big."[16]

Softbank would be Yahoo's gateway to the Japanese market, while Ziff Davis, which Softbank bought that very month, would lend its hand in Europe. The importance of the partnership to Yahoo was reflected in the addition of a Ziff Davis representative to its board, Chairman and CEO Eric Hippeau. And the benefits would flow both ways: After Ziff Davis swapped the *"ZD"* in *ZD Internet Life*, its one-year-old magazine, for *"Yahoo!,"* circulation quickly doubled to 200,000.

Sealing the deals with Softbank, Reuters, and Ziff Davis was a major feather in Koogle's cap. "I was incredibly impressed by how Tim Koogle came in and within weeks, he closed all these deals that were outstanding and locked in relationships with Softbank and Reuters," Haykin says. "His acumen brought everything together."

In its 1996 annual report, Yahoo reported a net loss of $634,000 on revenues of $1.4 million for 1995—a proud achievement compared to the performance of so many of its fellow dotcoms, which were burning through millions of VC dollars and racking up huge losses.

Chapter 3

Sunnyvale, 1996

Key Events

- April: Yahoo, Excite, and Lycos go public, cumulatively raising almost $120 million.
- April: Lucent Technologies' IPO raises a staggering $3 billion.
- June: Infoseek goes public, raising almost $42 million.
- October: Microsoft launches its MSN proprietary network, offering limited access to the Internet.

*I*n late 1995, Yahoo entertained a group of Goldman Sachs bankers at Pioneer Way. Goldman had already handled IPOs for a couple of Internet-access providers, Netcom in fall 1994 and UUNET in spring 1995, and was now ready to turn its attention to content. By then, there were about a dozen Internet service providers (ISPs), versus some 7,000 now, meaning the infrastructure was in place to spawn the next big generation of Internet companies: consumer services.

Goldman had been making the rounds to private search companies like Excite, Magellan, and SPRY. The purpose of this meeting was to suss out Yahoo's focus, and the bankers went away well satisfied. "Unlike a lot of companies in the same emerging space, Yahoo was coming at this from a directory perspective," says Goldman's Michael Parekh, the lead analyst on Yahoo's IPO. "Most of the other companies were started by engineers trying to build a better mousetrap in terms of search. Yahoo had a broader vision and a focused vision.

"I'd spent a lot of time with AOL. We'd been recommending those guys. What struck me was Yahoo had the opportunity to try to build AOL type of services without the focus on the access component." In other words, content and commerce.

Goldman's team, which included bankers Lawton Fitt and Brad Koenig, was also drawn to the intangibles. "You're making judgments on people and your perception of their ability to execute where a template doesn't exist amongst the group of companies," Parekh explains. "We were looking at the Yahoo people, and they were the only ones thinking about online services built on top of search and directory, and from day one, they were fixated on the consumer—whereas the founders of almost every company were thinking about this from a technology standpoint. Yahoo's people said, 'We'll just license whatever is the best technology and build services around it to take advantage of the traffic.' That's the model that resonated for me, because I'd seen it work for AOL and CompuServe. But these guys were trying to do it without having the capital-intensive part of the market where you have to build access networks."

Winning over Goldman, one of the most storied and successful investment banks in the world, gave Yahoo the Wall Street imprimatur it needed for its next phase of life. Two of Yahoo's competitors, Excite and Lycos, had announced plans to go public, so Yahoo had no choice but to move swiftly—especially if it wanted to preserve its precious first-mover advantage. "We didn't want to risk having the other guys go public while we didn't," Yang told Anthony Perkins and Michael Perkins, authors of *The Internet Bubble* (HarperBusiness, 1999). "Not only would they have the extra cash, but they could also use the stock as currency to acquire other companies. To have Excite and Lycos out there consolidating the market while we couldn't would've been a huge mistake. I also think the market at the time was clearly receptive to a story like ours."[1] That is, a story about an Internet media company, not a rant about tech.

In February 1996, Yahoo moved to new digs, only slightly more spacious and not much more glamorous than the old ones, at 635 Vaqueros in Sunnyvale, a misnomer for a deserted town with wide empty streets and ugly buildings. There, in conference rooms with names like Sneezy and Grumpy after Snow White's seven dwarves, Yahoo execs, VCs, and bankers held another powwow to strategize for the IPO and plan the month-long road show in March, a coming-out party for the public-company-to-be to meet its suitors, institutional investors. The bankers were already deluged with requests to buy, partly because, in a first for an upcoming offering, Yahoo had posted its prospectus on the Web. And the company's user base was growing relentlessly, with 6 million daily page views that month, twice its traffic in September.

Goldman wasn't the only entity looking to get a big piece of Yahoo. Softbank's founder and CEO, Masayoshi Son, decided his $4 million stake wasn't nearly enough. With revenues of some $1.7 billion that year, Softbank could afford to throw some more cash at Yahoo. Son flew to California to float his proposal in person: He wanted to buy the operation. But Yang and Filo were no more willing to sell out now than they'd been when AOL and Microsoft had come calling. Son countered with an investment offer of $100 million.

Yang and Filo agonized over the offer, which would require them to sell off a major chunk of their equity. They worried about future shareholders viewing this as a sign of lapsed faith, and that if Softbank owned the third of Yahoo it was demanding in return, it would exert too much influence on the company's culture, making it more structured Japanese and less freewheeling Silicon Valley. Then there were the less rational, more emotional arguments.

"It's like giving part of your kid away," Yang said. "It really feels like that."[2]

But the money would also mean more freedom for the kid, which would be less dependent on the proceeds from its IPO to scale up its business and freer to channel its resources into building its brand and adding content and services, through acquisitions as well as in-house development. Yang and Filo decided to accept, but only if Sequoia would sell an equal number of shares. Moritz agreed, telling the two they'd be foolhardy to tie their entire net worth up in Yahoo, no matter how much faith they had in its future. The three each sold Son about 10 percent of their 25 percent stakes, giving him a stake of 37 percent. Yahoo's former interim-management team also pitched in, selling a portion of their shares to Softbank to round out the numbers.

"We watched our competitors getting bigger allies and realized that to grow faster we needed some big trains," Mike Moritz said. "We wanted to avoid getting gauzumped by the competition."[3]

Not only did Son's money make gauzumping less likely, it made Yang and Filo instantly wealthy, to the tune of $12.5 million each—a pittance considering that Yahoo's shares reached a split-adjusted high of $237.50 in January 2000 but a fortune for them at the time. Still, no immediate lifestyle changes were evident. "Being a core part of a business that affects many people is different and takes some getting used to, but I am surprised at how little has changed in my life," Yang said in *Yahoo! Unplugged*. "Dave and I are still the same old guys who dress badly and drive beat-up cars."[4] In fact, Filo stayed in the same one-bedroom Mountain View apartment he shared with a roommate and, to this day, hasn't sold a share of Yahoo stock for his own gain—though at the end of 2000, he cashed in 100,000 shares worth $3.5 million to use as a gift. Yang eventually bought a house in upscale Los Altos and has sold several hundred thousand shares.

Son's investment in Yahoo whetted his appetite for Internet companies. He began snapping them up, buying all or part of dozens of companies, including I/PRO, E*Trade, and PointCast. Lately, he has paid the price for those acquisitions, as Softbank's stock has plunged from a high of about $600 during the height of the dot-com frenzy to about $16.80 as of January 2001.

◡

*I*t wasn't only Yahoo's offices that needed revamping as the IPO approached. Yahoo's PR handlers realized the cool, Net-savvy image they'd cultivated might actually be a detriment in wooing the Wall Street crowd. It was time for a PR makeover. "The idea of wild and crazy guys who sleep under their desks doesn't engender a lot of confidence on Wall Street," says Neihaus' Bill Ryan, who took over the Yahoo account after Melody Haller left. "We had to step up the gas on evangelizing the business model: running a business on banners, the monetization of eyeballs, and community."

Or as Yahoo's new brand steward, Karen Edwards, put it, "We needed to convince the press that advertising on the Internet was a viable business."[5]

Ryan started pitching the business press heavily, emphasizing Yahoo's experienced new management team and scrapping Yang's poster-child-of-the-Web positioning in favor of a mature Rupert-Murdoch-of-the-Internet image. In this first volley of the incipient portal wars, the challenge lay in differentiating Yahoo from Excite, Lycos, and Infoseek. "They were all based on search," Ryan says. "Yahoo had to get a different approach. We thought about it as a media company. Started describing it as a media company. The vision was to create a place that would connect anybody with anything they needed or anybody they needed." Stories appeared in publications such as *BusinessWeek*, *Advertising Age*, and *Marketing Computers*.

Karen Edwards sought out a brand-new San Francisco ad agency, Black Rocket—formed by two vets from Hal Riney and another from Goodby, Silverstein—to take Yahoo's message to the people. "She said enough to convince us the Internet was going to be a real business and would change our lives, and we should get into it early," says John Yost, a cofounder of Black Rocket—which later also designed campaigns for petstore.com, buy.com, and ourhouse.com—and former general manager of Hal Riney. "We spent a lot of time talking about what we thought was an opportunity for them to distinguish themselves from the others, not just on the basis of the product but on the basis of a personality they could develop for time.

"We saw the targeted audience moving well beyond the very narrow and small number of people who were actively involved in the Internet—the nerdy, geeky side of the Net. We saw this truly had mass-audience appeal, and we tried to imagine what the needs of those new people—'near surfers'—would be. They weren't currently surfing the Net, but we knew based on projections, they'd be the next to come into the marketplace. We knew they'd make decisions more on the basis of the brand, that they'd make choices on the Internet very much the same way they choose between different soap products or bread or anything that involves multiple choices. They'd be emotionally based, not just rational, decisions."

Yost, too, felt a sense of mission. "It was a new, emerging, fun, tech-driven but consumer-based business, and everyone was excited about that."

The Yahoo team had a sophisticated, nuanced view of what it takes for a company to stay ahead and an appreciation of the importance of intangibles like image, Yost says. "They understood that leadership can be both real and perceived. You can still be the perceptual leader of a category. They were ahead in enough of the product areas, either through acquisition or development of their own, to be able to convince consumers or the community or the VCs that they could stay ahead of the curve, that they were innovators."

Hungry for more first-mover points, Yahoo plunked down some $4 million (small change compared to the $50-odd million it spends on advertising today) for a year's worth of TV and radio ads aimed at winning consumers' emotional allegiance. The first

TV spots appeared during late-night and sports programming in the New York and San Francisco markets (since the budget wasn't big enough for national coverage) two weeks before the IPO and periodically afterward. Radio kicked in later that year. Each of the quirky, entertaining ads closed with the now-famous "Do you Yahoo!?" tag line and the signature yodel: Ya-hoo-oo-oo! Each spot offered a wacky problem-solving scenario. In the first to air, a man is fishing in a pond but having no success. He goes inside his house, logs on to Yahoo, and punches in the keyword "bait." A list of results pops up. The scene cuts back to the pond, where the man is fishing again, but this time he's surrounded by 30 or 40 500-pound tuna. As thanks for their ingenuity, the Black Rocket team, still Yahoo's ad agency today, was offered shares at friends' and family prices, and Yost took full advantage.

$$\backsim$$

*Y*ahoo filed for its public offering on March 7. During the road show, Koogle wowed his audience with his answer to the standard question, "What keeps you up at night?" He explained that though Yahoo's competitors numbered no fewer than five, the company was the only one of its class that had put the emphasis on creating a brand and an image as well as a service.[6] "We could see it was going to be a hot deal," says Lise Buyer, then an analyst at T. Rowe Price, one of the stops on the road show. Management's stellar performance helped trigger a frenzy for shares. As the IPO neared, a Goldman Sachs clerk reportedly received more than a hundred calls per hour from investors trying to get in on the action. The 11 pages Yahoo's filing devoted to delineating the risks of the Internet-directory business did nothing to dampen the enthusiasm.

The bankers wanted to cash in by charging $25 a share. "This was Goldman's first big Internet deal," Yang said. "They would have felt bad leaving money on the table because they knew if they kept their institutional customers happy, those clients would buy more deals down the line because they would have a sense of how to make money off the Internet."[7] But the normally reticent Filo put his foot down. He insisted that the individual investors get a fair shake. The more seasoned members of the team also had a less altruistic motive for keeping the price low: It would then be much more likely to rise steeply on IPO day, stirring lots of great buzz, and much less likely to subsequently slip below its IPO price. Since Softbank had just paid $13 a share for its private stake, the execs decided to use that number as their target offering price.

Just before the IPO, a curious occurrence illustrated just how charged the atmosphere had become: John Taysom was blackballed from Yahoo's board for allying himself with a competitor. Reuters had invested in Infoseek, and Taysom had decided to join that company's board. "It posed a conflict— people were pretty grumpy about that," Monego remembers. Just before Taysom parted ways with Yahoo's board, a new member joined, Art Kern, the founder of American Media and a Westinghouse vet. Taysom was impressed, since Yahoo could now leverage Kern's deep background in the TV ad business. The next addition to Yahoo's board, telecom VC and ex-Cisco CTO Edward Kozel, wouldn't arrive till 2000, contributing to charges of insularity.

In April, the portals hit the public markets, seemingly in one fell swoop. There was Lycos' IPO on April 2, followed by Excite's on April 4, and Yahoo's on April 12. Infoseek brought up the rear on June 11. While they all did well (Lycos' market cap reached nearly $241 million, Excite's $206 million, and Infoseek's $259 million), only Yahoo hit the stratosphere.

On IPO day, despite all the strategizing about price, the stock opened at $24.50, driven by the wild demand. Reporters from every conceivable sort of publication descended on the company. "Because many of our employees are young and inexperienced, we have to train them to become media savvy very quickly, so they won't spill confidential information to the press," Karen Edwards noted.[8] Not willing to take any chances, Yahoo locked the door to keep a lid on the hype, figuring it wouldn't help and might very well hurt. The company's aim was to distance itself from the glamour and send the message that it was in business for the long haul.

Each of Yahoo's 2.6 million new shares was swapped almost seven times that day. The stock rose 154 percent, climbing to $43 before settling back at $33, enough to bring the company's valuation to $848 million—more than 120 times its expected 1996 revenue—and to beat Netscape's 108 percent first-day gain. In fact, that 154 percent was good enough for third place in the all-time first-day-gain standings. Yang and Filo were each worth about $130 million on paper. Softbank profited by close to $200 million. And the investing public made out well, too. If Yahoo had chosen to issue its shares at $25 each, it could have raked in at least $30 million more, but instead that money was transferred to investors.

Some who had scoffed at the hoopla were surprised at how well Yahoo's IPO came off. "Yet Another Highly Overhyped Offering" and "the deal from hell"[9] is how Manish Shah had described it in his newsletter, *IPO Maven*. But, he says, "the stock did far better than I anticipated. It was a puzzle I couldn't solve until I found out that most of the investor base was individuals. Yahoo did manage to accomplish many goals: It got the early branding, early success in building a navigational directory, and early on also built Yahoo Finance, which was the reason many people reached Yahoo. It put out lots of information for individual investors free of charge."

In Sunnyvale, Yahoo's 40-odd employees rang in the company's new status with a bash. Srinija Srinivasan called the day "just a total rush,"[10] but others were more subdued. The full import of being beholden to investors was dawning on Yang, who said he felt "panic—no, not panic, but anxiety."[11]

In any case, reality soon set in. The stock was down to $18 by mid-summer, where it more or less stayed put for the rest of the year, waiting for the promise of the Internet to produce more tangible signs. But unlike that of its competitors, Yahoo's stock never dipped below its IPO price. By October, Lycos, Excite, and Infoseek were all trading at a fraction of their offering prices.

Yahoo's IPO success was reflected in some tried-and-true ways. Yang replaced his Oldsmobile Cutlass with a four-wheel-drive Honda Passport. Others went further.

"In early 1996, I was looking around with another colleague of mine at the cars in the parking lot—Nissans, Toyotas, middle-range cars—and I said to my friend, 'I bet this is going to change,'" says Alex Alben, then VP of business affairs at Starwave and now a public-policy exec at RealNetworks, who did a content deal with Yahoo that year. "Next time we were back there was within six months, and I noticed the Porsches, Mercedeses, and other high-end sports cars."

Though the IPO raised plenty of cash, Eric Hall faults his successor, Gary Valenzuela, for not milking the capital markets as aggressively as he could have during this relative boom time. "They did their IPO, but it was also a time to raise some very cheap capital via syndicated credit agreements, public and private debt offerings, etc., to take advantage of opening up sources of capital other than the equity markets," Hall says. "You should always finance to the worst-case scenario. This was a common failure of a lot of dot-com CFOs. They forgot that the capital markets can also be tight."

⌇

*B*ut Yahoo didn't waste any time in taking its act overseas, where 35 percent of its traffic already originated. Just 10 days after going public, it announced the launch of Yahoo Japan as a joint venture with Softbank, taking 40 percent and 60 percent stakes, respectively. Going global would connect Yahoo to more users so it could sell more advertising at higher prices. The move carried some risk of leaving the company with higher costs it couldn't cover. But by penetrating foreign markets early, Yahoo could also once again seal its first-mover status and increase the likelihood of its becoming the dominant brand in the area—exactly what ended up happening in Japan. Besides, partnering with Softbank in Japan and then Ziff Davis in Europe cut Yahoo's risk, since it could tap those companies' existing infrastructures (everything from their offices to their sales reps), content, and knowledge of the regions, reducing its cash outlay.

For Koogle, accepting Softbank's money was tied to a realization of what Softbank could do for Yahoo abroad: "We sat down with Son and said, 'You know, we want you as an investor to help us capitalize this company, but the business relationship also means leverage in international markets.' " Koogle said he was thinking, "Maybe, if we structure this thing right with Softbank, we can go and launch properties in other parts of the world, in partnership with those guys. Make use of their infrastructure. Not have to invest in that. When we invest we invest light, but we invest in the people who are actually adding value from day one."[12]

The peculiar restrictions of the Japanese market made having a partner particularly important. "In Japan, it's a whole different beast—you almost have to do a joint venture to be really successful in business," says Gloria Gavin, Yahoo's director of international business development from 1997 to 1998. "It's very much a closed environment. You'd have to partner up with an already-existing partner because localization and language are much bigger issues."

Softbank set up an office in Tokyo and hired a manager, Masahiro Inoue, to run the show and put together a local staff of producers, surfers, and salespeople. "We didn't just try to take an American product and put it out there," Gavin says. "We built a whole new directory on top of the core Yahoo and hired local people." And each foreign site was in the local language.

In the first effort by an American Net guide to establish a foreign outpost, Yahoo beat Infoseek, Lycos, and Excite as well as the local competition to the Japanese market. Yahoo Japan would prove to be one of the company's most profitable enterprises. Its low dependence on dot-com advertisers—which made up only about 25 percent of total ad revenue versus 47 percent for its parent at the pinnacle—and growing business from old-line companies like retailers and restaurants have helped shield it somewhat from the debacle. "Yahoo Japan's business model from the profitability standpoint is much better than in the United States," says Thomas Rodes, director of Nikko Salomon Smith Barney in Tokyo. (Still, things had gotten muddier by the third quarter of 2000, when concerns about the effectiveness of online advertising began to take hold.)

Despite the advantages of having a partner with local clout, Yahoo didn't benefit as much from Yahoo Japan as it would have had it retained a larger stake, a fact that certainly didn't escape the company's notice. "They kind of avoided doing joint ventures after Yahoo Japan," Gavin says. "It was more profitable to maintain full control."

In fact, Yahoo did just one more minority-share joint venture after Japan, partnering with the media conglomerate Rogers Communications in Canada. "It was a really bad deal," Gavin says. "Rogers had the majority share but didn't do much with it. They were slow. We ended up renegotiating that deal and starting fresh. It was the only time a partner was more of a liability than an advantage."

For its next major international foray, the ownership roles were reversed, with Yahoo grabbing 70 percent and Ziff Davis 30 percent. Yahoo Europe kicked off in the United Kingdom, Germany, and France, which, along with the rest of Western Europe, harbored some 8 million Internet users. The potential looked endless: Forrester Research was estimating that the European market for online services would be the fastest-growing in the world over the next two years, with annual growth rates exceeding 80 percent. Yahoo's international push attracted first-class advertisers like IBM and Hewlett-Packard, which chose Yahoo to launch global online campaigns, and garnered higher fees: On average, advertisers paid a robust $45 per thousand impressions—cost per mille (CPM), in industry parlance—compared to $20 to $25 for the main domestic site.

In a perk of its partnership with Ziff Davis, Yahoo inherited

Heather Killen, now 42, an Australian and former member of Salomon Brothers' media and telecom corporate-finance team. She'd been handling Ziff Davis' online-business development in Europe and would now oversee Yahoo's international efforts. "She was a really tough driver," Gavin says admiringly. "She worked really long hours, and she really understood the different markets."

The big hurdle abroad was that old-line companies such as Deutsche Telekom and France Telecom, repositories of the yellow pages and white pages Yahoo coveted, weren't convinced yet that the Internet would be central to their business. They weren't in a hurry because they controlled the country's Internet connections. Initially, most of the money to be made from deals came from ad-revenue splits, just as in the case of Reuters. The nature of the deals evolved as the business evolved. "We were all kind of making it up as we went along in terms of what the deal was and how do we make money at this," Gavin says. "A lot of times, it was a revenue split. Sometimes it was about whoever drove eyeballs—it was all about paying for eyeballs. Sometimes it was a little bit of both—not that I pay you, but we pay each other depending on who's delivering value."

The dynamic of Yahoo having to coax reluctant European companies to do deals changed as it began to woo away their users. Then Gavin began signing up all the big European media companies and their music and magazine divisions. Soon those companies were paying Yahoo for its ability to steer traffic their way. Finally, they were paying just for the promise of what Yahoo could deliver. "As Yahoo started stealing share from the large ISPs, as it became less search and more portal, they started talking because they had no choice," Gavin explains. "There was this huge fear factor as Yahoo became a destination. It was a huge competitive threat to all these companies.

"Once Yahoo became a huge portal with a huge amount of traffic, then we were commanding huge fees for people to have placement on the sites. When I started at Yahoo, we had a lot of these revenue-sharing deals where as we drove traffic, they were paying for clicks. Maybe it was in the tens of thousands, up to a couple-hundred-thousand type of deal. By the time I left, we were commanding multimillion-dollar fees, everything from $5 million to $20 million, and it was kind of a combination, not just paying us for click-throughs or results but just paying for the privilege of having a button up there because we could drive so much traffic to your site."

⌒

While Yahoo was busying itself abroad in 1996, it also began building local communities in the United States, launching one city guide after another, in San Francisco, Los Angeles, New York, Chicago, Washington, D.C., and Boston. Each guide had dozens of partners like TV stations and newspapers contributing local content: news, classifieds, sports scores, weather reports, information on entertainment and businesses, yellow pages, white pages, and interactive maps. Yahoo's Get Local service took the concept one step further, allowing users to plug in any of 40,000 zip codes and retrieve the same features offered by the local guides in 30,000 cities.

An abrasive deal maker from LATimes.com with an M.B.A. from Stanford, Ellen Siminoff, now 33, was hired to oversee business development for the community sites, which opened up whole new vistas of potential advertising clients looking to target users in their areas. For the targeting capacity of its local sites, Yahoo raked in CPMs of $30 to $40. By the end of October, its San Francisco site alone had 25 advertisers. Classifieds drew the most traffic. Yahoo made deals with national aggregators of classifieds in order to avoid having to chase individual advertisers and local newspapers that resisted giving away their classifieds for free. Similarly, it would get a national weather feed and divvy up the content locally.

"Anything with a local feel was very labor-intensive," says Elizabeth Collet, whom Ellen Siminoff hired out of Harvard Business School right after Yahoo's IPO. "You were much better off to get a national-weather feed by zip code—it was a way to take national content and divide it up locally and create local content for every city in the country with a lot less effort. It wasn't all hand-designed like Yahoo San Francisco with a San Francisco icon, the Golden Gate Bridge, laboriously chosen. Cost-benefit was really a huge trade-off. Initially, we tried to do classifieds locally by phoning all the employers and car dealers in each city. It turned out to be more effective to do business-development deals with big aggregators and use their content."

The content on Yahoo's main site was also burgeoning. Besides headline news, it added a welter of services—among them stock quotes, weather reports, horoscopes, events calendars, travel information, and maps—through partnerships with other companies. To improve its pure search capability, it licensed AltaVista's search engine, once again demonstrating that proprietary technology wouldn't be its focus. The new content set off an explosion in Yahoo's weekly page views, from 21 million in fall 1995 to 42 million in spring 1996 and 100 million the following fall.

Yahoo introduced My Yahoo, a customizable home page, to

cement its relationship with those millions of users and extract the sort of priceless personal data—name, birth date, e-mail address, zip code, occupation, interests, and permission to notify them of special offers—for which it could charge advertisers an arm and a leg. By letting users choose their own news, stock quotes, weather reports, sports scores, favorite Web sites, areas to bookmark, and other features, Yahoo effectively turned them into repeat customers. The service launched with a bevy of prestigious advertisers—including Lexus, IBM, and MCI—all keen for insights they could use to reach an audience that had plainly identified its interests (and kept identifying new ones every time they plugged in a search keyword). In comparison, the simple demographics supplied by TV and print outlets looked outdated and one-dimensional.

TV and print also didn't have access to click-through rates, which could definitively show how many people had seen a given ad. Click-through exemplified the promise of advertising on the Internet. "Yahoo had a luxury and a drawback," says Manish Shah, who advertised his investment-news site, 123jump.com, on Yahoo. "The Internet is so precise that advertisers can demand how many people came to the site, downloaded a banner, and clicked through. They have to deliver that information to advertisers. That became the downfall of virtually every Internet company. No TV or print company will have to say, 'I guarantee you 3 percent of people who buy the newspaper will read your ad,' and they get away with it. We never know the response rate for TV or *New York Times* ads. That works in their favor."

And TV and print wouldn't get embroiled in the privacy debates that rocked the Web later, especially after online ad firm DoubleClick started a huge controversy in 2000 by trying to merge offline and online data that would make it possible to identify individual Net users. DoubleClick also drew ire by requiring that consumers "opt out" if they didn't want their personal data collected. To avoid similar problems, the portals favored "opt in" policies that took the onus of exempting themselves off consumers and put it on the portals to request permission to collect data. Posting privacy policies became de rigueur. "Yahoo! will not sell or rent your personally identifiable information to anyone," Yahoo's policy promised. But the company reserved the right to "send"—not "sell"—personal information under certain conditions—among them, when the consumer had okayed it ("permission marketing") and when the information was necessary to provide a product or service the consumer had requested. Indirectly, of course, Yahoo *was* selling the information, since its access to it let the company charge advertisers a premium to target consumers. In fact, Yahoo was so gung-ho about the future of permission marketing that in 1998, it bought a company devoted to it, Yoyodyne, founded by marketing personality and author Seth Godin.

But Yahoo was careful not to do anything that privacy advocates could finger as intrusive. "It became important to prove you weren't abusing the data in the context of users' desire for privacy," Parekh comments. "This is an opposition in theory that AOL and Yahoo have, but [Yahoo has] chosen to not use the data as aggressively as they could to not infringe on the privacy of users." AOL, however, deluges its members with e-mailed special offers.

Still, Yang recognized early on that selling targeted advertising could give Yahoo a big boost: "Most sites sell banner advertising based on the fairly uneducated notion that if you stick a banner in a high-traffic site, then people will imprint them. A golf area may get only 10,000 hits a day, but they would all be from people interested in golf. I think that's more effective than putting some banner on the home page. . . . Our next step is working on more context-sensitive ads. The more qualified of a demographic we can provide, the better."[13]

Yahoo began forging strategic partnerships to draw more eyeballs and thus more advertisers that could be won over with fine-tuned data. "Our strategic goals are to get advertising and get in front of every browser in as many channels as we can," Yang said. "We want to build strategic relationships with two types of people: the ones who own the eyeballs—the online services, the ISPs, and the Netscapes of the world—and the content providers. A lot of publishers are realizing that they should be developing relationships with us. How we manage those content relationships is really the core of our business."[14]

This meant striking deals with other Web sites to provide a link to Yahoo. "We're on Prodigy, we're on eWorld, we're even on Microsoft Network's new Explorer page," Yang said. "We've been talking to them about relationships."[15] Netscape had informed Yahoo in December 1995 that it planned to rent the directory button that had pointed to Yahoo for free for almost a year. In the early days, anyone stumbling onto the Net needed Netscape's browser to navigate, so most of Yahoo's traffic had been generated through this link. Now, with multiple browsers and lots of sources sending traffic to Yahoo, it didn't depend on the Netscape link. Still, like many of the other search companies, Yahoo decided a link on Netscape was worth the big bucks it commanded and paid $5 million a year to be a "premier provider" through 1998, when it reevaluated and dropped out of the program.

Why would competitors like Netscape, Microsoft, and

Prodigy want Yahoo in their midst, anyway? "There are a lot of reasons why these people want to work with us," Yang explained. "One is performance and quality—it's much better for them to have us on-site. More importantly, they want to secure a relationship that will be here today, not gone tomorrow. Directories are so strategically important to a lot of online services that they require that peace of mind. In Microsoft's case, they're behind in terms of launching a product, and they need the leverage we provide. They want to see more Internet, whatever that means. We're not the only choice—they license Lycos, for example—but we are one of them."[16]

Yahoo's "independence and impartiality" enabled it to partner with all the services it wanted, Tim Brady pointed out, unlike competitors AOL and Microsoft, which made exclusive deals with other companies. "One of the problems Microsoft Network has in terms of building an index is people's perception that they would be pointed towards Microsoft stuff," Brady said. "Perception of independence is pretty important."[17]

Yahoo sealed deals with big multinational and small niche players alike. "Not only are we linking users to content," Koogle said, "but we're tightening and tightening and tightening the relationship between Yahoo and other companies who are trying to find eyeballs."[18]

So, the goal was to develop relationships with companies that went beyond advertising. "What we tried to do was do partnerships," says Mike Nelson, one of the first salespeople Yahoo hired.

But that goal didn't always pan out. An "interactive promotional campaign" with Procter & Gamble, in which Yahoo splashed P&G banner ads across its site, appears to have been little more than a typical advertising deal. Yahoo didn't disclose how much it had been paid by P&G, one of the nation's largest advertisers and therefore one of the most desirable, or even if P&G had paid at all. Having P&G on the site would give Yahoo credibility. "P&G and Pepsi were paying, but nowhere near what you and I would pay if I called and said, 'I want to advertise,' " Shah says.

For Yahoo's early content partnerships in the United States, just like those abroad, money didn't always change hands. Some providers were happy to swap their content for a chunk of Yahoo's traffic or, in the case of a glamorous partner like MTV, a share of its ad revenue.

Alex Alben helped negotiate two content-for-traffic deals with Yahoo, first in his position at the Web-site producer Starwave and then later at the media-player company Real-Networks. When Starwave site ESPN SportsZone wanted help generating traffic, Yahoo seemed like the best candidate. SportsZone started feeding Yahoo sports headlines in late 1995. "The economics in this kind of Web deal weren't spelled out," says Alben, echoing Gavin. "We'd sit around tables and say, 'Should we pay you, or should you pay us?' There was no precedent."

As a result, both sides agreed on a reciprocal deal. Yahoo would receive headlines that linked to SportsZone articles once or twice a day. Although those links ended up being a major driver of Starwave's traffic, the arrangement still created a sense of unease. "There's always tension in these types of relationships because everyone wants the eyeball, and they want to retain the eyeball," Alben explains. "Yahoo wanted the traffic to stay on their site, and we wanted to drive traffic to our site. I think portals understood they'd get X number of page views and then lose the eyeball. But they still built out their content sections in order to retain the person visiting the site as long as possible."

RealNetworks still profited from Yahoo's development of its movie section in early 1998, when RealNetworks' film.com site supplied Yahoo with links to movie trailers. "Film.com got very significant traffic from Yahoo, and we monetized that through advertising revenue," Alben says. And RealNetworks also benefited in another way: Its deals with Yahoo helped gain support for its formats. "It was very important for companies like Real-Networks to make sure Yahoo was supporting their formats," Alben says. "RealNetworks did a number of deals to make sure Yahoo would support Real audio and video, which they do today. It's a mutual relationship, because Real has 200 million Real players installed."

Unfortunately, though, the charges of arrogance and mismanagement that would plague Yahoo later first surfaced in some of its early deals. In one of the more acrimonious of these, Yahoo teamed up with MTV to create unfURLed, a music search engine. "Yahoo felt like the most brand-appropriate for MTV—it had the most brand personality," recalls Matt Farber, then senior vice president of programming and new business for MTV and now founder of consulting company Wilderness Media & Entertainment. "It always felt like the leader in its category, and we wanted to be with the leader in the category."

Farber says MTV bought into a vision to create the ultimate cobranded music search engine and blames both companies for failing to fulfill that vision. Both neglected unfURLed, he says, because they were too busy developing their core businesses, and it died about a year after its launch in January 1997. "It had the potential to be a defining brand on the Internet," Farber says. "But neither party ever really made it a priority. We were still building mtv.com and doing experimental things, and this was only one small piece of Yahoo. In some ways, it was a bastard stepchild for both companies."

But there were extenuating factors that hastened the demise of the partnership. In midstream, Yahoo switched strategies, according to Farber. "There was a seismic shift in business, and they decided to create Netcenter powered by Yahoo," he says, referring to the short-lived Netscape Guide by Yahoo, a version of Yahoo that resided on Netscape. "They're all good people and their hearts were all in the right places, but what they planned to do and what excited them one month, they may have changed another. We got very upset, because you're now associating the Yahoo brand with another music brand. Our brand wasn't part of that deal. In looking at the deal we had with them, there were discussions about whether that was a violation of our agreement. It was hard to make agreements that contemplated three months down the road. There was no real loyalty, and unless you wanted to sue, in some ways your deal was only as good as . . ." He trails off.

Farber doesn't lay all the blame on Yahoo but also fingers the accelerated pace of deal making at the time and the rapidly changing marketplace. "They had to look at what was good for their business first, even though it might be frustrating for their partner," he says. "They were moving so fast they had no choice but to be reckless."

The rampant "coopetition"—companies trying to claw their way past each other and at the same time angling to strike mutually beneficial partnerships—created a supercharged atmosphere. "There was no such thing as true partnership," Farber says. "Yahoo was best at seizing every opportunity at that moment. Sometimes partners that were really dependent on them for their livelihood got left in their wake. What they did made them successful but also made them dangerous and difficult. I wouldn't have wanted to depend on them as a partner."

ABCNEWS.com also ran into problems with Yahoo, when at the height of its bargaining power, it tried to convert a long-standing content-for-traffic deal into a paid relationship. "We're giving them a bunch of tech stories a day, and in return, they're giving us traffic," says an ABCNEWS.com source who requested anonymity. "A year or two years ago, in addition to demanding content, they were demanding pay. We never really got to it. Six figures they wanted. I'm pretty sure CNET was paying them for content placement. The *New York Times* has a deal with them, and if they're not paying them, they may have had to buy advertising space. Every time we had negotiations, they wanted us to spend money on buying advertising on Yahoo. As a result of that, I don't believe we got premiere placement in some places. But it's a business, and you have to run your business the way you think it makes sense."

In addition to having to figure out how to run the business, Yang and Filo had a lot more content to worry about categorizing from all the partnerships. "Keeping up with the Web is going to be our biggest challenge," Yang said. "The social-engineering side will soon outweigh the technological maintenance side, if it hasn't already. Do we call it 'pro-choice' or 'anti-life,' where do we put homosexuals? Dave and I can go on for hours talking about these things."[19]

They solved one of those conundrums—placing homosexuals—in one of their very first partnerships, a content-for-traffic deal with the niche portal PlanetOut, which still supplies Yahoo with syndicated news about gays and lesbians. "It was important from a traffic standpoint and also for a baby company to be able to say, 'We have a partnership with Yahoo,' as we tried to establish ourselves," says Megan Smith, vice-chairman of PlanetOut's board and former CEO, sounding a note common to the many dot-com advertisers that threw money at Yahoo and ended up paying a steep price. "We got the business benefit of credibility and help with VCs"—fortunately, for free, which may partially explain why PlanetOut is still around.

By the fourth quarter of 1996, Yahoo had been rewarded for all its content building with 550 advertisers, among them many Fortune 500 companies and major brands like Wal-Mart, Coca-Cola, BellSouth, and Nabisco. To fuel its expansion, Yahoo opened sales offices in San Francisco, Los Angeles, New York, Chicago, and Dallas, and hired its own direct sales force, rather than continuing to rely on Softbank Interactive Marketing. But in mid-1996, up to 75 percent of Yahoo's potential ad space was still going unsold, according to Sue Decker, then an analyst at Donaldson, Lufkin & Jenrette and later Gary Valenzuela's replacement as CFO of Yahoo. Clearly, there was a lot more work to do.

In the first and fourth quarters, Yahoo also recorded small but symbolic profits, of $81,000 and $96,000, respectively. But the 1,300 percent increase in its revenues, to $19.7 million in 1996 from $1.4 million in 1995, was a lot more than symbolic. Meanwhile, its net loss grew to only $2.3 million from $634,000, less than analysts had predicted. Traffic was up to 14 million page views per day during December 1996. And the company was poised to weather the occasional storm with $100 million in cash on its balance sheet. In fact, in every major metric—stock price, market cap, cash, revenue, number of advertisers, CPMs, and total page views—Yahoo dwarfed its competitors. (See Table 3.1.)

Plus, the company had spent just $3 million in all of 1996 to achieve this record. "Amazingly, [Yahoo] has adhered to our Internet mantra of 'get big fast' without spending heavily to do

Table 3.1 Search Directories: Analysis of Comparable
Industry Metrics

Company	Excite	Infoseek	Lycos[a]	Yahoo
Ticker	XCIT	SEEK	LCOS	YHOO
Fiscal Year Ended	December	December	July	December
Stock Price 11/6/96	$6.00	$10.38	$11.50	$18.00
Market Capitalization ($MM)	$72.00	$263.53	$158.59	$472.68
Cash and Equivalents ($MM)	$30.42	$50.58	$44.14	$100.79
Most Recent Quarter Revenue ($MM)	$4.0	$4.0	$2.7	$5.5
Number of Advertisers	160	193	160	340
Average CPM	$18.00	$20.00	$19.00	$22.50[b]
Traffic: Average Page Views per Day (MM)	6.0[c]	3.5	4.0[d]	14.0

[a]Lycos analysis is based on company's most recent quarter, Q4 ended July 31, 1996.

[b]Estimate based on average of $20 to $25 CPM rate.

[c]Includes performance of acquired service, Magellan.

[d]Hambrecht & Quist estimate for October.

Sources: FactSet Data Service, company's financials/press releases, and company management.

Adapted from "Yahoo: Extending Its Brand Across the Internet and Beyond," company report, November 6, 1996.

so," [20] wrote Paul Noglows, an analyst with Hambrecht & Quist, in a fourth-quarter report on the company in which he raised his recommendation to a "strong buy."

With the number of Web users worldwide predicted to shoot from some 50 million to 200 million by the year 2000, and Web advertising expected to surge from $200 million to $3.5 billion, Yahoo's future looked golden.

Chapter

4

Santa Clara, 1997

Key Events

- May: Amazon.com has the year's best-performing IPO, raising $54 million and bringing its market cap to $438 million.

- June: CNET launches its Snap portal.

- September: Netscape launches its Netcenter portal.

- October: The U.S. Justice Department accuses Microsoft of antitrust violations for bundling its Internet Explorer browser with its operating system, Windows 95.

- November: AOL membership reaches 10 million.

With its content burgeoning, its local and international sites rolling out, and its new direct ad-sales force busy bundling multiyear, multimillion-dollar deals, Yahoo was ready to turn its attention to e-commerce. And itching to put her stamp on it was Elizabeth Collet, Ellen Siminoff's hire. Just having come off the failed Netscape Guide by Yahoo (see Chapter 6 for more details), Collet was eager for a new challenge.

It took a while for Yahoo to get comfortable with the blatant commercialism of e-commerce. "They grappled with the idea that commerce would add to revenues but wanted to make sure it was the right thing for the users," Collet explains. As a result, "at first Yahoo was adamantly opposed to position-placement deals like AOL did. They knew they could make money that way but started off focusing on making shopping just another piece of content. It's a tool." And even after Yahoo accepted such deals, it had to get used to the idea of multiyear versions, which Collet thought looked "desperate."

As a result of its dithering, the company was late entering the arena and already had plenty of competition in the form of AOL, Excite, and the year-old online bookseller Amazon.com when it took the plunge in August 1996 and established the Yahoo Marketplace as a joint venture with Visa. Problems with Visa from the start slowed the project down even more and, finally, killed it. "It never got going," Collet says. "Yahoo and Visa had very different goals. We'd agreed to this 50–50 venture, which meant neither of us had control."

While Visa was looking to promote only merchants using its new credit-card encryption technology, Yahoo wanted to be much more comprehensive. The Marketplace's president, Scott Randall, resigned in frustration. The project never proceeded beyond the planning stage, and Yahoo bought back Visa's half of the deal in spring 1997.

As part of the terms for shutting down the Marketplace, Yahoo agreed to put Visa's logo on its shopping site for three years, but Visa would no longer have any editorial control over the relaunched venture, called the Visa Shopping Guide by Yahoo. "We thought this was a win-win, that having the Visa logo would be a confidence booster for consumers," Collet says.

With a skeleton crew of Collet, a part-time engineer, and a part-time surfer, Yahoo launched its first commerce effort. It started out as a listing of online and offline merchants integrated with Yahoo's yellow pages and classifieds, so consumers could type in their zip code and find products in their area. But you couldn't buy stuff on Yahoo. "It was done on a shoestring," Collet says. "That's very much Yahoo's style—they'll dip their toe in the water, then if it works, they'll invest in that topic."

The shopping section got enough traffic over the 1997 holiday season that Yahoo decided to invest some serious dollars in staffing it up and getting it off the ground. By the next holiday season, it was called Yahoo Shopping, it handled transactions, and it had more than 3,000 merchants. Yahoo's mall concept had taken shape. The mall let each user shop across a wide selection of stores using one shopping cart and one credit-card transaction, with the information securely stowed in the user's electronic Yahoo Wallet. Collet claims the company was the first to offer a shopping cart across merchants, which proved a difficult technological feat. Product guides and consumer reports referred users to various merchants. "You're going to Yahoo because it's a gateway to all the stores," she says. "It's an aggregate. You don't have to go to each store to find out if they carry a specific item. You can go to Yahoo, and we'll search all of them."

Ultimately, though, you were buying from the merchant,

not from Yahoo—one reason the company began to institute commissions per sale and charge a fee for membership in its mall. In the beginning, "we were trying to aggregate and include anybody who had valuable content," Collet says. "We were thinking it was content for our users." Not everyone paid for the privilege of being included. But Yahoo eventually moved to a system where every merchant paid rent ($100 and up, depending on the number of items for sale) and, if they elected to participate in Yahoo Shopping, 2 percent of monthly sales over $5,000.

Still, the transaction portion of Yahoo's revenue stream from shopping was insignificant compared to the real jackpot: multimillion-dollar fees for multiyear placement on "buttons" on the shopping pages. The first button taker was Amazon.com, which ironically turned out to be an e-commerce archrival of Yahoo's after it, too, morphed into an all-purpose mall. Online music retailer CDnow soon followed. In a sign of how much these deals could cost, Yahoo's two online vitamin partners, Greentree and PlanetRx, later crashed, as did many other dot-coms that advertised on Yahoo.

"There was a land grab. It was no one's fault, but lots of companies were overinvesting and trying to grow too fast," Collet says. "It's hard to blame Yahoo for that—but sure, we were right there, taking the money." In the third quarter of 1997, 12 percent of Yahoo's revenues came from e-commerce placement deals and transactions, with the bulk from the former, according to Goldman's Michael Parekh.

Still, unlike AOL, Yahoo never milked the opportunity for all it was worth by doing exclusives. "The cardinal rule at Yahoo was we'd never do exclusives," says Collet, who headed business development and strategic planning for all of e-commerce—including Shopping, Auctions, Classifieds, Small

Business, Yellow Pages, Autos, Real Estate, Careers, Business to Business (B2B), and Finance—by the time she left Yahoo in 2000. "AOL would sell exclusivity. They'd say, 'You are the only music store or bookstore.' In exchange, they'd ask for very high dollars. I think that's a horrible user experience. The user should be able to decide and shouldn't have to use whoever paid AOL the most money. They should be able to search across merchants. We didn't care if we'd make more doing the wrong thing for the user. We thought if we did the right thing for the user, we'd make more money in the long run. That was a very fundamental difference between us."

But it's a philosophy that hasn't borne fruit, since AOL enables many more billions' worth of e-commerce transactions than Yahoo. And doing the right thing for the user didn't extend to keeping comparison-shopping technology that might send the user off Yahoo to other e-commerce areas of the Web (see Chapter 6).

⌐

Collet loved working at Yahoo. Yahoos were fiercely loyal (at least, before they cashed in their stock options and left), because the company gave them so much individual responsibility. "It was great for morale," she says. "It allowed the company to be nimble. You'd hire someone who was a sports expert, and they were given the autonomy, told, 'Go for it. Run that.' Everyone felt like they were running their own business. I think it was critical to the company's ability to be successful and stay ahead of the competition. It also allowed you to attract much more self-motivated, bright people who were self-starters, who wanted to run their own piece of the world"—qualities, she admits, that aren't so great once a company scales up and needs more accountability. Besides fully vested stock options, the shift to a more structured environment helps explain why so many old-timers have left Yahoo in the past year.

In 1997, management's role was still to coach and give input. "Management was so likable. T.K. had great style—he was very sexy in that way," says Collet, referring to Tim Koogle's trademark black turtleneck and black trousers. "He was very friendly, always stopping people in the halls and laughing and chatty. I'd almost have felt rude walking by his office and not stopping in to say hi."

People looked up to Jeff Mallett: He was *"the* guy," with no traces of the arrogance he'd later be skewered for, while Yang was "the philosophical leader." Collet spent many a late-night brainstorming session with Yang when e-commerce was being rolled out, "thinking about how far down in the transaction you'd carry Yahoo." Of course, the answer turned out to be all the way down.

Koogle, Mallett, and Yang sat in cubicles, in a row; only lawyers had offices, for confidentiality purposes. "You could go in around 7 A.M.—they'd be there, bantering around," recalls Collet, who at just 30 cashed in her options at $160 apiece and made substantial wealth. "If Jerry and Jeff disagreed, Jerry would back down. He'd be vocal, but in the end, he'd respect [Jeff]."

⤳

*T*he number of Yahoo's employees quintupled to 200 from early to late 1996 and, by the end of 1997, approached 400, leading to several more office moves, starting in August 1996. The spacious new digs at 3400 Central Expressway in Santa Clara featured fat chairs in signature Yahoo purple and yellow in the lobby and row upon row of cluttered beige cubicles upstairs, occupied by the twenty-something staff and the odd pet tarantula. In early 1998, Yahoo added more space at nearby 3420. The fanciful conference-room tradition continued, with the 3400 group named after the Ten Plagues (think Locusts, Boils, and Hail), and the 3420 group called Decent, Consistent, and Competent so people would be forced to say things like "I'm in Competent."

The addition of 3420 was difficult for many on the tight-knit staff, since people who'd worked side by side and become good chums were split up between the two buildings. "We would bump into people who worked in the other building and would say, 'Wow, it feels so different—I miss you!' " Collet says. "It was one aspect of growth that was really painful emotionally for lots of us. Being in two buildings for the first time was when we finally started saying, 'Wow, we are a big company.' "

∽

*M*ike Nelson was a salesman at Lycos in October 1996 when Anil Singh called him with a tantalizing offer to head up Yahoo's Dallas sales office. Within months, Nelson was also overseeing the Chicago and Detroit offices and, by 1999, a 20-state central region.

The companies in Nelson's region were of the traditional sort, like airlines and beverage companies, that needed a bit of convincing to make the leap to the Web, especially since their online-advertising "budgets" were typically dollars siphoned off from print and broadcast. But Nelson was just the sort of talented, tireless pitchster who could make them see the light. "We were making 10 sales calls a day, every day, and flying to every little city in our region. One day you're in Oklahoma City, then you're in Kansas City," Nelson says.

The idea was to convince these companies to do more than just buy banners. "Yahoo was a big player, so getting a meeting wasn't difficult," Nelson says, "but if you were just asking for ad dollars, you were just like any other ad salesman." Instead, Yahoo sold prospective clients on the unprecedented power of the platform and all the synergies they could reap from it if they were smart enough to get on board. This approach helped Nelson bag a big fish, Sabre, owner of the travel site Travelocity, which provided booking services for Yahoo's travel section.

With such a partnership, the clients "would pay us a lot of money in advertising, but that would be more than banner ads," Nelson explains. "It would give them links and a presence." In the case of Travelocity, its millions bought it ubiquity on all of Yahoo's travel pages.

Together, Singh, Nelson, and two other regional vice presidents—Jeffrey Zink on the East Coast and Tim Rielly on the West Coast—built Yahoo's U.S. sales force. By the time Nelson moved to international sales in early 2000, the domestic force was 200 strong. "We spent an enormous amount of time talking up the company and recruiting," Nelson says. "We needed people to support our very fast growth."

The sales team's grueling hours were more tolerable because upper management walked the talk. "Anil Singh and Jeff Mallett had the most incredible work ethic, and that pushed down into the sales organization," Nelson notes. "If anyone had any idea how hard these people worked. . . . You didn't mind having a conference call on Saturday, because they were having a conference call on Saturday, too. I've never worked as hard in my life as I did for four years at Yahoo."

Nelson found Singh, a big man with an aggressive manner who eventually became chief of sales, particularly impressive. "He's an incredible human being—one of the smartest people I've ever met. He is the very best in the business."

Nelson may have thrived on his never-ending workdays at the time, but he did eventually burn out on them. After he switched to the international division, the schedule of constant overseas travel following three years of constant domestic travel soon did him in. Ten months later, he resigned to spend more time with his family—a line one sees often in Yahoo's announcements of exec departures—even though his stock options weren't fully vested.

～

While Yahoo's targeted-advertising offerings were growing more sophisticated, the audience that enabled the targeting generated a major milestone: one billion page views a month. In June, the company added one of its "stickiest" services, designed to make those users linger longer: online trading. E*Trade and Datek signed multimillion-dollar deals for trading buttons. When users saw a stock they liked, they could click on one of these buttons, go right to their account, and buy it. Or they could sign up for an account. Stock-quotes pages were among the most lucrative on Yahoo, since people check finance information regularly, generating lots of page views to sell.

"Stock quotes generated good CPMs on volume," says Collet, who took over business development for Yahoo Finance in 1999.

Deals usually bundled together a number of different formats, such as keyword searches (where an ad for a BMW, for example, would pop up if the user plugged in "car"), run-of-category ads blanketing a specific section, and less targeted (and cheaper) run-of-site ads. Although advertisers could choose to buy just one keyword, they typically bought very long lists. They could buy keywords per month, but they usually bought them for 6 or 12 months. One thing that was still *verboten* at Yahoo, according to Collet, was selling search results, now a common practice among search engines like Inktomi and LookSmart, and almost all the portals—including Yahoo.

"Feedback grew over time as we had the ability to track which ad placement was getting a higher percentage of click-throughs and which search term was performing better," Collet says. And that feedback was instant, in contrast to TV and print, where gathering data took time.

In 1997, the online-ad market hit $906 million, according to the Interactive Advertising Bureau, with Yahoo taking about a 7.5 percent chunk of the total. Interactive-media agencies began springing up, while traditional ad agencies launched interactive divisions. But, Nelson admits, agencies sometimes still got the runaround because of speed-to-market concerns. "Many players were trying to get established with ads, and the ones that got in early had a better shot," says Nelson, using Travelocity as an example of that first-mover success. Going through an agency added another layer to the negotiations and inevitably slowed things down.

"These companies viewed Yahoo as being a kingmaker," says Derek Brown, an analyst for W. R. Hambrecht & Co., one of at least eight firms that picked up coverage of Yahoo that year.

"With the right placement on Yahoo, company X could become a household name."

Amazon was the first company to pursue online advertising in a big way, according to Brown, signing deals with both Yahoo and AOL. "It was all about location, location, location," Brown says. "If you're a home lender getting the largest, most prominent position within Yahoo's real estate section, that was viewed as a gateway to success—and at the same time, you could block your competitors from that same position." When companies that were about to go public talked up their deals with the portals, AOL and Yahoo were the names Wall Street wanted to hear. And private companies that had just received funding often turned around and handed a big piece of it to Yahoo and AOL for promotion, creating a fat pipeline from the VC community to the portals.

Yahoo's rising clout didn't go unexploited by the company, whose reputation for hard-nosed negotiating began around this time—not so coincidentally, the same time its stock began to really move. "The stock has experienced a blistering 386 percent run-up in its price year-to-date," Hambrecht & Quist's Paul Noglows wrote in his third-quarter 1997 report.[1] The shares had rocketed to the mid-50s by October. By the end of the year, the stock had shot up a total of 511 percent. At a peak of $71 a share on December 30, with a market cap of $3.9 billion, Yahoo was the most valuable Net pure play in the world—not to mention, the site with the largest audience, according to Mediamark Research, with an average of 25.4 million unique visitors a month, or 63 percent of all U.S. adults using the Internet.

Smartly, Yahoo began capitalizing on its stature by making its partners agree to keep their content within its network, instead of bouncing users over to the partner's URL when they clicked on a link. "One thing Yahoo did differently from a very early stage was when they did partnerships, they kept the brand name," says Lise Buyer, who left T. Rowe Price in fall 1997, moving from Baltimore to Silicon Valley, the epicenter of the action, to be a Net analyst for Deutsche Morgan Grenfell. "You'd go to Yahoo's auto page or Yahoo's finance page. Competitors shared the credit with partners. On Excite, you'd go to Quicken Finance or ABC News or whoever it was. Yahoo insisted it had to be their brand and only their brand. Sure, it alienated people—it absolutely alienated people, but at the end of the day, size was what mattered, and that's what Yahoo had." The company also broke out its search results into a prominent section called "Inside Yahoo Matches" that kept users from straying outside the network, while nonproprietary "Web Site Matches" were listed in the wasteland below.

While Yahoo broadened its distribution through deals that put it on the desktops of Compaq and Gateway PCs, it continued to add features to enhance its stickiness, including Yahoo Chat, Yahoo Classifieds, Yahoo Travel, Yahoo Sports, and more regional and international Yahoos.

The goal, according to Yang, was to create a one-stop shop on the Web. "You're a search engine—once they've done the searching, why do they need you?" Yang asked on TechTV's "Big Thinkers" program. "One, make ourselves stickier; two, as long as you have content out there that is changing all the time, your habits are changing all the time. You're always going to go back to something you have a relationship with.

"How do you add these value-added things that no one else has if the Web is open and free? If we stuck to our guns and kept ourselves as a search-engine company, you wouldn't be talking to me today. Instead of going to five search engines, you may only want to have one e-mail address, one buddy list. . . . You don't want multiple identities and multiple places and experiences down the line. How do we make sure our shopping experience and commerce experience are as integrated? So, the key for us has been you package this all together. . . . You have a one-stop shop in which all your basic Web needs can be met."[2]

And, of course, Yahoo got the chance to put those loyal users to work for it—and turn itself into a one-stop shop for advertisers, too. "They'd say, 'We have a registration process on Yahoo Mail—would you like to buy women who are unemployed or seniors who are interested in entertainment?' " says Maggie Boyer, vice president of media for Avenue A, an interactive agency and third-party online-ad server. "They'd sell demographic information at anywhere from a 10 percent to 100 percent markup, depending on how specific that information was. You could get everything but name and address. One of the great things about Yahoo from a media-marketing standpoint is if you want a certain type of demographic, because they're so huge, you can pretty much get it. You can find very niche or broad advertisers."

Of course, you paid through the teeth for that privilege. "The nice thing is Yahoo really can be a one-stop shop for you," Boyer says. "You're very likely to find those users on smaller sites for a fraction of the cost, but you run risks when you work with less credible sites. Yahoo has very credible content and very credible users."

Avenue A has found that Yahoo's direct e-mail campaigns yield the best results of all its ad formats—but are priced accordingly. "You're buying a person's name and sending a direct message right to that person," Boyer notes. "E-mail isn't measured on CPM. They don't say it's $200 per CPM, because you'd

choke and fall off your chair. They say it's 10 cents per name—
but it ranges vastly depending on who you're targeting."

⌒

Yahoo's acquisition of Four11 gave it the stickiest application
of them all: e-mail, which, along with chat and instant messaging, accounts for the vast majority of collective time spent online today. "Any time we had an opportunity to get you to enter
your own data, we did, because you'd be coming back more often to check addresses, calendars, etc.," Collet says.

When Yahoo decided to add e-mail, Four11 was the obvious
place to turn because the portal already had a deal in place with
the online-communications company for cobranded white
pages. Four11 also had a free e-mail service called RocketMail.
Yahoo wanted Four11 to develop Yahoo Mail, but soon the companies' conversation turned to acquisition, with the deal closing
in October 1997. Yahoo Mail was launched the same day, October 8, that Yahoo announced the acquisition.

The man behind every Yahoo acquisition was J. J. Healy, Yahoo's resident investment banker, hired in November 1996. After
Yahoo had looked into buying a yellow-pages directory called
BigBook in summer 1996, the portal realized it needed its own
M&A specialist. During T.K.'s long tenure at Motorola, he'd
come to a strong understanding of the strategic value of acquisitions. "No one knows your business like your employees," says
Healy, a Thunderbird business-school graduate who'd worked
in M&A at First Boston. "T.K. wanted to develop that business
in-house so we could use acquisitions as a strategic weapon."

Healy was teamed up with Yang, who was always the first
to appraise new technology. Healy was always the first to vet
the company. Between 1997 and 2000, before he was transferred

to head up Yahoo's new acquisitions program in Europe and shortly afterward quit to "get a life back," Healy handled 12 acquisitions. "There's a rule that's 60 percent to 40 percent," says Healy. "Sixty percent of the opportunities come over the transom. Companies and investment bankers would call us, and as soon as you start becoming fairly acquisitive, those things go crazy. Sometimes even 80 percent of deal activity comes from outsiders." The rest came from internal sources, often bubbling up from the producers of various areas.

Unlike some of his peers at other companies at the time, like Mike Volpe at Cisco, Healy tried to keep a low profile to avoid being inundated with offers, many of them totally off base. "A lot of us stayed under the radar, especially me," says Healy, who avoided any press. "Mike was more public—he regretted some of that. In our business, the more you're known, the more you can get swamped with potential opportunities."

Healy, Volpe, and the other M&A players in the Valley networked constantly. "We'd talk about different deal structures and how things were getting done, what kinds of technology were coming down the road," Healy says.

He'd get anywhere from 5 to 15 outside inquiries a week and followed up on all of them, looking for that elusive needle in the haystack. As a result, the work hours were hellish. And the competition to get there first was cutthroat. "Every acquisition has its challenges and has its ugly parts," Healy muses. "If you step back and say, 'What kind of environment are we in?' we were in a very time-condensed competitive environment. We were in competition with Excite or Lycos or AOL, and had to move very quickly."

Those companies were all interested in Four11, along with Microsoft. "We always had a bias about being acquired by Yahoo," says Gloria Gavin, who came with Four11, where she was director of international business development. "They were more entrepreneurial than Microsoft. We had a great cultural fit—it made a lot of sense."

Other potential acquirees apparently often felt the same way. "We had a number of companies come to us first because they really liked the management," Healy says. "They liked what we had to say, and they didn't like AOL and Microsoft—it's known as the Evil Empire around the Valley. With AOL, a lot of the people in the Valley don't want to move back east, and they haven't heard great things about AOL." So Yahoo was offered first looks at Hotmail, which Microsoft eventually bought for about $400 million, and Mirabilis, maker of instant messenger ICQ, acquired by AOL for about $288 million. Yahoo passed on both because it didn't want to pay what they were asking. The Four11 deal closed at $94 million, marking the start of the portal land grab and the huge sums paid out for each piece of turf.

In any deal, the first question Healy asked was always, "Should we build, buy, or rent?" If the asking price seemed too high, Yahoo would consider whether it could build the same service less expensively itself. The trade-off was losing speed to market. The main reason to buy things was gaining speed to market. "You say, 'If we don't have it in two, four, or six months, what is that going to mean to our market position?' " Healy says. If the answer was "a lot," money would be spent.

"E-mail was a classic example of that, where Hotmail was growing at thousands and thousands of users per week," Healy says. "We did an analysis. For us to build, it would have taken four to six months, and by then, so many users would have had an e-mail account. The speed to market was critical."

Right after the Four11 deal closed, Yang dropped in to

Four11's Menlo Park offices, "giving a very inspirational talk about how Four11 had built a great company and a great technology that would now be out there for the whole world," says Katie Burke, then director of marketing and business development for Four11 and a key player in the acquisition talks. Yahoo HR staffers handed out Q&A sheets, benefits comparisons, mugs, and T-shirts.

In the three months before Four11 moved to Santa Clara, "Yahoo was impressive in the way they handled people's issues and concerns," Burke says. "They made everyone feel welcome, and they communicated a lot of excitement."

When Burke herself expressed reservations to colleagues about moving from a 30-person company to a 300-person one and adding 40 minutes each way to her commute, word got to Mallett. He called her and invited her to breakfast in Portola Valley, a charming town settled by Spanish missionaries and one of the nation's wealthiest, near Menlo Park. There, Burke got a taste of Mallett at his best. "It was a great meeting," she says. "He got me really jazzed about Yahoo and instilled confidence that I could accomplish a lot there. I signed my [employment] agreement that afternoon."

After the move, according to Burke, Yahoo was equally impressive, spreading Four11ers throughout the company and finding good job fits for them. Almost the entire former Four11 staff is still at Yahoo, a testament to the success of the integration. Two exceptions are Four11's CEO, Mike Santullo, and its VP of business development, Steve Victorino, both of whom left after a few months. "It was pretty clear the management team was set, and it was going well," Gavin says. "It was less tough for me because I was at the director level. It was harder for my boss, the VP of business development, and our CEO."

The dynamic of an acquired company's staff staying while

its management hit the road would become a pattern in all of Yahoo's acquisitions, underscoring the insularity of its own management. "I can't think of a CEO who was asked to stay," Collet says. "Or who stayed."

Burke herself stayed a little over a year as a senior producer working on products such as Yahoo People Search, Calendar, and Address Book as well as Yahoo Delivers, the direct-marketing program. "Products were getting launched every other week," Burke recalls. "You could be certain some product team was pulling an all-nighter each night. I was extremely excited about the culture, as one of my bigger fears in going to Yahoo was an absence of this kind of 'fly or die' start-up environment."

One ever-present element of that environment was Filo. "I saw him up at 2 A.M. on occasion, and he could still occasionally be caught sleeping under his desk," Burke says. "You could send him an e-mail at any hour on any topic and would get a very quick response." After all, Filo was managing the precious home page, rotating in different properties. He participated in every product launch, testing the product and overseeing its exposure on the home page. Anybody who wanted to make a change on the home page had to go through Filo or Tim Brady.

Despite Burke's high praise for Yahoo, she left the next December to start the Web-site and file organizer Desktop.com, which folded after just a year, with Four11's founder, Larry Drebes.

⤳

*T*he hiring of Fabiola Arredondo, now 35, as managing director of Yahoo Europe in December 1997 revved up the pace of international development. Arredondo, a native of Madrid who'd attended Stanford as an ungrad and worked at JP Morgan and

Bertelsmann, gave the Yahoo sites across Europe a unified look and further localized the content. In Italy, for example, the sports section was built out to satisfy rabid soccer fans. In Great Britain and Ireland, the bolstered music headlines drew plenty of clicks. Later, localization encompassed a karaoke chat room in Taiwan (yes, people would sing online), a horse-racing section in Hong Kong, and a cricket section in India.

The pace of deal making was slower in Europe and the rest of the world, just as other countries were slower to embrace the Internet, and the hurdles to entry were higher. People in the rest of the world still accessed the Internet mainly through unwieldy wireless devices rather than through PCs; large companies resisted giving away anything, including content, for free; and people spent less time e-mailing each other since dialing up in many countries saddled them with the cost of a local call. Bureaucratic red tape didn't help matters, either. In France, for example, the tax on stock options was as high as 50 percent by 2000, real estate regulations were restrictive, and it was nearly impossible to fire someone.

The large telcos in Europe had an advantage over an upstart like Yahoo because they could cross-promote their portals, like France Telecom's Wanadoo and Deutsche Telekom's T-Online, with the Internet access they controlled. As a result, Yahoo's bargaining power was weak until it started to hit the telcos where it hurt by stealing away their users.

But to really reign overseas, Arredondo needed more help from home than she was getting, according to observers. In fact, the obstacle she faced in Santa Clara—lack of full support—reportedly culminated in her resignation in 2001. "She's a very intelligent person. She said it was invigorating to work there but very frustrating," says analyst Manish Shah. "She thought the U.S. parent didn't understand Europe's different content structure. There's less community, less commerce, and less content in Europe. Yahoo had enough content to aggregate in the U.S., but there's nothing to aggregate in Europe and Asia. They wait for someone else to create content and then partner with them without paying them something or paying them a very minimal fee, so Yahoo's success is destined to be limited abroad. It will never happen. You have to reinvent yourself in Europe, and they failed to do so."

One of the reasons for this failure was doubtless the rapid-fire pace of Yahoo's international expansion. By the end of 1997, the company had added Australia/New Zealand, Korea, Denmark, Norway, and Sweden to its list of outposts.

Gavin also was frustrated by some of the conditions abroad. A case in point: her experience with France Telecom. "They were interested enough to talk to us—the challenge was to convince them they should give us their data," says Gavin, then Yahoo's director of international business development. "I had done a white pages [deal] with Wanadoo. They were using Four11's directory, so we piggybacked off that deal and tried to extend it with Yahoo, not just using Yahoo for People Search but doing a much bigger deal, since they were controlling the Internet traffic. We wanted to talk to them about a joint venture. But they had so many different divisions looking at Internet strategy—they had conflicting strategies. They moved just too slowly. Yahoo couldn't afford to move that slowly. There were local search engines, Nomad and Wanadoo and others, popping up in France. In the end, we did a small deal with France Telecom for white pages and search, but we were going it alone, while Wanadoo had all the users in terms of connectivity. A lot of their customers were coming to Yahoo for content like the Finance site. Then Yahoo started building up its own reputation."

Building it up enough, in fact, that by early 2000, Yahoo was the leading player in the United Kingdom, France, Germany, and Japan, and was among the top three in Spain, Italy, Denmark, and Norway. In an interview with BusinessWeek Online in January 2000, Arredondo noted one big advantage Yahoo had in these countries over AOL. "We are lucky," she said. "Our brand name, Yahoo, is phonetic and transfers well across Europe. America Online has a much bigger problem there."[3]

In January 1999, Gavin transferred to U.S. business development, where she encountered a frustration of a different sort, Ellen Siminoff, who cranked out a lot of deals but also alienated potential partners. "She was kind of unusual," says Gavin, obviously choosing her words carefully. "If you met her face to face, you'd say she didn't seem corporate in her dress or her demeanor. She was a little rough around the edges. She wasn't afraid to say in a meeting with a large telecom company, 'I don't have time for this' and just walk out."

Not that Siminoff wasn't modeling her behavior on that of other impatient top Yahoos, like Mallett and Singh. "At that time, Yahoo had the luxury of walking away from deals," says Gavin, who worked on the precursor to Corporate Yahoo toward the end of her tenure. "They were interested in doing deals quickly and dealing with people who were ready to do deals."

And why not? The strategy was paying off. In 1997, Yahoo's advertising base shot to 1,700 from 550, while traffic also almost tripled to an average of 65 million page views per day. That growth fueled a 257 percent rise in revenues to $70.4 million from $19.7 million in 1996, beating all the analysts' forecasts. After taking one-time charges for its Yahoo Marketplace restructuring and its acquisition of Four11, Yahoo posted a net loss of $25.5 million, or 29 cents per share. But Wall Street analysts didn't pay attention to those one-time charges, so why should anyone else? The analysts preferred to stick to pro-forma, or hypothetical, accounting methods, by which Yahoo actually showed net income of $2.2 million, or 4 cents per share.

"Yahoo's story has never been stronger," Noglows wrote in fall 1997. "Yahoo is increasingly well-positioned competitively and will prove one of the best vehicles for investors seeking to exploit the long-term growth of the Internet."[4]

No doubt about it: In 1997, it was great to be Yahoo.

Chapter

Staying Put and Scaling Up, 1998

Key Events

- February: GoTo.com launches a search engine with paid results.
- February: Lycos acquires Tripod, with 1.5 million member home pages.
- May: The U.S. government and 20 state attorneys sue Microsoft for antitrust violations.
- June: NBC buys a stake in CNET's Snap portal.
- June: Disney buys a controlling interest in Infoseek and creates the Go Network.
- June: AOL acquires Mirabilis, maker of the popular ICQ instant messenger.
- September: eBay goes public, gaining 163.2 percent and raising $63 million on IPO day.
- November: AOL acquires Netscape.
- November: Theglobe.com's IPO soars 605.6 percent, taking its market cap to $622 million.

*B*y fall 1998, all of Wall Street had jumped on the Yahoo bandwagon. The press was touting the stock's amazing performance just as more shares were becoming available after two stock splits, in July 1997 and again in August of the next year. During Yahoo's IPO, only 10 percent, or 2.6 million, of its shares were offered to the public, while Yahoos and other insiders held the remaining 90 percent. But some insider selling and various acquisitions that required more stock to be issued had brought the float to above 10 million shares by spring 1998. (After a third stock split in February 1999, the float stood at about 80 million shares.)

"By December 1997, you couldn't ignore the tremendous performance of the stock," says Lise Buyer, who picked up coverage of Yahoo in January and moved to Credit Suisse First Boston with Deutsche Morgan Grenfell's entire tech group in July. "Mutual fund investors were asking, 'Why don't you own these stocks? What's wrong with you?' The real catalyst was the publicity of the stock's performance that resulted in wide knowledge of these great stocks and the limited ownership, which prompted many institutional investors to throw in the towel and start buying the stock in '98."

Even a few months made a big difference in the desirability of the shares. "When I was first visiting corporate accounts to talk to them about the stock, right through early '98, people really didn't care about these things," Buyer recalls. "They wanted to hear about Intuit and Electronic Arts. Those were companies with real profits, revenues, and assessable funds— and these Net stocks didn't go berserk until later that year."

And go berserk they really did. By the end of the year, Yahoo, for one, had gained 584 percent. Another dot-com star, Amazon.com, surged 540 percent, and in the four months following its September IPO, eBay jumped 509 percent.

"I said, 'These things are going up, and if you want to play a momentum game, buy them,' " Buyer says. "I had to be able to demonstrate that the stock is undervalued based on current performance. I was clear about saying the stock was going up because it had momentum, but the fundamentals never worked. I was *very* clear about saying these were unsustainable valuations, but they had been for two years, so people who stood on the sidelines had dramatically underperformed. The challenge was to get in early and get out. At the end of the day, investors don't care about what the stock should do but what it *does* do."

Enter the age of relative valuation, when Net stocks were compared to each other, traditional metrics like price-earnings (P/E) ratio went out the window, and companies with 7-figure revenues sported 10-figure market caps. "You can't have a P/E ratio if you have no 'E,' "[1] *Fortune* writer Joseph Nocera proclaimed, aptly recapping the craziness. With negative earnings for 1997, Yahoo fit the category of an "E"-less company. And while its revenues would barely have qualified it for a Fortune 10,000 list, its market cap put it in the company of old-economy stalwarts like Humana and Estée Lauder.

Analysts began to invent new—and in hindsight, outlandish—measures to talk about this new breed of company. There was customer mind share, number of engaged shoppers, discounted cash flow, price-to-eyeball ratio. Mary Meeker, the high-profile Morgan Stanley analyst dubbed "Queen of the Net" by *Institutional Investor* magazine, who initiated coverage in April, would cite upbeat "usage metrics."[2] A self-aggrandizing Internet.com analyst whose equally fast rise to prominence and fade into obscurity mirrored the bursting of the bubble, Steve

Harmon liked to calculate market-cap/monthly-page-view ratios, market-cap/potential-market-share ratios, and various other measures that sound more like witchcraft than high finance today. By August 1998, 20 analysts were following Yahoo, and 14 were rating it a "buy." With Yahoo's gross margins of 88 percent, just off Microsoft's 92 percent, they asked, how could you go wrong?

In five weeks during the summer of 1998, Yahoo's shares ran up 82 percent, taking its market cap from $5 billion to $9 billion, Filo's stake to more than $1 billion, and the now-married but prenup-less Yang's to about $987 million. "I've never seen anything as dramatic as that in terms of a company—taking the fact that these guys couldn't afford lunch, and a couple of years later, these guys are billionaires," says entrepreneur Randy Adams. "It's mind-blowing."

The stock's precipitous rise prompted one of Yahoo's biggest cheerleaders, analyst Paul Noglows, to put a "hold" on it on July 9. The stock was expensive even in relative-valuation terms, trading at 37 times estimated 1999 revenues while its competitors were trading at 14. Briefly, Noglows' move looked inspired, since Yahoo dove 30 percent in late summer along with other Internet stocks on concerns about the Russian economy. But the stock took off again that fall, hit a split-adjusted $104 in January before another two-for-one split, and was holding steady when Noglows finally upgraded it in March. It was an even more remarkable performance given the fact that thousands of Net stocks remained in the doldrums, trading 25 percent or more off their recent highs.

"When I downgraded Yahoo, I thought, this thing has a bigger market cap than Viacom," Noglows says. "We had valuation concerns. We realized the company was a hypergrowth story. I was right for a while—then it became very clear it didn't matter. The Street was going to do what it was going to do."

And the supply-demand imbalance was going to keep moving the stock. Buyer made no bones about that. "We won't even pretend that there is a correlation between the discount value of the earnings stream of the companies and the current price of the stock,"[3] she wrote.

Mutual fund managers were coming under increasing pressure to beat the Standard & Poor's 500, which had been growing at a 20-percent-plus rate for several years. For most of the Street, that meant time to get in on the action. And more than any other company, Yahoo symbolized that action.

"The greed factor on Wall Street was rising right along with the S&P," says David Ganek, who runs the Internet portfolio of the multibillion-dollar hedge fund SAC Capital. "Now comes this newfangled part of the Internet of which Yahoo is a huge symbolic part, and the investing public goes absolutely crazy. Everyone sees blue-sky opportunity."

The rising greed was drawing more and more people into the market just as online trading made it more accessible to the masses. By 1999, nearly half of U.S. households owned stock, up from about 30 percent in 1990, according to the Securities Industry Association. "You have all this momentum—then Yahoo comes along," Ganek says. "Other than eBay, Yahoo was the company that seemed to be meeting the opportunity of the Internet." Ganek bought Yahoo stock for his fund in 1998, made $25 million on it, and began to short it in the second quarter of 2000.

Abel Garcia, then manager of Waddell & Reed's Advisor Science & Technology fund, had jumped into Yahoo in 1997. He was particularly taken with its strong and growing operating margins of 25-percent plus, meaning any profits fell straight to the bottom line. "It was amazing—I'd never seen anything like it," says Garcia, who joined AIM Funds as manager of its Global Telecommunications and Technology fund in April 2000. "It was the ultimate growth stock." He, too, made many millions on Yahoo, peeling back his position in early 1999.

Garcia and Ganek had plenty of company as the biggest funds in America—funds managing people's retirement money like Fidelity, Janus, and Alliance Capital—dipped into Yahoo, along with banks like Chase Manhattan, Mellon, and State Street. But since Yahoo's float had been tiny for so long, shares weren't readily available in the big blocks of 20,000 and up favored by institutions. So when it came to Yahoo, large numbers of individual investors—38 percent of Yahoo's total by the end of 1998, while institutions made up just 4 percent—were "playing the mo," as the Street put it. These individuals were the ones with the most to gain and, ultimately, the most to lose.

⌒

*I*n 1998, Yahoo and all the other online-search companies got an official designation: "portal." Suddenly the p-word was on everyone's lips. It meant a gateway to the Internet, the entry point through which travelers could discover the many wonders of the Web, much the way the wardrobe served as a portal to the magical land of Narnia in C. S. Lewis' famous children's series. In a September 29 report, Forrester Research analyst Chris Charron summarized some of the characteristics shared by the most successful portals: broad functionality, wide distribution, and brand identity.

In fact, as the competition heated up among the major players, they were starting to look more and more alike. They all had e-mail, instant messaging, chat, clubs, news, weather reports, sports scores, stock quotes, personalization, shopping, search, and so on and so on. Even their home pages were eerily similar. Whatever differences remained were subtle and disappearing fast, but people still had their personal favorites. Some favored Lycos' and Infoseek's sophisticated search capabilities. Others chose Excite for its Web-site reviews. Yahoo acolytes extolled its user-friendliness.

"All the companies had the same products, but Yahoo integrated them flawlessly," says Max Drucker, chief information officer (CIO) of the now-defunct online insurance company eCoverage. "They were the pioneer of the single-user account and single point of entry that would enable you to access personal stuff across the entire property. With horoscopes, stock quotes, weather, mail, calendar, you could get this stuff on the other sites, but it felt like they were built piecemeal and poorly integrated. It was like an addition on a house that was really obvious."

Buyer felt much the same way. "What really differentiated Yahoo was the wonderful ease of use of the service, not particularly the content, which was standard commodity stuff for the most part," she says.

But with all the existing competition, plus powerful new entrants in the form of Microsoft's MSN and Netscape's Netcenter, Yahoo could hardly afford to rest on its laurels. Instead, the portal made sure it was as ubiquitous in the real world as it was becoming in Wall Street portfolios. Call 1998 Yahoo's Year of Branding, the year Karen Edwards and her Buzz Team went into overdrive.

"We want a name that will stand the test of time," Edwards told *BusinessWeek* in 1998.[4] Certainly, she seemed to be doing everything possible to make that a reality, including planting the seeds, literally, in her own garden in the form of purple petunias and yellow gladioli.

Suddenly the Yahoo logo was everywhere: on the Zamboni at the San Jose Sharks' arena, on Visa cards, on Indy 500 cars, on parachutes, on employees' Yahoo-mobiles, on Ben & Jerry's ice cream lids, on kazoos, on yo-yos, and on Slinkys. It was even tattooed on the butt of Yahoo exec John Briggs. Starting with staples like boxer shorts, the Yahoo Gear area on the site branched out into Yahoo golf balls, caps, watches, backpacks, umbrellas, and glow-in-the-dark pens.

None of the other portals, certainly, had their names on a magazine, like *Yahoo! Internet Life*, which could now be found in every airport in America. That intense exposure, though, came with a price tag. "People thought of it as Yahoo's magazine, so it became a little bit of a liability if there was something negative in it or if it had trends in it that Yahoo didn't advance," Gloria Gavin says. "As the company matured, it wasn't necessarily a huge plus because there was zero control or feedback as to what went into the publication."

The list of idiosyncratic surfaces bearing Yahoo's name has grown over the years to include rickshaws, Internet-enabled taxi-cabs, billboards, a high-speed Internet kiosk in New York's Times Square, and two cow-osks in CowParade New York 2000, an out-door exhibit of more than 500 cow sculptures—all of which sends the message that this quirky, irreverent company has a marketing attitude to match. Yahoo may have a yen for silly marketing, but it's extremely serious about its silly marketing.

While the cabs, kiosk, and cow-osks certainly helped create

the impression that Yahoo was everywhere, and that Internet access had gone mobile, it's debatable that they served much of a utilitarian purpose. A New York City Yahoo cab that was recently flagged down, for example, had been stripped of the handheld Palm VII that was supposed to reside in a little compartment in the rear—with the driver none the wiser. Asked how many passengers actually went online before the theft, driver Bill Bernitt said, "Very, very few."

But utilitarianism isn't the point of such marketing, according to Black Rocket cofounder John Yost. "What that adds to Yahoo and to the world that sees Yahoo is the feeling that everywhere you turn, there's a little bit of Yahoo," he says. "Over time, it reinforces Yahoo's accessibility and friendliness."

And Yahoo's global platform provides the opportunity to send that message simultaneously in many different countries. "Karen Edwards is a great believer in integrated, consistent communication, and she made sure that people in the various countries didn't dilute the brand by interpreting it in different ways," Yost says. "Even the French have come around, if reluctantly. They've acknowledged that 'do you Yahoo?' doesn't have to translate directly to be meaningful."

∽

While Yahoo's brand equity was growing, so was its reputation for arrogance at the bargaining table. "They were still playing the strategy of pushing the envelope in the sense that 'we're the biggest guys, and we have the largest audience, and we have our terms by which we do business, and you'll live with our terms whether you like it or not,' " Manish Shah says. "They had internal thinking that came from Jeff Mallett, that 'the old-economy guys don't get it, and we're here to change the world.'

It was that revolutionary zeal that was driving the whole enterprise and, in some ways, rightly so." After all, Shah points out, in 1998, Yahoo was getting better results than the 1 percent to 2 percent response rate of junk mail.

Yahoo was an equally demanding customer—again, because it could afford to be. Just as Yahoo served as a kingmaker for advertisers, it could crown customers category leaders. Akamai, a company that streamlines content delivery over the Web, had to develop a new service for Yahoo. Unlike other leading Akamai customers, like Disney and CNN, Yahoo refused a system that would have required its users to leave its network and enter the Akamai network. Instead of distributing Yahoo's content on Akamai's network, Akamai had to devise a way to use its network to point to Yahoo's servers. "Yahoo was the most demanding customer," says Todd Dagres, a general partner at Battery Ventures, the lead investor in Akamai. "If you could satisfy Yahoo, you could satisfy anyone. But they were a great customer, because they challenged us and made our service better."

Yahoo also exploited its cachet to the max. "Their attitude was, 'We're Yahoo, and we get the best price,' " Dagres says. "It was early, and they were important. It was worth giving it to them."

⌒

A host of distribution deals Yahoo struck in 1998 broadened its existing base and pushed it onto the wireless platform, which was being hailed as the next big thing. Companies like Lucent Technologies and AT&T were developing ways to deliver interactive content and services to wireless devices through Internet Protocol, the same standard used for the Web.

Finnish cellular phone maker Nokis was rolling out Internet-equipped phones, and sales of 3Com's PalmPilot handhelds were off the charts.

In its first wireless deal, Yahoo partnered with 3Com to bring Yahoo People Search to Palm VII devices. Through Yahoo's Internet-access deals with MCI and AT&T, the first thing new users logging on to the Web saw was the Yahoo home page. The MCI partnership, which came first, upped the pressure on Yahoo's rivals to strike copycat deals. MSN took the bait, signing up to be AT&T WorldNet's content provider. A similar arrangement with British Telecommunications expanded Yahoo's reach in the United Kingdom. And through a contract with the Internet service provider and telco IDT, Yahoo delved into Net telephony, charging as little as 5 percent of the average long-distance service.

Yahoo also launched its instant-messaging feature, Yahoo Messenger, to keep its users lingering, and its clubs offering, a gold mine for targeted marketing since membership in a given club could be construed as a declaration of interest in the subject. To step up targeted marketing, Yahoo paid $29.6 million in stock to acquire the interactive direct-marketer Yoyodyne, along with its database of customers who had agreed to receive direct e-mail solicitations. Yoyodyne founder Seth Godin spent a little over a year at Yahoo as VP of direct marketing, leaving in January 2000. "Really smart people doing their best in an incredibly turbulent environment" is all Godin would say about the experience.

Yahoo's $30 million purchase of WebCal in July allowed it to launch its Calendar feature—yet another way to keep users logged on longer—and stay a step ahead of the other portals, which were hot in pursuit of this new must-have. A companion service, the Address Book, featuring compatibility with Palm handhelds, soon followed.

But Yahoo reserved its most aggressive push of all that year for e-commerce. After all, online retail sales were expected to grow to $12.1 billion by 2000, a 404 percent leap from $2.4 billion at the end of 1997. To poise itself to take advantage of this growth, Yahoo expanded its initiatives mightily through its launch of Yahoo Shopping and Yahoo Auctions, and its $49 million June acquisition of Viaweb, which created software for building and operating online stores.

"Negotiations were relatively straightforward and smooth," says Steve O'Leary, a managing director for Broadview Associates, an investment bank specializing in M&A that handled the deal for Viaweb. "J. J. Healy was a very hardworking, very ethical, very driven guy. Jeff [Mallett] struck me at first glance as being awfully young for the role he plays. But he's very bright, a very well organized operations guy. You could tell the guy had the business under his thumb.

"The Yahoo people had a can-do attitude. They were commonsense guys. We have a phrase: There are people in the industry who are last-nickel guys. Those are the ones who fight for every nickel on the table. These weren't last-nickel guys."

The deal was memorable for other reasons, too. "There was a 10-times return for those who had the shares," says O'Leary, referring to the all-stock deal. "The stock took off like nothing I've ever seen. One guy went on vacation in Spain after the deal closed, and when he came back two weeks later, he was worth twice what he'd been worth before he left. One Viaweb director tells the story that the escrow ended up being worth more than the original price. They called it the happily-ever-after deal."

Viaweb had a thousand clients when Yahoo bought it, and management worried that it might not be able to handle a deluge of thousands more once Yahoo Store was launched. "They were wondering what happens when you get 5,000 or 10,000 users—will everything still work, and how much it would cost per user, and how much of that cost was fixed," says Paul Graham, who was president of Viaweb and has a Ph.D. in computer science from Harvard, like the company's three other cofounders. "A Yahoo store still costs the same amount for a merchant as it did then. It's pretty damn cheap to run server-based software."

And it turned out the system handled the load beautifully. For $100 a month, any store, no matter how small, could have an Internet presence. By the following May, 5,000 merchants had signed up. Testimonials from transformed businesses abounded.

- Chris Gwynn, owner of Fridgedoor.com, a retailer of magnets, and a former B2B analyst for the Yankee Group: "Every year, sales have doubled! It enabled me to quit my job at the end of 1998!"
- Jim Painter, president of Oakville Grocery, which dates back to 1881: "Web sales were up 300 percent in 1999!"
- Russ Halley, president and CEO of MagazineCity.net, which launched on Yahoo in 1998: "Ninety-eight percent of our sales are Internet-based! Gross sales are eight figures! Sales will grow at least 250 percent this year!"
- Through its site on Yahoo, AAPS Alternative Power Systems landed a contract "worth $100 million in business easily!" says James Hart, manager of client services. As a result, AAPS didn't have to raise funding to build its business as it prepares for an IPO.

But if the arrangement was great for the stores, it did little for Yahoo's bottom line. Finally this past fall, to try to wring more revenue out of Yahoo Store, the company rejiggered the payment structure, adding a 10-cent commission per item per month, a 50-cent commission per transaction, and a 3.5 percent commission on transactions that originate on Yahoo's network.

Yahoo Store added lots of content to the site, but the program also caused the company a lot of headaches. "There's a quality-control problem when you're dealing with that many merchants," Elizabeth Collet says. "These are mom-and-pop stores. When mom goes on vacation for a week and doesn't check order status, how do you differentiate that from Yahoo? Who gave you the bad experience? There was expense and headache associated with it. You had people calling all the time, merchants and customers. Any time you're the front representing 5,000 merchants, you're going to have issues."

Graham stayed at Yahoo for a year after the acquisition in the role of Technical Yahoo, developing software for Yahoo Store. He was jazzed, then ultimately disappointed by the atmosphere. "It was pretty impressive to work there," he says. "A lot of start-ups have one smart guy, and everyone else is obviously inferior. At Yahoo, the whole group of VPs is very smart."

Anil Singh was "terrifying," Graham says. Tim Brady "thought about nothing except Yahoo from the moment he woke up until he went to bed at night. He was just like an obsessive mother. If you wanted to make a change on the home page, it was only Tim Brady and David Filo who could do it. Tim Brady would fire up a text editor. It showed you how devoted they were and how engaged the first group of people were in the company, even when it had a valuation of about $50 billion and a thousand employees."

But that devotion was both a boon and a bane. "Yahoo was still run by the core group of people who'd started it," Graham says. "I wasn't one of the club. I was very frustrated—I had ideas that wouldn't get implemented. I felt like I was out of the loop." Luckily, since Graham had sold plenty of his shares early on, work was purely optional for him.

Most of the 20-person Viaweb staff still works at Yahoo, though. One of those, Viaweb cofounder Trevor Blackwell, was a Technical Yahoo until the summer of 2001, despite the freedom Viaweb's sale gave him. "It was the best place I've ever worked," he says.

When Blackwell moved from Viaweb's Cambridge, Massachusetts, offices to Santa Clara, he brought along his Bogometer, a contraption he'd built that had eight dials, powered by model-airplane servomotors. The Bogometer was hooked up to a master computer that the e-commerce Web servers sent reports to every second. If the e-commerce servers went down, there was a *swoosh*, and the Bogometer's dials—which measured such criteria as orders, traffic, and page views—would fall to zero.

The Bogometer got its name from a comment by Blackwell, who initially thought the idea of measuring e-commerce activity every second was "bogus." But the results turned out to be more illuminating than he'd imagined. "We'd come in in the morning and the dials would be low, and at lunchtime they would go up, and then they would peak at three or four and start to go down," he says. "Sometimes something would go wrong—the server would be down, or there was network trouble, or maybe we released some software that wasn't quite ready—and we could see the dials go down from across the room, and we'd race back to our desks."

The Bogometer's name became official the day after it was mounted on the wall near Blackwell's desk in late 1998, when Yang was giving a tour of the Santa Clara offices to some California congresspeople. "He came around to our area, and there was the Bogometer," Blackwell recalls. "We'd been up all night running the wires up to the ceiling and down the wall. We wanted to put it somewhere visible. He said, without breaking stride, 'And this is our Bogometer.' After that, the name pretty much stuck."

⌒

*T*he year was also notable for an acquisition that didn't happen. It certainly wasn't Yahoo's most notable nonstarter acquisition, a role reserved for eBay. This one also would have changed Yahoo's destiny but, as it turned out, probably not for the better.

Talks with the now-bankrupt Excite started in December when, after being at each other's throats for so long, the two companies finally put their competitive spirit aside to contemplate how a combination could potentially give them an unbeatable lead. Yahoo had that vast audience, and Excite had developmental skill and database and marketing technology that could have been an advantage for Yahoo.

Koogle, Mallett, and Yang met with Excite CEO George Bell, President Joe Kraus, and Executive VP Brett Bullington at an athletic club near Yahoo and then sporadically afterward to evaluate what a combined company could do. Conversations started out awkwardly, with a corporate version of "I'll show you mine if you show me yours."

Kraus recalls, "We'd say, 'Tell us where you think you're

going, and we'll tell you where we think we're going.' It's strange. You're hesitant. You need to kind of ride the line between revealing too much and also revealing too little, so there's interest. I remember being nervous about riding that line."

Yahoo was hesitating, Healy says, because it would have had to make the combined company profitable within a year, and if it didn't, "Wall Street would have taken off our head." The talks ruined Healy's Christmas that year. "We decided to go really hard at each other's business and see if it made sense to combine," Healy says. "T.K. said, 'J.J., go get 'em,' so we did our analysis. Every acquisition has its time span. You dance and dance and dance, and then say you're looking pretty good."

Only they weren't. Yahoo got a clue that Excite wasn't as serious as it pretended to be when CEO Bell stopped showing up for meetings. And in January, it became apparent why. Cable operator At Home announced it was buying Excite for $6.7 billion. Excite's content—free e-mail, chat, instant messaging, and all the rest—would be distributed over At Home's cable infrastructure. Both firms had been funded by Valley kingpins Kleiner Perkins Caufield & Byers. As a result of its independent status, would Yahoo now be shut out of growing high-speed networks, like that of Excite@Home, as the new company was called? At the end of 1998, At Home had 331,000 subscribers, but by the end of 1999, it had 1 million.

~

*T*hough Yahoo mainly focused on enterprises closer to home in 1998, it launched two more international properties, Yahoo Spain and Yahoo Chinese. By the end of the year, it was in 14 countries and 9 languages and was estimating that nearly 30 percent of its traffic came from outside the United States. But the take from the international sites was disproportionately small, at about 10 percent of total revenues. And Yahoo's competition abroad was heating up, as more local players got into the game and Lycos gained on Yahoo's record with sites in 11 European countries.

        ~

*I*n 1998, Yahoo finally reported an "E": earnings of $25.6 million, or 14 cents per share, on revenues of $203.3 million, nearly three times the $70.4 million of 1997. But a year later, when the company restated its 1998 earnings, that "E" vanished. After acquisition-related and other charges, it turned out, the company actually showed a loss of $12.7 million, or 6 cents per share. Yahoo was still spending money faster than it was making it. Luckily, a $250 million investment by Softbank in the company in July 1998 helped give Yahoo's balance sheet a rosy glow and bring its total in cash to $1.7 billion.

Traffic now averaged 167 million page views per day, and registered users—those precious repeat customers—hit 35 million. Advertisers numbered more than 2,500. The vision Yang later articulated in a speech to the National Press Club was in full swing: "We offer everyone on the site a free business model, one where the consumer continually gets better and better services and content for free, and at the same time, we offer better and better marketing to clients."[5]

Lise Buyer shared Yang's optimism. "If we throw caution and rational thought to the wind, and let ourselves be swept up by Internet exuberance, we could forecast $1 billion in revenue and $4.50 per share (pre-split) [in 2002] or, what the heck, in 2001," she wrote in the report in which she initiated coverage, qualifying that she still couldn't "make a compelling valuation-based pitch."[6] The first half of her prediction turned out to be not just rational but actually conservative. Yahoo reached that $1 billion milestone in 2000.

Still, amid all the good news at the end of 1998, a cloud hovered. Yahoo still had the highest reach (49.6 percent) of all the portals among users at work, but for the first time, it had slipped behind AOL in numbers of users at home, with 43.7 percent, according to Media Metrix. Even more alarming, in combined home-work reach, Yahoo's ranking fell from No. 1 to No. 3, behind both AOL and MSN. If Yahoo's standing could slip during such a period of expansion for the company, what might happen in a less forgiving time?

Chapter

The Portal Wars, 1996 to 1998

"At Hotmail, we called them trailer-park businesses. The portals were tornados, looking for a trailer park to sweep up."—Scott Weiss, Hotmail's director of business development in 1996

*B*y early 1996, there were so many search engines that a couple of opportunistic companies tried to cash in on the trend by offering engines that did metasearches—in other words, you could use their software to perform a single search across multiple search engines. *BusinessWeek* quipped that since there were already more than 30 search engines on the Web, we might one day need a search engine to find the right search engine.[1]

To stand out, search companies needed something different. They began adding extra services, like yellow pages or white pages directories. Instead of thumbing through a phone book, you could type in the name of the person you were looking for and get a phone number in return. Search engines started adding maps. One site, InfoSpace, would even let you click to see a map of the area where the person you were looking for lived. It was a little creepy, but people were eager to show off what their inventions could do.

The race to add services like these marked the start of what became known as the portal wars, and the combatants were Yahoo, Excite, Lycos, Infoseek, AltaVista, and the myriad others that sprang up. Curious users, seeking information about electronic music or fishing tackle or body art, would go to one of these sites, type in what they were looking for, and get back a list of links to peruse. And the stakes were high: By the end of 1995, 9.7 percent of U.S. households were online, according to Jupiter Media Metrix. Jupiter expected that percentage to almost double, to 18.1 percent, in 1997, and to reach 34 percent by 2000, as more and more users discovered the wonders of the Internet. For once, Jupiter was too conservative: By 2001, more than half of U.S. households were online.

Even though Yahoo was a directory of human-classified Web sites, it got lumped together with the search engines, which used technology to scour Web sites for keywords. In the end, these nascent online services all did something similar: They helped users find what they were looking for.

But the problem with the word "portal" is that it implies you go through a door to some other destination. You search for something, find a result, and click to a new Web page. That isn't what was happening, though.

The portals began adding more and more features to get their visitors—whom they not-so-affectionately dubbed "eyeballs"—to hang around longer. Because the space was so competitive, once one site added a feature, like chat, all the others had to have it, too.

And adding all those services took serious cash. Yahoo and the other portals had obviously noticed how gaga the investing public was for Netscape. They raised cash by going public, too—in a very short period of time. By the end of 1996, the top four at the time—Yahoo, Excite, Lycos, and Infoseek—had raised $162 million via initial public offerings. The first search engine to go public was a Canadian company called OpenText, but it never became a major player. Next up, in April 1996, was Lycos. Two days later, Excite became a public company. Then it was Yahoo's turn, followed by Infoseek in June.

Lise Buyer, who covered the Internet for Deutsche Morgan Grenfell at the time, quipped in the *New York Times*, "Why do they do IPOs? Why do rock stars marry models? In part, it's because they can." She added, "The market is willing to accept deals when business models are still in their infancies. These companies would be silly not to take access to capital while they can."[2]

Yahoo executives repeatedly said they didn't spend time thinking about money, but they were clearly influenced by Netscape's attention-getting IPO. And when Yahoo went public on April 12, 1996, its 154 percent gain in the first day outdid Netscape's. Shortly before the IPO, Softbank invested $100 million in Yahoo (becoming its largest shareholder), so Yahoo wasn't desperate for money. "I really wanted a few more quarters [before going public]. I wanted to be sure we could deliver our numbers consistently and ahead of [Wall Street's] expectations," Koogle said in *Fortune*.[3]

The competitive landscape changed his plans. Lycos and Excite had announced they were going public, so Yahoo needed to go public, too. "We couldn't afford to be boxed in," Koogle said, "so we took the risk."[4] In other words, Yahoo had to have the same access to capital so it could compete against the other portals for acquisitions, so it could build out its site with features that would attract the growing number of new Internet users going online each month.

There was one thing Yahoo recognized that the other portals seemed to have missed (except Excite, with its rowdy "Are You Experienced?" advertisements): The race wasn't just about adding features. It was about creating an experience that included loyalty to a brand. It included—*gulp*—emotion.

"People attach an emotion to our service. If we don't have that emotion, we're just like every other service," said Jerry Yang. "We don't get people to come to the site by saying we have 10 million Web sites and our competitor has 9 million. We're not going to get them here by saying our response time is one nanosecond faster than our competitors'. We're going to get them based on an emotion, based on the idea that they're going to have fun, or that they're going to solve a problem they've never been able to solve before.

"We had to invest in brand so that people could see us as more than just technology. That was important, even though the expense of the investment meant that we couldn't develop some new product as fast as we wanted or hire as many people as we wanted."[5]

To the outside world, Yahoo didn't seem to be hamstrung in any way. It continued to add service after service, often beating its competitors.

~

*T*hings really started heating up when Web-based e-mail hit the scene. E-mail had been tied to the PC, where the application resided. But with Web-based e-mail, you could send or receive e-mail from any PC on which you could launch a browser. You could be in an Internet café in Thailand or a friend's house down the street and still read or send e-mail. This was the start of a revolution.

Not only was e-mail the "killer app" at the time, but it was an application that took time to use. You could sit and compose and read messages for hours—exactly the type of service that made Yahoo salivate. If it could get those eyeballs to hang around longer, it could sell more advertising. And e-mail was a great way to differentiate. The search engines were becoming commodities. They were starting to look more and more alike, as each one copied the others, and it was simple for the user to switch. But e-mail was intrinsically more valuable. Once you registered your name at Yahoo.com, you'd be less likely to cavalierly switch to another portal's e-mail service—especially after the advent of instant messaging, when knowing other people's e-mail addresses and having others know yours could translate into instantaneous contact. Plus, think of the free advertising and brand building!

Suddenly, all the search engines—not just Yahoo—wanted to offer their audiences free e-mail. The question was, should they buy it from someone who had already created it? Or should they build it themselves? As J. J. Healy said, this question came up again and again, as new services were invented in rapid-fire succession over the next several months.

Hotmail made history on July 4, 1996, when it launched the first free Web-based e-mail service, and it almost immediately caught Yahoo's attention. Scott Weiss, who knew No. 3 Yahoo Tim Brady from their Harvard M.B.A. days, was looking for a start-up to join in the summer of 1996. In an e-mail, Brady suggested his friend take a look at Hotmail. "He said he wasn't sure about the business model, but he said it looked interesting," Weiss recalls. "I went over there on his recommendation." Weiss joined Hotmail as director of business development.

Yahoo had several meetings with Hotmail, but didn't buy the company or license the technology because it was worried about scalability and reliability. If a search engine comes up with a bad link, no problem; you do another search. But if you go to access your inbox and your e-mail is gone, "you want to torch someone's house," Weiss says. Yahoo kept looking around, mulling its options.

In the meantime, Four11 decided to get into the free e-mail business. Four11 started out by putting white pages and yellow pages listings online. It then licensed its product to several of the portals, like Yahoo, and would-be portals, like Hotmail. Since Four11 and Hotmail were both funded by the same venture-capital firm, Draper Fisher Jurvetson, they had a close relationship. The two companies took things a step further by sharing information: Hotmail would have a link for sign-ups on Four11's home page, and Four11 would get access to new Hotmail users' e-mail addresses, helping Four11 have updated and more complete directories. As new users signed up for Hotmail, it sent those e-mail addresses directly over to Four11. Hotmail had been trumpeting that 6,000 new users were signing up for its service a day, but nobody believed it. Four11, however, had the evidence and was amazed at Hotmail's popularity. Four11 recognized a new opportunity immediately and decided to build its own free e-mail service.

When Hotmail learned its partner was going to be a competitor, it confronted Four11, but Four11 denied it was developing free e-mail. Then Hotmail saw that Four11 had licensed new domains with names like yahoomail.com, excitemail.com, and lycosmail.com. When confronted again, Four11 'fessed up.

Suddenly, the partners were competitors. Four11 launched RocketMail in March 1997. While Hotmail was appealing directly to consumers, Four11 executives thought they could do with free e-mail what they had done with their directories: license it to several companies, including Yahoo. "Yahoo was, of course, top of our list for a similar relationship with our e-mail technology, not just because it was the largest fish, but because of the solid, preexisting relationship," says Katie Burke, who was director of marketing and business development for Four11.

She set up a meeting with some Yahoos through her close friend Tim Brady, a former classmate of hers at Harvard Business School. A couple of weeks later, she dropped by to see Brady at Yahoo with a lava lamp in the shape of a rocket—and a proposal for a Yahoo e-mail service. Discussions got heated, because Yahoo didn't want RocketMail to be available to certain of its competitors (who, once they got wind of the talks, would want the same service). Yahoo wanted to "preserve uniqueness in their service and a first-mover advantage in the portal e-mail space," Burke says.

Yahoo also was nervous about Four11 hosting its users' data and e-mail, from both a security and a quality standpoint. "It was a topic with which they could never get comfortable," Burke says. And the company worried about what would happen if the deal unraveled. By August, Yahoo had made it clear it thought Web-based e-mail was too important to license, and it would have to build the service itself, or buy it outright from Four11—or another company.

Then things grew frenzied. Burke called a friend at Infoseek. Another Four11 executive called Lycos. "One day I picked up the phone, and it was someone from Microsoft inquiring about our service," Burke says. Within a week, Four11 had meetings or phone conversations with six of the top Internet companies. Some were more interested in licensing the service; others wanted to buy the company. "It was clear they were talking to our competitors as well. Yahoo was talking with our competitors, too—they told us so, and we found out through other channels." And there were plenty of competitors to talk to. They were popping up like mushrooms after a rainstorm, companies like WhoWhere, Mail.com, and USA-Net.

Complicating matters even further, Four11 had no idea how much it should ask if Yahoo wanted to buy it. Tim Draper, who was on Four11's board and whose VC firm had funded Four11, told its founders they shouldn't take a penny less than $400 million. Tim Koogle and Jeff Mallett had in mind a much lower price—less than $100 million. Then, while Yahoo was negotiating with Four11, an unsolicited bid came in from someone else. When Koogle learned about the bid, he wasn't amused. He let Four11's founders know he didn't want to get into a bidding war. But Yahoo was also negotiating with Hotmail. Tensions were, to say the least, high.

"I believe we quoted them a billion [dollars], but they were thinking in the neighborhood of $100 million," Hotmail's Weiss says. "So, that's how it went." Yahoo decided to buy Four11 instead in October 1997, for $94 million. No problem for Hotmail. Microsoft acquired it in January 1998 for almost $400 million.

Lycos bought WhoWhere, and Netscape picked up free e-mail by licensing it from USA-Net.

This scenario—where a new technology or service would emerge and become a must-have for the portals—happened monthly and, at its height, almost weekly. "At Hotmail, we called them trailer-park businesses," Weiss says. "The portals were tornados, looking for a trailer park to sweep up."

Yahoo started out with its directory, or guide. It added Yahooligans, a site for children, local guides in several countries, and then cities. Excite followed suit, focusing on local and then international content. They both added personalization, which meant you could choose how you wanted your home page to look.

In January 1997, Yahoo added chat—the ability for multiple people to post messages to each other simultaneously. A month later, in February, Yahoo added online classifieds, a service built by a team of Yahoos. In October, Yahoo added the all-important e-mail via its acquisition of Four11.

Then the pace quickened. In November 1997, Yahoo launched a travel section. In December, it was sports. Three months later, in March 1998, Yahoo introduced a games site. In May, it was Yahoo Movies. June? Real Estate. In August, Yahoo debuted three services: Yahoo Calendar, for its growing audience to track their own schedules and see what was going on in their communities; Yahoo Clubs, where people of like minds could band together and share files and chat; and Yahoo Small Business, a suite of communications tools and B2B services.

It kept going from there. In September, Yahoo opened Yahoo Auctions, Yahoo's answer to eBay's person-to-person sales behemoth. In November and December: Yahoo Employment, Yahoo Shopping, and Yahoo Address Book. It's a wonder anyone who worked at Yahoo ever got a chance to sleep.

The Portal Wars, 1996 to 1998

❦

Silicon Valley is an insular place, and word spreads fast when new trends are born. If one Web calendar company was incubating, you could bet that half a dozen others were coming together in dank garages and apartments throughout the region. Word would spread via entrepreneurs and their friends, and through venture capitalists who entertained pitches from companies that dreamed of being the next Hotmail or Four11.

And if Yahoo was talking to a Web calendar company, then Microsoft, Excite, Netscape, Lycos, and Infoseek were probably talking to it, too. This scenario played itself out over and over during the portal wars, as portals got ideas for new services that would lure users to hang out at their sites longer—that would make their sites stickier.

In Yahoo's first meeting with start-up When.com, a small company that was building a calendar that users could access through their browsers, it found a roomful of people who had different goals for the meeting than it did. "The conversation was fairly strange," says Joe Beninato, a cofounder of When.com. "We went in there looking for distribution partnerships with these guys, and very quickly the conversation turned to them buying us."

The strangest part of the story is that When.com hadn't even launched a product yet. "We didn't really have anything. We were a couple of months old," Beninato says.

The time was early 1998, and Yahoo was also talking to Web-Cal, another small company that already had a Web-based calendar application. And Yahoo was talking to Jump Networks, then a tiny start-up developing an application that would take My Yahoo stats—stock quotes, weather, news, and so on—and transfer them to a handheld device. After the meetings, Jump

131

decided to switch its focus to building a calendar application, says Bill Trenchard, who was CEO of Jump. "My whole goal was to get acquired by Yahoo," he says. "We were pitching them anything that could possibly get acquired."

Trenchard, all of 23 at the time, was just out of Cornell University. He knew if Yahoo wanted something, all the other portal players would, too. A few months after its meeting with Yahoo, Jump raised $1.5 million in venture funding from Idealab Capital Partners. After another few months, with its beta application finished, Jump launched its calendar. Several other players got into the game, including companies with self-marketing names like SuperCalendar and SmartCalendar.

Yahoo ultimately acquired WebCal for about $30 million. Yahoo Calendar launched in August 1998. A short while later, other portals were willing to pay much more to add calendars to their checklists: AOL ended up buying When.com for about $225 million in April 1999. Microsoft bought Jump for about $60 million at the same time, a nice payoff for Jump and its venture capitalists. "Even in fantasyland, it was nice," Trenchard says.

There was no time to stop and look in the rearview mirror—only time to accelerate to the next deal, so you could get there before your competitors. There often wasn't even time to figure out whether a particular new feature made sense to add. Did users really want online calendars or online bill paying? No matter—if your competitor had them, you had to have them, too.

In spring 1996, Pete Budlong had just joined Classifieds2000 as the first employee after the founders. Within weeks, Excite made an offer to buy the company. The way the offer came about illustrates the Wild West atmosphere of Silicon Valley in 1996. Founding brothers Sani and Karim El-Fishawy were having dinner with Excite President Joe Kraus at Osteria, a low-key

Italian restaurant in Palo Alto. Kraus said he wanted to buy the brothers' company. Since Classifieds2000 had three employees, Kraus asked, how would $6 million sound? He scribbled the offer on a napkin and gave it to the founders. Budlong recalls that when he found out about that, he thought, "What an amazing time this is when a 24-year-old founder of a public company can make a deal like that."

The deal soured, however, after Excite announced it was buying the McKinley Group's Magellan Web guide in June 1996. Wall Street didn't like the deal, and Excite's already-sliding stock took a hit and on June 28 closed at less than half its IPO price. Classifieds2000 decided to move forward instead with a plan to create a service that it could license to several companies. It would customize the look and feel of the service for each customer, but all the customers would share the same classifieds listings. The model resembled the one Four11 had used for its white pages and yellow pages directories, except that in the case of Classifieds2000, users could add their own listings for free, so the number of listings multiplied exponentially as each partner was added.

The arrangement was a no-brainer for most of the portals. They had to fork out little or no money up front. Classifieds2000 would build each portal a site, and the portal would get up to 50 percent of the ad revenue generated by the classifieds, after expenses. But Yahoo wanted more. It wanted to control its own listings and user information.

For Classifieds2000's first meeting with Yahoo in April 1996, Budlong and the two founders went to Yahoo's low-key Vaqueros headquarters in Sunnyvale. Jerry Yang was busy being interviewed by a Japanese television crew. When he finished, he came into the conference room wearing a T-shirt, shorts, and just socks on his feet.

Besides Yang, Jeff Mallett and Ellen Siminoff were there. They said they were studying the classifieds market and debating whether to develop their own service internally or partner with someone. After sharing their vision for the classifieds space, Yang and Mallett left the three Classifieds2000 employees alone with Siminoff. Along with her charge to build the local sites, she was responsible for yellow pages and classifieds.

"I remember Ellen saying, 'Maybe we could just bring you guys in,' and soon the talk turned to the what-if of how the closest kind of partnership might look," Budlong says. He recalls that when asked what value Yahoo would place on the company, Siminoff said, "Anything approaching $20 million would be out of the question." Budlong and the Classifieds2000 founders had thought $20 million would be a good starting point, but regardless, Budlong says, "we realized Yahoo had already made up its mind to build its own classifieds."

For one thing, Siminoff had told them they should know Yahoo had an internal group evaluating classifieds that might go off and build its own. "In their view, the listing quality and user experience were just too important to entrust to someone else," Budlong says. "We were just three guys. We had a lot of listings, but they could get a lot when they launched. They didn't need us for that. I think they wanted to keep us guessing and slow us down potentially."

Yahoo launched its Classifieds section in February 1997. Classifieds2000 became the engine for most of the other portals. Even after Excite bought the company in April 1998 for $48 million, Infoseek, Hotmail, Lycos, and others continued to license their classifieds technology from one of their closest competitors.

〜

*E*ventually, just about everything you could think of got lumped into the portals—even greeting cards. Yahoo and the other portals had a secret-intelligence source: their own traffic. They could see which areas of the site—as well as other topics on the Web—were most popular by watching where their users flocked and what they searched for. Greeting-card sites were cropping up on the Web, so Yahoo decided it needed its own.

However, Yahoo prided itself on being as cheap as possible. Elizabeth Collet, then director of business development for e-commerce, decided to hire an intern in the summer of 1999 to build out Yahoo's electronic-greetings offering. The intern inked deals with artists, who got exposure plus the chance to sell their art to people who saw it on Yahoo's greeting cards. "At the bottom of the card, it would give credit and tell people where to find the artist," Collet says. The total expenditure to launch the site? "Probably $10,000," Collet says. "It was such a Yahoo way of doing it. It wasn't the elegant or expensive way—it was a roll-up-your-sleeves-and-be-entrepreneurial way."

Two months later, when Excite@Home announced it was buying Blue Mountain Arts, a fairly cheesy greeting-card site, Collet says she chuckled. The price tag was $780 million. To be fair, Excite was largely buying the site because it was the 14th-most-popular site on the Web at the time, with 9 million unique monthly visitors. But Yahoo was the traffic leader. By that time, it didn't need to buy sites for their traffic.

Besides Stanford University, Netscape was Yahoo's biggest incubator as Yahoo was hatching. It seems strange today, when Microsoft's Internet Explorer is by far the most widely used browser, but in the early days of the medium, the vast majority of people clicking on to the Net were using Netscape's Navigator. Its toolbar had buttons for "Search," "What's New," "What's Cool," and "Directory," and the latter button took surfers directly to Yahoo. "They were just kids in school," says Mike Homer, explaining why Netscape gave Yahoo the free publicity and loads of free traffic. But Homer also thought Yahoo was the best directory available.

About a year later, in late 1995, Netscape realized how valuable those links were and, in early 1996, started charging companies like Yahoo a fee in the neighborhood of $5 million a year for all the traffic it was sending them. Netscape added a search button on its home page, which search engines had to pay to be part of. Yahoo was one of five options that got cycled through for the fee.

But Netscape and Yahoo continued their close relationship. Netscape approached Yahoo with an idea: Why not create a Netscape Guide by Yahoo? That way, Netscape's brand would be on the directory, and Yahoo would still get traffic from Netscape. "We thought that Yahoo could build that out for us in a way that would begin our path towards beginning a portal, but with little cost to us," Homer says. Besides, Homer thought, such a deal would bring in new revenue: Yahoo agreed to pay Netscape $20 million over two years for that prime real estate on Netscape's home page, Homer says.

Although people didn't consider Netscape.com a portal per se, it was quickly becoming one. In 1997, it raked in $100 million from advertising and sponsorships on its home page, which it had dubbed Netcenter. That gave Netscape portal revenue that was second only to Yahoo. Another surprise: Netscape was third-largest in terms of reach, Homer says.

Suddenly, Yahoo and Netscape were competitors in the portal business. And both parties realized the Netscape Guide by Yahoo deal wasn't working out the way either had envisioned. Yahoo thought the guide would bring it a lot more users, and thus revenue, and had already made a $5 million down payment to Netscape for the privilege. But the Netscape Guide saw less than half the traffic that Yahoo and Netscape had expected. "They probably thought we didn't promote [the guide] enough, and from our perspective, the content [a limited version of Yahoo] wasn't desirable," Homer says.

To Yahoo's credit, it agreed to back away from the deal, and though Netscape had been guaranteed $20 million over two years, it agreed to settle for only the $5 million first payment. "When both parties found out it wasn't working, we came to the table like mature adults and appropriately wound down the deal," Homer says.

Meanwhile, Netscape had officially launched Netcenter, which was now a full-fledged portal with free e-mail, personalization, news, and the like. Netscape needed its portal revenue stream to flourish, since its core browser business was being hacked away by Microsoft. In a harbinger of the consolidation to come, AOL revealed in November 1998 that it was buying Netscape for $4.2 billion. AOL was still largely a proprietary online service that only subscribers could access. The Netscape deal would jump-start AOL's move to the Web. Yahoo's competitor Netscape would become part of an even more formidable competitor: AOL.

⌒

*A*s long-standing relationships became more tangled and partners jockeyed for position, things started getting really interesting. For example, AOL had a stake in Excite dating back to November 1996, when AOL chose Excite as its search partner and invested in the company. AOL's chief executive, Steve Case, joined Excite's board. But as Excite started becoming an online service, Case resigned his seat on Excite's board, and AOL sold some of its stock in Excite. A former Excite employee says Case would find himself in a board meeting and a topic would come up that was too close to home. Excite was planning to offer software, called Pal, that would notify people when their friends were online and let them exchange instant messages that resembled typed phone conversations, rather than e-mail. But Pal would be a competitor to AOL's Instant Messenger, so Case had to leave the board meeting. Still, despite their rivalry, AOL continued to use Excite's search software to power AOL NetFind, AOL's search option.

Deals that had come together often unraveled. In November 1997, Yahoo and a small Silicon Valley start-up called Junglee paired to offer a service that would help consumers comparison-shop for products carried by Yahoo merchants. Yahoo had turned to Junglee's technology because another potential partner Yahoo liked, Netbot, had suddenly been acquired by archrival Excite. Excite was preparing to officially launch its new comparison-shopping service, Jango, which Netbot had built, when Yahoo preempted its announcement by two days. Yahoo got a slap in the face less than a year later when Amazon scooped up Junglee. Spurned on all sides, Yahoo ended up creating comparison-shopping technology of its own.

But perhaps Yahoo and Excite didn't give enough thought to whether a comparison-shopping service was such a good idea. Customers liked the service, but advertisers didn't appreciate it when the portals' comparison shoppers would find another merchant that sold their product for less. Eventually, both Excite and Yahoo quietly put the kibosh on their comparison-shopping services.

As if competition among the start-ups weren't hairy

enough, traditional mass-media companies started dipping their toes in the Web waters. When NBC announced it was investing in Snap, a portal created by technology-news site CNET, all the other portals stood at attention. On June 9, 1998, NBC paid $5.9 million for 19 percent of the fledgling portal, which CNET had launched to mixed reviews. NBC took a small stake in CNET as well.

The power of the deal was obvious: Even though Snap wasn't all that special, its relationship with NBC could set it apart because the network could tap the cumulative power of its television properties to advertise Snap. Such a deal could offer a huge advantage over the other portals. Sure, Yahoo had TV advertising, but if Snap were pitched during an episode of *Friends*, what would that do for its reach? Just nine days after the announcement of the Snap deal, Disney said it was buying 43 percent of Infoseek, a deal that eventually culminated in the creation of the failed portal Go.com.

Soon all the portals were talking to media companies. "We were talking to the remaining media companies, meaning Time Warner and Fox," Homer says of Netscape. "There was this feeling that Excite was everywhere we were—they would come in the door and we would go out."

In addition to talking to the media companies, the portals were talking to each other. Yahoo and Excite met to hash out whether they should merge. Several talks took place—one in an athletic club in the Valley, others in the offices of the Venture Law Group, Yahoo's legal counsel at the time.

Excite was also having secret meetings with Netscape. A few months before the media companies came knocking, Netscape chose Excite to be its portal provider, meaning it would manage the content and plumbing of Netcenter. There was a lot of money involved. Excite promised to pay Netscape $90 million—$70 million up front—for the traffic it expected to reap. And Netscape and Excite considered deepening the relationship even more, through a merger.

But after weeks of discussions, Excite surprised both Yahoo and Netscape by agreeing to be acquired by cable operator At Home. And Netscape was acquired by AOL.

Luckily for Yahoo, the early portal-media partnerships didn't pan out the way their investors had hoped. Disney leveraged its ownership of ABC and plastered Go.com's logo all over television. But instead of capitalizing on its strengths, it lost ground by trying to copy Yahoo and AOL. "It was pathetically misguided," Lise Buyer says. "Disney had all these wonderful properties and characters that people would have flocked to see online, but Disney was so protective of its brand that it wouldn't put them up. All these companies looked at Yahoo and Excite and said we want to be just like that instead of trying to leverage their own space. It was just dumb."

Despite their hoards of capital and the exposure traditional media companies like NBC and Disney gave their portal partners, they lost to the pure Web start-ups: Yahoo, Excite, and Lycos. And among the Web pure plays, Yahoo emerged the winner.

By 1998, AOL, Yahoo, and MSN were bringing in 43 percent of total online advertising revenue. The rest of the portals combined (AltaVista, Excite, Go.com, Lycos, and Snap) attracted 19 percent of advertising spending, while the vertical portals (niche-oriented sites, like Amazon and eBay) garnered 24 percent. That left 14 percent being spent on all other Web sites.[6]

As the portal victor, Yahoo found itself competing in a new arena: against AOL, and gradually MSN. These giants began throwing their weight around, amassing more impressive revenues. Since they were Internet service providers as well as portals and had millions of "members" with whom they had a billing relationship, they could charge advertisers a premium just for being associated with them. Case in point: AOL began the push toward multimillion-dollar-placement deals when it made Tel-Save its exclusive long-distance provider in February 1997. Tel-Save agreed to pay AOL $100 million for the privilege of offering discount long-distance service to AOL's 8 million subscribers.

The AOL–Tel-Save deal was "head-turning," Buyer says. "No one had done anything like that. That kicked off the deal race."

Soon, Yahoo began charging its advertisers hefty fees for being the premier music retailer or bookseller. Yahoo was becoming more and more like AOL: able to charge huge partnership fees and distribute an advertisement to millions of viewers. But one thing it didn't have was a billing relationship with the customer.

While AOL subscribers paid a monthly fee to get Internet access and, along with it, all of AOL's content and services, Yahoo's customers—if you could call them that—were accustomed to getting everything for free.

But as the dot-coms started to collapse and the advertising market shrank, Yahoo had to find ways other than advertising to make money. It started charging for some existing services, like auctions and personals, and introducing new paid services, like extra storage space for e-mail and photos, registration of personal domain names, and tools for building personal Web pages. Yahoo hopes that some percentage of its users will continue to use the services they used to get for free and pay for the new ones. It's a model that for Yahoo, so far, is unproven.

⌐

Yahoo's main competition continued to shift—from the portals to e-commerce players to AOL and Microsoft. "We are scared of a lot of people," Yang said. "We watch out for AOL, Microsoft, Excite, and Amazon—they all want to eat our lunch in one form or another."[7]

And there was one more seemingly benign but nonetheless insidious threat to Yahoo: a directory that listed many more Web pages than Yahoo and let anyone license its content for free.

Some companies have built entire businesses around licensing their technology or content to others. Reuters, Yahoo's first big partner, grants Yahoo a license to post its news stories in exchange for traffic and a share of the resulting advertising revenue. An early Yahoo competitor, LookSmart, built a directory like Yahoo's that it licensed to other companies for use on their Web sites.

Then, in June 1998, along came Gnuhoo (pronounced newhoo), a guide compiled by volunteer editors instead of paid surfers.

Four Sun Microsystems engineers and an attorney friend of theirs ran Gnuhoo in their spare time. Frustrated by Yahoo's inability to keep pace with the rapidly expanding Web, they decided to make Gnuhoo an open-source project, which meant anyone who they determined wasn't a quack or a threat could create categories and index Web sites. They named the directory after Gnu, a piece of open-source software, but thankfully, soon changed its name to NewHoo!. Without much effort on the five founders' part, the project quickly took off. People passionate about topics like thyroid glands or amusement-park machinery indexed sites, and NewHoo!'s directory listings multiplied.

Rich Skrenta, a cofounder of NewHoo! and now a director of engineering at Netscape, says he helped start NewHoo! because he thought Yahoo, once the greatest directory on the

142

Web, had changed for the worse. "It seemed like they were focusing more on marketing-ish things, like cobranded Visa cards and putting up entertainment pages. What had made them great was the directory, and they were ignoring it," he says. "It was irritating."

Following the open-source philosophy made sense, Skrenta says. "That was the way the Internet was built—you had these amateur people creating Web pages and mailing lists and discussion forums. It makes sense if someone is into unicycling, they'd be better [at indexing sites about unicycling] than a generalist living in Santa Clara, California."

For a while, Yahoo didn't seem to be threatened by NewHoo! and a host of other Yahoo copycats (some of which were parodies, like Robohoo!, Shoparoo, and Trekhoo). Yahoo even created a category for Yahoo imitators that offered links to their sites. But then it started sending cease-and-desist letters. Apparently someone at Yahoo didn't like the fact that some of the sites were using the syllable "hoo." Or maybe it was the exclamation point or the cartoonish lettering some used in their logos. NewHoo! ultimately changed its name to the Open Directory. And that Yahoo category for Yahoo parodies? It's gone.

Five months after NewHoo! launched, Netscape acquired it for $1 million, according to Homer. By then NewHoo! already had 100,000 sites indexed by the more than 4,700 editors who had signed up. At the time, Yahoo had about 70 surfers cataloguing and indexing the Web. Even though they had salaries and stock options, it had been only a matter of time before their efforts were eclipsed by those of NewHoo!'s volunteer editors, just because of the sheer numbers dedicated to the effort. Today the Open Directory (www.dmoz.org) has more than 40,000 editors who have indexed more than 3 million sites, and every online service from Google to Lycos to AOL uses its directory content on their sites.

At one time, LookSmart got a large percentage of its revenues from licensing its directory to companies that incorporated it into their Web sites. That business has dwindled. "We kind of wrecked that model," Skrenta says. For Yahoo, too.

Try as they might, the portals chasing Yahoo simply couldn't catch it. Excite tried everything, including, in the early days, confrontational advertising. "We were definitely the underdog, willing to take some more aggressive tactics," Joe Kraus says. An early Excite marketing campaign, in 1996, asked the question: "Are you still with the same old Yahoo?" Kraus says, "If we stayed with the status quo, we weren't going to win. We had to do things that were different."

Excite even lost to Yahoo in a friendly softball game between the two companies, despite snagging San Francisco Giants outfielder Barry Bonds as a ringer on its team.

In those early days, before Yahoo execs learned to play politic, the pressure they were under from the assaults on all sides sometimes seeped out.

In a 1995 interview with *Red Herring*, Jerry Yang dissed the look and feel, and even the technology, of Excite (then called Architext). "I think they can make certain parts of their product work very well and make some parts of it look really bad. That's the nature of search engines. The product must speak for itself over time. I think they've gone through several business plans. They have openly stated that they want to compete with us. I'm not sure if I'd do that if I had their technology."[8]

Despite such slights, the competition rarely criticized Yahoo. Yahoo was too good. "They were an amazing group to compete against because of their ability to deliver quality products all the time," Kraus says.

How much did Kraus respect Yahoo? In early 2001, about a year after he left Excite, when he was no longer forbidden to do so, he bought Yahoo stock. At first the shares were in the $40 range. He kept buying as they dropped to the $30 range. A few weeks later, as the stock continued to plunge, he gave up, and sold his stock—in the $20s. "It's not good, but it's not all bad," Kraus says. "At least they gave me a capital loss."

Even Yahoo isn't the leader it used to be, at least not in the stock market.

The Euphoria, 1999

Key Events

- January: Cable-modem provider At Home acquires Excite for $6.7 billion.
- February: USA Networks bids for a controlling interest in Lycos.
- May: USA Networks and Lycos scrap merger plans after shareholders balk.
- May: Napster enables music-file sharing.
- July: Disney buys the rest of Infoseek and spins out Go.com as a tracking stock.
- September: CBS and Viacom combine in a $35 billion merger.
- December: VA Linux sets a new opening-day IPO record, soaring 708 percent above its offering price and closing with a market cap of $9.6 billion.

Silicon Valley circa 1999 was like one giant crack frenzy. The venture capitalists, entrepreneurs, and investors day trading Internet stocks were high out of their minds on insane company valuations. In hindsight, after the bubble burst, pundits laid some of the blame for the fanaticism on venture capitalists for opening up their pocketbooks to hundreds of new start-ups, many of them with questionable business plans. They poured $56.9 billion into mostly high tech start-ups in 1999, more than twice the $22.7 billion they had disbursed the previous year, according to Venture Economics, a VC-market researcher. Some of the blame also went to investment banks, which took an average of 191 tech companies public each year from 1996 to 2000. In 1999 alone, 318 companies went public, according to Net Queen Mary Meeker. In contrast, during the summer of 2001, Meeker predicted there would be only 20 tech IPOs by the end of the year.[1]

Add to that frothiness the irrational exuberance of day traders, a new breed of investor who would buy stocks and sell them hours or days later after a quick run-up, rather than invest for the long haul. There were an estimated 5 to 7 million online day traders in the first quarter of 1999, and their numbers were expected to jump to 10 million by the end of the year, further fueling the craze.[2]

Against this backdrop, announcing a dot-com strategy could make even an old-economy loser suddenly seem fresh and promising. Witness the marvel of Ktel, a music retailer known for its cheesy late-night TV come-ons for disco or country compilations. When Ktel announced it was going to launch ktel.com in early 1998—instantly transforming it, at least in the public's eye, into an Internet stock—its shares soared to $49.50 from $6.25 within a couple of weeks. In 1999, when Ktel signed a pact with Yahoo competitor MSN to market its wares on the rapidly growing online network, its shares almost doubled in a day.

Similarly, *Individual Investor's* shares rose more than 36 percent on the day in February it announced the simple news that its Web site would be linked from the popular Yahoo Finance site. Investors assumed the Yahoo link would drive buckets of traffic, and traffic was one of the few ways to measure value, since few Web sites were actually profitable. Delia's, an online clothing store for girls, had seen a similar boost two months earlier: Its shares increased 67 percent in a day when it said it would open a store on Yahoo.[3]

But in the beginning of 1999, none of this seemed irrational, because the Internet industry and Yahoo in particular were humming along. Stocks were going nowhere but up. Yahoo's stock had jumped 584 percent in 1998. At the beginning of 1999, its market cap was $23 billion; three months into the year, it had already ballooned to $35 billion.

Still, along with the Net industry's high came extreme paranoia, especially among the entrepreneurs and venture capitalists. Things were changing so fast that it was by no means certain who was winning, or even exactly what the game was. From month to month, so many new users were going online that Yahoo, the leader until 1998, was overtaken by several of the competitors circling around it—first AOL and MSN, then briefly Lycos. In April 1999, Lycos had a 51.8 percent reach, just besting Yahoo's 50.8 percent reach, according to a report released by Media Metrix.[4]

Yahoo had to be nimble in order to regain its leadership by winning the majority of new Web users—and keeping the ones it already had from straying to a competitor. The best way to do this at the time was to add the best new services—thus, the steady stream of exploratory talks with upstarts and even competitors, like Excite.

Since Excite had decided to merge with At Home, suddenly analysts and shareholders were wondering whether Yahoo would make such a pairing. At an investment conference in Snowbird, Utah, in March, Tim Koogle told analysts that Yahoo wasn't looking to merge with or acquire a major media company. The company "doesn't have any intention of purchasing offline assets, if you will," he said.[5] He added that Yahoo was planning to focus on building its business through acquisitions and cross-promotions with content providers.

At first, the pairing of Excite and At Home was worrisome for Yahoo, which revealed in one of its regulatory filings that the deal could threaten its new relationship with AT&T's WorldNet ISP, in which WorldNet customers got Yahoo as their default home page.

But the Excite@Home deal started showing cracks in its foundation almost immediately. In August, AT&T, Excite@ Home's largest shareholder, sent a letter to the Excite@Home board, calling for it to break up its cable and content assets and foreshadowing its later demise, good news for Yahoo as it sprinted to stay ahead.

⌒

*Y*ahoo's next generation of deals were geared toward getting its expanding cadre of services in front of more new PC users. In early January, Yahoo and Hewlett-Packard (HP) inked a deal for My Yahoo to be the start page on new HP Pavilion PCs. A week later, Yahoo and IBM announced a similar deal for new IBM Aptivas. Distribution deals with Toshiba and Micron followed.

Meanwhile, sales and earnings continued to impress financial analysts. In mid-January, Yahoo revealed results for the fourth quarter of 1998: Revenues were $76.4 million, and more impressively, earnings per share after various charges were 16 cents. Yahoo's revenue was growing even faster than its page views (167 million per day in December), prompting analyst Lise Buyer to point out that Yahoo was not only growing phenomenally but was monetizing the new traffic it had amassed in 1998, a year of rapid growth. In the fourth quarter, the number of customers who had registered their personal information with Yahoo grew to 35 million from 25 million—a growth rate of 40 percent! And Yahoo added 275 new advertisers to its stable and increased its retention rate to 94 percent (from the 90 percent it had reported in the previous quarter). Operating margins increased to 26 percent in fiscal 1998, and Buyer estimated they would increase to 34 percent in 1999, 36 percent in 2000, and ultimately beyond 40 percent.

"We remain tremendously impressed with the fundamentals of Yahoo's business,"[6] Buyer said. "We also believe that Yahoo is one of the best run, best managed entities in the 'Internet' arena, and arguably is to the Internet what Cisco is to networking or Dell is to the PC industry."[7] No wonder Tim Koogle and Jeff Mallett both got promotions: Koogle added chairman to his CEO title, and Mallett became president as well as chief operating officer.

About two weeks later, Yahoo unveiled its latest plan to stay near the top of audience-rating charts: It would spend $3.6 billion to acquire GeoCities, a Marina del Rey, California, provider of personal home pages. GeoCities boasted some 3.5 million "homesteaders" who'd spent the time to create their own personal sites, with photos of their kids, pets, and favorite entertainers. And those sites, hokey as many of them were, attracted more than 19 million unique visitors, making GeoCities the third-most-trafficked site on the entire Internet in December 1998, according to Media Metrix. Just think: millions of new folks to whom Yahoo could market its growing stable of services. And even though GeoCities wasn't profitable—in fact, it had lost $32.1 million on sales of $23.3 million in its short four-year life span—Yahoo saw great value in the deal. Most important, by combining the two companies, Yahoo believed it would reach into the homes and businesses of about 58 percent of Web users.

Yahoo's relationship with GeoCities started out as an investment in late 1997. "On things we thought we might need to own, we'd date the company before we were married," says Yahoo's former M&A head, J. J. Healy. As part of a deal to offer GeoCities' free home pages to Yahoo customers, and free Yahoo services like e-mail to GeoCities customers, Yahoo handed over an undisclosed sum to GeoCities. In December 1998, Yahoo owned 2.1 percent of GeoCities' stock, according to a regulatory filing.

Sitting on the sunny deck of his Woodside home, with Sade piped through outdoor speakers, Healy explained Yahoo's thinking. "It was a frothy time," Healy said. He would vet each of the 5 to 15 solicitations Yahoo received each week because he knew that if these companies were approaching Yahoo, they were likely approaching Yahoo's competitors, too. If an important company fell through the cracks and was bought by someone else, "we were screwed," he said.

Yahoo heard that AOL was exploring GeoCities, too. A GeoCities acquisition could tighten AOL's grip on the lead position. Though the price Yahoo was willing to pay for GeoCities, about $3.6 billion, might seem high, Healy says, it wasn't in the context of the currency of the times. Yahoo had about 200 million shares outstanding at the time, and GeoCities cost 5 percent of that, or 10 million shares. "It was not insignificant, but not huge," especially since the point was to "keep that out of the hands of AOL." And in the bargain, Yahoo bagged a big group of Web diehards who had used GeoCities tools to build their home pages. "You couldn't uproot your home page and move it somewhere else. . . . Therefore, they were very sticky and loyal to the GeoCities platform," Healy said. It was a classic example of acquisition as "strategic weapon."

But GeoCities wasn't a great fit with Yahoo culturally, insiders say. "It's hard to underestimate a cultural organization," Elizabeth Collet says. "They were a top-down organization. Yahoo was more distributed." When the deal went through, about 200 of GeoCities' 300 employees lost their jobs, and Yahoo took a $68 million charge against second-quarter earnings. Analysts saw no problem: Yahoo was still raking in the dough.

By now, several influential analysts had started covering Yahoo, including Merrill Lynch's Henry Blodget and U.S. Bancorp Piper Jaffray's Safa Rashtchy. It was about time for Yahoo to preach its gospel to these influencers, so it staged its first analyst meeting at its Santa Clara offices in early March.

The main message? Yahoo is more than a portal: It's a global media company that will make itself accessible not just from Net-connected PCs but from cell phones, pagers, handheld devices like the PalmPilot, and all manner of forthcoming wireless gizmos. And it's cheap. (Perhaps the best illustration of this point: Yahoo told analysts at the meeting that it runs its entire network on a free version of the Linux operating system.)

Analysts ate up the message. At least one, Paul Noglows, even raised his rating on the company from "hold" to "buy."

꙳

The morning of April 1 started very early for Tim Koogle, Jeff Mallet, Jerry Yang, and the other top Yahoos, who were getting ready for a 5:30 A.M. conference call that would announce to Wall Street Yahoo's newest strategic weapon: the acquisition of Broadcast.com, a four-year-old start-up that broadcast audio and video over the Internet.

Broadcast.com had boasted a lot of firsts since launching in September 1995: It had carried the first live Internet broadcasts of a radio station, a sporting event, a corporate quarterly earnings call, and a stockholders' meeting. Still, Broadcast.com wasn't the pioneer of enabling audio and video over the Internet—that was RealNetworks, with its RealAudio player. But Broadcast.com founders had had the foresight to recognize that aggregating audio and video would open a market for someone to be the Yahoo of audio and video. And that's what Broadcast.com did, though it went further: It rounded up programs from radio and television networks—the largest collection of audio and video content available on the Net—and distributed its partners' content on the network it had built. At the time of the acquisition, it hosted streams of content from 400 radio stations and 450 sports teams, and tons of live or recorded press conferences and corporate meetings. Like Yahoo, Broadcast.com was duplicable, but it had done it first.

Yahoo knew text and graphics. But audio and video was a whole new world, and the Yahoos were wowed by Broadcast. com's prowess. At the time, only about 4 percent of U.S. households had the broadband or super-high-speed connections that made viewing rich-media content anything except frustrating. But analysts predicted that by the year 2002, 20 percent of households, or about 20 million, would have broadband connections.

In the early-morning conference call, Koogle could barely contain his excitement. "We're really stoked about this combination," he told analysts. "Take two leading companies? Combine them? Powerful.

"This is not one plus one equals two. We favor deals that have different math than that," Koogle said, laughing.

The Broadcast.com acquisition had originated similarly to the GeoCities deal: Yahoo dated Broadcast.com before deciding whether to pop the question, investing $1.2 million in early 1997, according to Broadcast.com founder Mark Cuban, who became a billionaire and bought the Dallas Mavericks basketball team. "We didn't do it because we needed the money," Cuban says. "We ended up spending the same amount in advertising with them. So it wasn't about cash. It was about developing relationships."

Cuban says Broadcast.com was always going to be the little guy looking up at the majors from an overall traffic and size perspective. Yahoo had more than 100 times Broadcast.com's traffic, and there was no financially prudent way for Broadcast.com to catch up, even though it dominated its space. So it let Yahoo in the door to see how it operated and perhaps develop a closer bond in the future. Of course, having Yahoo as a partner had other benefits: "It also helped to have them on our resume as an investor if and when we decided to go public," Cuban says.

Which it did, in May 1998. Broadcast.com was a concept stock, and investors liked the concept, but it was hemorrhaging money. When it went public, it had an accumulated deficit of $12.5 million. Just before Yahoo acquired the company, that figure had climbed to $30.7 million. In late February 1999, Cuban put together a presentation for Yahoo. His pitch: "The Net was not always going to be about text and graphics, and there was going to be a need to leverage that fact to create new revenue streams beyond advertising. They liked that less than that 20 percent of our business came from ads and the rest came from services." Yahoo had already begun thinking about diversifying so it didn't have to depend entirely on advertising.

〜

*B*efore the nuptials, Broadcast.com did entertain other suitors, including NBC and AOL. During one phone call, Cuban was turned off when Steve Case didn't seem to know what Broadcast.com was. "They felt like they needed this space, but we were too committed to Yahoo and liked working with them too much," he says.

Once things got heated with Yahoo, the deal came together within 30 days.

There was a problem, however. Within an hour of the last Broadcast.com negotiation, when the parties were hammering out the final price at the offices of the Venture Law Group, BusinessWeek Online had the story on its Web site, in much detail, including the agreed-upon price of $130 a share. Broadcast.com's stock had closed the day before at $118, which meant Yahoo was paying a 10 percent premium for the company, or $5.7 billion. But since rumors had been swirling for more than a week and the stock had already shot up more than 30 percent, the premium was closer to 40 percent when compared to Broadcast.com's average price for the previous month.

Yahoo execs were furious, according to an insider. How had the news gotten out so fast? But none of that rancor was apparent the next day, April 1, when the happy engagement was announced. "This is probably one of the worst-kept secrets in the industry," Koogle quipped, as the call began. Lise Buyer pressed execs during the call, asking whether the leaks had cost Yahoo shareholders. Koogle said no, sounding like he meant it.

The deal, Mallett told analysts, was all about leverage. Broadcast.com had grown to attract 1 million customers a day, totally organically. Imagine how it could grow when placed before Yahoo's 50 million registered users.

Todd Wagner, Broadcast.com's CEO, explained how his company could enhance Yahoo's advertising proposition: It could offer audio and video ads, plus there would be pay-per-view opportunities and new commerce applications (ShoppingVision, a streaming-video infomercial for Yahoo Shopping launched in 2000, proved to be an example of the latter).

Wall Street loved the deal. The next trading day, April 5, the shares rose $39.4, or 22 percent, on very heavy trading.

Soon after the Broadcast.com announcement, Jerry Yang made a trip to Washington to call on the chairman of the Federal Communications Commission (FCC), Bill Kennard. "It struck me as one of those unique moments in time," says Jamie Daves, who was special assistant to the FCC chairman. "He was going around to put in courtesy calls to the powers-that-be."

The meeting was a bit unusual: Picture the 30-year-old Asian-American leader of one of the fastest-growing media companies in the world with the 40-something African-American FCC chairman—not the typical older white guys in suits.

Yang was very unassuming and charming, Daves says. "And hopeful. He said something to the effect of, 'Yeah, I hope it works out, too.'"

Kennard was reaching out to other new-economy leaders, like Marc Andreessen of Netscape/AOL, hoping to gain support for competition. "The deals they were doing were impacting telecommunications policy," Daves says. "We wanted them to be voices to encourage competition."

There were no specific regulatory issues that would have prevented the merger from taking place, but Yang was playing the role of Internet evangelist, a role he would fill for years to come.

Yang and Kennard clearly thought alike in one way: They

both favored openness and competition rather than the consolidation that was becoming the norm. Long before the AOL Time Warner behemoth would threaten Yahoo's way of life even further, Yahoo was increasingly coming under fire for remaining independent. Rather than partner with a major media company, like Infoseek did with Disney, or an infrastructure provider, like Excite did with At Home, Yahoo vowed to stay solitary.

In an interview on cable station TechTV's "Big Thinkers" show, Jerry Yang said that Yahoo's philosophy was neutrality. "We don't tie ourselves to any platform, either cable or another platform. We don't tie ourselves to any one source of content, meaning that we only get stuff from one studio or other. Our core belief of the Internet is it's very open, very accessible from anywhere."[8]

Ever humble, he added, "We don't have critical mass. In my opinion, you don't want to do anything that cements anything—certainly not legislatively, in a way that's natural for growth." But he also revealed his trademark paranoia: "I do worry about having faster pipes that Yahoo doesn't offer services on."[9]

But wouldn't it help to have a big media or infrastructure distribution partner? "I don't think we need an exclusive partner. If you look at our landscape, look at what we need to compete with, we'd be crazy to lock ourselves out of another 50 percent of the market. Our shareholders would say, 'Wait a minute, you have more than 50 percent share—you do this deal so you have *less* than 50 percent share? Why did you do that?'"[10]

In contrast to its typical mode of operation, Yahoo allowed Broadcast.com employees to stay in Dallas, where they were based. At first the integration of the two companies seemed smooth. But soon, says Cuban, who joined the combined company in April 1999, Yahoo tried to "Yahoo-ize" the company.

"Rather than leveraging the expertise that we had, they tried to fit us into their mold, and that hurt the combination. Hindsight is 20–20, but my guess is that had they let us go and push like we had since day one, we all would have been happier."

Not one to hold back his opinion, Cuban made no attempt to tone down his bull-in-a-china-shop personality, telling it like it was. "Several times they got mad at me for making the point that Yahoo wasn't No. 1 or the qualitative best in most of their categories. The biggest upside, beyond even the business-services side of our business, was to be able to combine the size of their audience with our content to create audiences that were bigger on the Net than on radio or TV. We had streaming-audio stations and events that approached radio and small cable-network sizes. If they had focused on the promotion of any of these, they could have possibly—it wasn't a slam-dunk, but possibly—completely tilted the balance of power of media. The combination of their audiences, our ability to stream in size, and the multicast network we were building has amazing possibilities to this day.

"They lived off of the Super Bowl effect. People pay premiums for getting the biggest audience in one bite. But when the ad market collapsed, they had nothing they could depend on. They weren't great at anything but being big, which isn't enough."

Perpetuating the traditional scram of top execs from acquired companies, both Cuban and Wagner left Yahoo within a year.

౿

A month after its big event to woo analysts, Yahoo was courting them again, this time with the revelation of its sales and earnings in the first quarter. Revenue had climbed to $86 million, up 13 percent from the previous quarter. And earnings? Yahoo reported net income of $16.4 million, compared to $3.3 million for the same quarter a year earlier. Its operating margins soared to 38.3 percent. But these numbers didn't tell investors how the pending acquisition of GeoCities or the just-announced acquisition of Broadcast.com—two expensive, money-losing deals—would affect the bottom line.

Softbank, Yahoo's largest shareholder, decided to cash in on some of its gains. In its earnings report in May, it revealed that its sale of 3 million Yahoo shares gave it a nice income boost. Without that hike, Softbank would have reported a loss in its publishing unit.

Yahoo continued its acquisitions spree, though by no means on the same scale as its GeoCities and Broadcast.com buys. In May, Yahoo paid $130 million for Encompass, a maker of software that facilitates access to the Internet by walking users through the process of getting online. The two companies had already collaborated for a year to bring new PC users online and into the Yahoo fold. In June, to further its "Yahoo Everywhere" strategy of making Yahoo accessible from a range of wireless devices, it scooped up Online Anywhere, a small company that created software to enable people using TV set-top boxes, handhelds, and other non-PC devices to access online content like e-mail, calendars, and address books. That acquisition cost about $80 million. And it wasn't until Yahoo made a quiet regulatory filing in May that anyone noticed it had spent $9.9 million in January to acquire log-me-on, an application that would add Yahoo-personalization features to Web-browser toolbars. Yahoo later marketed the personalized toolbar as Yahoo Companion, a way to transplant Yahoo permanently to your browser window.

In-house development also continued apace. Small teams inside Yahoo were constantly throwing together new services: Corporate My Yahoo (precursor to Corporate Yahoo), a partnership with Hewlett-Packard to build customized corporate portals; Yahoo Radio, which let you listen to broadcasts of offline and online radio stations; Yahoo Messenger, a beefed-up version of Yahoo's instant-messaging software that let users hear each other's voices when communicating; Yahoo Health; Yahoo Companion; Yahoo Greetings; Yahoo Wallet; Yahoo Pets. And several foreign Yahoos, including Yahoo Brazil, Yahoo China, and Yahoo Mexico. Yahoo really *was* everywhere.

Yahoo Briefcase was another service Yahoo launched that summer. Like so many other services, it raised the "build or buy" question.

By early 1999, several companies were offering storage space online. Instead of backing up letters and spreadsheets to your PC's hard drive, why not back them up in cyberspace? Among the companies duking it out to gain mind share in this nascent industry were idrive, Driveway, and Xdrive.

Yahoo saw online storage as yet another service it could offer its growing audience. In typical fashion, it thought about whether it should build the service itself or buy a young company and more quickly bring the service to market. It met with several companies, including idrive and Driveway, to suss out the market.

To Jeffrey Bonforte, CEO of idrive, Yahoo's motivations were a little suspect. "We weren't sure how hard they were considering us," says Bonforte, 28 at the time. "My limited experience is that Yahoo uses partnerships and acquisition talks to research an area and educate internally, à la Microsoft." Bonforte says Yahoo didn't want to pay what he thought his company was worth.

One former Driveway employee, whose company also was rejected by Yahoo, says the explanation was simpler: Yahoo decided to build its own online-storage service because none of the start-ups had a massive user base. Under those circumstances, it wasn't worth spending a lot of money to acquire technology Yahoo could build quickly.

J. J. Healy defends Yahoo: "That seems more sinister than it really is. When you go through that process, you see some things and say, 'Well, this really isn't that hard,' and you end up building it yourself."

Yahoo didn't waste any time doing just that. In August, it introduced Yahoo Briefcase, a simple service that gives users 20 megabytes of free online storage space to back up important files.

The main motivation behind both the GeoCities and Broadcast.com buys was this: to expand Yahoo's audience so it had more eyeballs to monetize. At that time, the main way to monetize eyeballs was through advertising. And Yahoo was adding hundreds of new accounts each quarter. From the second quarter to the third, it landed 450 new advertisers, for a total of 3,150. Not that gaining new advertisers in 1999 was all that difficult. Start-ups, fattened with venture capital, were spending a huge portion of their cash on advertising in the game of growing the fastest and becoming the perceived leader. One of the best ways to do that was to partner with a portal—the bigger, the better. An announcement that you were the preferred drug-and-sundries seller on Yahoo could help you nab more venture capital, and an investment bank with a better pedigree when the time came to go public.

Drugstore.com announced in March 1999 that it was entering into a partnership with Yahoo that included the purchase of advertising banners on health-related pages and accessibility through a merchant button. Together, the two companies planned to run several promotional campaigns. The value of the deal wasn't disclosed.

Just two months later, drugstore.com filed to go public, touting its relationship with Yahoo and other portals. Drugstore.com also pointed out the downside of such deals in its regulatory filing: "To promote our brand, we will need to commit substantial financial resources to creating and maintaining brand loyalty among customers. This includes continuing our advertising efforts on major Internet destinations such as Amazon.com, America Online, Excite, and Yahoo and other Web sites our customers are likely to visit, as well as other forms of media such as television and magazines."

In a filing in June, drugstore.com laid out just how significant those deals were. As of April 4, 1999, the company had $38 million in cash and cash equivalents, and its principal commitments were marketing agreements with Web portals totaling about $25 million. Drugstore.com wasn't unusual in this kind of spending, however. In 1999, the brilliant minds on the boards of most Internet companies thought this was the way to win the game.

And three years later, drugstore.com was struggling to stay afloat, with its stock sunk to below $1 from around $50 per share at the time of its IPO.

Living.com was another upstart that wanted to be the premier online outlet for furniture and other home-decor items, and entered into deals with several portals, including Yahoo. Perhaps its splashiest was with Amazon, which it agreed to pay $145 million over five years. But Living.com is no longer alive: It closed shop and filed for bankruptcy in August 2000.

There were so many online pet stores vying for leadership that in their desperation to differentiate themselves, some committed to ridiculous terms that could never pay off. Petstore.com spent $150,000 a month advertising on Yahoo. "We were wasting millions of impressions in numerous areas, and there was no way to make the deal any better," said Seth Baum, director of marketing for Petstore, before its assets were bought by Pets.com in June 2000.[11] Baum said it cost $200 to acquire a single customer on Yahoo, but for the math to work, that figure should have been closer to $20.

⮑

*I*n 1999, the heyday of the Net, Yahoo didn't have to strain itself to sell ads. It hired 20-something ad-sales reps, whose job consisted of picking up the phone and taking orders. Not that Yahoo was any different from the other portals. There was so much venture capital to go around that companies were spending their way into the hearts and minds of customers. "Not only [was Yahoo] included in just about every media plan, they were one of the most powerful publishers," says Marissa Gluck, senior analyst at Jupiter Media Metrix. "The publishers were the ones in control. They were commanding $20 to $30 million portal-tenancy deals, which were essentially just ad deals."

Before the Net start-ups arrived on the scene, ad agencies were loath to get their customers into contracts with long terms. But since the cash-rich start-ups like Amazon, drugstore.com, and CDnow were signing multiyear contracts, the agencies began to play along. "Some would do it simply for the boost in the stock price, for shareholders, not for economic sense," Gluck says. "They entered into [campaigns] without testing how the campaigns worked."

Advertisers were flocking to the portal: In 1999, the figure spent on online advertising was $4.6 billion, one-eighth of which went to Yahoo. Some advertisers felt they had no choice but to deal with Yahoo. And as its clout grew, so did its reputation for smugness and arrogance. "If you look at the term sheet, maybe you have a guaranteed number of impressions, but you also have 9 million impressions in a chat room tangentially related to your product," says Aram Sinnreich, senior analyst at Jupiter Media Metrix. "There was nothing you could do about it. They were inflexible on these deals."

Jim Meskauskas, chief Internet strategist at online media-buying firm Mediasmith, says 1999 was a banner year for buyer's remorse. "I've had clients that have entered into long, extensive multimillion-dollar buys, and then they'd have buyer's remorse a week later, and then try to optimize or cancel the contract," Meskauskas says. "Yahoo has a vicious legal team that tries to prevent that from happening."

One of his clients, Petopia, yet another online pet-food seller that is now defunct, signed a number of million-dollar-plus deals with several portals, including Yahoo. "Immediately, they wanted to try to find a way to get out of them," Meskauskas says. "We were able to get out of all of them except for AOL and Yahoo. Part of the reason they went under is because they tried to fund these deals."

The results of this backlash wouldn't really register until later.

Yahoo did occasionally go out of its way to woo potential advertisers. When 1-800-flowers.com was weighing its online-advertising options, it considered Yahoo. "Obviously, they were the force in the online world," says Christopher McCann, president of 1-800-flowers.com. "They had a lot of users, traffic, all of that." But McCann didn't think Yahoo's approach to e-commerce paid enough attention to building brand, except, of course, its own.

In January 1999, McCann ran into Jerry Yang in Miami at the Super Bowl festivities. While they were guests of Visa, McCann and Yang met in a tent and then on a bus to the game. "How come you're not a big advertiser with us?" Yang asked him. "How can we get you to be?" The two talked about how Yahoo and 1-800-flowers.com could work together, but McCann felt his objectives and Yahoo's didn't match up. "We would have wanted key placements," he says, and Yahoo already had preexisting agreements with other companies that stood in the way.

To Yahoo's credit, its reps and execs kept trying to entice McCann with sweet-smelling incentives, and he finally decided to give the portal a try. His company spent several million dollars on Yahoo between October 1999 and June 2000, but the placements it tested didn't work. "We saw they could deliver traffic—it's just we weren't getting sales," McCann says. He and Yahoo reworked the deal to give 1-800-flowers.com anchor positions in the shopping and flowers categories. That turned out to be the key. "We built a nice little business. So, it went from very little revenue to a very nice, lucrative package that produced millions of dollars at an appropriate expense level."

Still, 1-800-flowers.com's relationship with AOL was twice as beneficial, McCann says. Later in 1999, 1-800-flowers.com entered into a four-year deal with AOL, agreeing to pay $37 million over that period. "Our relationship with AOL is a home run and has been from day one," McCann says. "With Yahoo, it took a while to get going. We stumbled in the beginning, but now because of the diligence of their account team, we managed our way to a partnership that works well for both parties." And, he says, he learned that "Yahoo was a very good partner."

⌒

*I*n a more comprehensive effort to soothe ruffled advertisers and sell its platform, Yahoo launched a program called Fusion Marketing Online in March. The pitch: Advertisers weren't merely bagging banner ads—they were participating in complex media buys that would give customers a one-stop shop for building their online presence. Procter & Gamble was one of the first to take advantage of the new program by promoting its Pringles potato chips in the games area of Yahoo and Pepto-Bismol in a special "Hot Summer Relief" hub site designed to highlight "what's hot this summer."

The program proved popular. When Yahoo reported its third-quarter revenues, management pointed out that its average contract size now was $49,000, up 81 percent from the previous year.

⌒

*D*espite Yahoo's late entry into the fray, its e-commerce business also was heating up. By the end of the year, more than 9,000 merchants had joined Yahoo Shopping, including top brands like Barnes & Noble, Brooks Brothers, Eddie Bauer, and Gap.

"E-commerce continues to be a key area of management focus," wrote Michael Parekh, the Goldman Sachs analyst, in November. "Consequently, we believe that Yahoo, much like America Online, will increasingly be viewed as a premier shopping destination with its unrivaled Web audience of 105 million [unique] monthly visitors, up from 80 million the previous quarter alone."[12] Parekh also lauded Yahoo's new Yahoo Points program—through which users collected points to redeem for gift certificates or use for special auctions—for encouraging repeat business and increasing shopping volume.

News from the company just kept improving. "Perhaps they should change the underlying meaning of the name to Yet Another Higher Operating Profit Occurrence," Lise Buyer had quipped after Yahoo released outstanding second-quarter results.[13] Now its third-quarter performance—revenues of $155.1 million, versus $115.2 million in the second quarter— was blowing analysts away again. And in perhaps the most significant sign of the company's striking growth, between the first and third quarters, it almost doubled its head count, to 1,728 from 920.

⌒

The giveaways just continued: In December, Yahoo announced that in partnership with Kmart's retail site, BlueLight.com, it would give the gift of free Internet access. The provider was Spinway, a start-up that offered Net connections in exchange for its users viewing advertisements. Users of BlueLight.com's Internet service would be greeted by a cobranded BlueLight.com–My Yahoo home page. The retail site would gain lots of new Net-savvy customers, plus promotion on Yahoo Shopping. Yahoo would get yet another distribution platform. The ambitious plan called for Yahoo and Kmart to pass out CD-ROMs providing Net access in Kmart's 2,177 stores across the United States by February 2000. More than 10 million CD-ROMs ended up being distributed through Kmart stores.

In fact, the plan smacked of AOL's grand global-domination scheme, in which the company distributed countless CD-ROMs offering hours of free Net access. But Yahoo and Kmart were going one better: Not only would you get e-mail, calendar, chat, and all those other portal services for free, but you could avoid paying for an ISP, like AOL.

It seemed that Yahoo could do no wrong.

Chapter

8

The Unraveling, 2000

Key Events

- January: AOL buys Time Warner.
- April: Tech stocks drop precipitously, bringing the entire market down.
- April: AltaVista cans its IPO.
- May: Prominent dot-coms start failing.
- October: Spain's Terra Networks completes its merger with Lycos.

*O*n the first trading day of the New Year—and of the new millennium—Yahoo continued to wow. Its stock closed at $237.50, a new high, giving it a market capitalization of $128 billion.

About a week later, the company reported results for the fourth quarter of 1999 and the entire year. For the first time in its history, Yahoo had had a profitable year, showing net income of $47.8 million on revenues of $591.8 million, almost three times its 1998 take. Fourth-quarter revenues also were stellar: Yahoo registered sales of $201.1 million, up 120 percent, after an amended filing, compared to the same quarter a year earlier. And earnings were astounding: The company made $44.7 million, even taking into account acquisition-related and other charges.

All its metrics were soaring: The number of unique monthly users had grown to 120 million during December 1999, twice the figure for December 1998. Yahoo's 39.7 percent operating margins were the highest ever for the company. It had pumped up its advertisers to 3,550 from 3,150, and revenue per advertiser had increased to $59,000 from $49,000 just three months earlier. For the first time, Yahoo broke out its international revenues, saying that 13 percent of its sales came from outside the United States. Thirty-five million of its unique users were international, meaning that the revenue per user outside the United States fell far behind that of U.S. customers. But instead of interpreting that as a negative, analysts saw potential upside in international markets for Yahoo in the future. To top off the good news, Yahoo announced its fourth, and final, stock split.

But despite all this bounty, the stock was already falling. The day of the earnings announcement, it closed at $198.68; the next day it dropped to $178.87. The stock would never surpass the high it reached on January 3.

A month later, it dipped into the $150s. The news that caused the most shareholder unease, and triggered the sell-off, was the announcement on January 10 that AOL was buying offline media giant Time Warner for $160 billion. Time Warner had a stable of venerable and valuable properties: New Line Cinema and Warner Brothers film studios; Warner Music; more than 60 magazines, including *Time*, *Fortune*, and *People*; Time Warner Cable, the nation's second-largest cable operator; and a slew of TV stations and cable networks, including HBO and CNN. Despite its relatively short history of showing a profit, upstart AOL was buying an institution. AOL and Time Warner painted the merger as almost a marriage of equals: AOL shareholders would own 55 percent of the company, while Time Warner shareholders would own 45 percent. But the combined company's ticker symbol said it all: It would trade under AOL.

While Yahoo boasted more than 100 million unique users, the combined AOL Time Warner had more than 100 million actual paying customers, from AOL's dial-up subscribers to Time Warner's cable and magazine subscribers, according to AOL's chief financial officer, Michael Kelly.[1]

Time Warner's Internet efforts had included several flops. In 1994, the company started Pathfinder, a hub site for all of Time Warner's magazine and news properties, but it found that people gravitated to the individual brands, not Pathfinder.com. While TW was trying to build a new brand, Internet users were flocking to start-ups like Yahoo instead. In April 1999, Time Warner announced its plan to shut down Pathfinder.

But AOL had already acquired Netcenter and successfully built out its Web presence, and analysts saw a match made in heaven. Industry watchers immediately posited that Yahoo should do the same: take its $100-billion-plus market cap and buy a traditional-media partner. Disney's market cap at the time was about $68 billion. Yahoo could afford to scoop it up.

Yet Yahoo's top executives, hunkered down in one of those funky purple-and-yellow conference rooms at Santa Clara headquarters the morning after the stunning merger announcement, sealed their fate: They would remain independent.

"These guys have never allowed themselves to be distracted by the hoopla over the stock," said Michael Moritz, the venture capitalist who first funded Yahoo and was also a board member. "They've always understood they are building a business and not promoting a stock. In all the conversations I've had over the years with Jerry and the guys, I don't think we've spent five minutes talking about the stock. Not five minutes."[2]

Perhaps they should have. That stock value gave Yahoo vast buying power. It could have swallowed up a company with years of operating experience and profits. Observers were already wondering what crazy math was at work, giving dot-coms like Yahoo such huge valuations.

"How could Yahoo, even considering all its earnings, audience, and momentum, be worth more than Disney and CBS combined? Maybe someday, but surely not in January 2000," writes Bob Davis, the former CEO of Lycos, in his memoir, *Speed Is Life* (Currency Doubleday, 2001). "In fact, for a company that executed well on so many fronts, I suspect Yahoo's failure to use its $130 billion-plus market cap to create a transforming event will be looked back upon as one of the greatest missed business opportunities of all time. Yahoo could have purchased virtually any business it chose, yet its determination to remain pure to an Internet-only model deprived the company of the chance to build scale on a grand dimension.

"Only time will tell," Davis writes, "but I believe the company left a massive opportunity on the table and will ultimately be owned by one of the old-economy companies it should have acquired."[3]

At that time, though, it wasn't clear whether AOL's move was brilliant or blockheaded. Or whether Yahoo was making the right choice or a huge mistake. But in hindsight, the answer appears to be the latter. "We used to call it 'wampum,' " says Mike Homer, then general manager of Netcenter and now chairman, CEO, and founder of Kontiki, a start-up that delivers digital media. "What you were doing was trading wampum for cash."

Homer says AOL's move to buy Time Warner is similar to a lesser-known deal that accomplished the same thing: Gemstar's purchase of *TV Guide*. Gemstar's cofounder, Daniel Kwoh, invented the VCR Plus+, a remote-control device that assigned a code to a TV listing. Kwoh began to license those codes to makers of digital program guides for television set-top boxes. At one point, after Gemstar went public, its market capitalization was about $30 billion. Kwoh used that wampum to buy *TV Guide*, a magazine with one of the largest circulations in the world.

"He traded Internet wampum, in this case, digital TV, for a real business that had taken 30 years to build," Homer says. Now the vast majority of Gemstar's revenues come from *TV Guide*, just as the bulk of AOL's revenues come from the Time Warner media properties. "Anybody that had a lot of wampum and didn't trade it, in hindsight made a mistake," Homer says. "But who really knew at the time?"

Even some Yahoo executives disagreed with the pure-play strategy. Mark Cuban thought Yahoo should take advantage of that once-in-a-lifetime buying power. "They knew I felt that they should leverage their stock valuation to buy as much hard earnings as they could," Cuban says. "I was a big fan of [the proposed] USA-Lycos [merger] for the same reason from a Lycos perspective. But they chose not to, for reasons that I can only guess were related to Yahoo culture. They truly believed that they were different, and it showed up in the way they did business. They had a culture where everything had to be done by consensus, which meant you got mediocrity rather than excellence."

Attacks were coming from all fronts: In February, several prominent Web sites, including Yahoo and Amazon, were shut down for hours due to mysterious denial-of-service attacks, where a computer or several computers send so many false requests for services that the Web site is overloaded and bona fide users can't access it. Some sites, like AOL, had a backup plan to keep such an attack from taking the site down. Not Yahoo. It lost three hours of business before its engineers could reroute traffic and make the site available to users.

While the attacks weren't that serious—the sites were down for only a few hours—they highlighted the vulnerability to such freak incidents of businesses that rely on the Web. When users can't access a site, there's no audience to deliver ads to. Still, analysts decided the service interruptions were negligible and wouldn't hurt Yahoo's earnings.

In April, a 15-year-old Canadian boy, identified in the press only as "mafiaboy" because police wouldn't release the minor's name, was arrested for the attacks. He was sentenced to eight months in detention. Yahoo was sentenced to the knowledge that a 15-year-old could disable its entire operation.

Though Yahoo was determined not to merge with an old-media company, it did toy with the idea of joining forces with another Internet star to create an even more shining Net pure play. In late March 2000, Yahoo execs held discussions with eBay, the online-auction leader. A merger with eBay would boost Yahoo's nonadvertising revenues, which accounted for just 10 percent of Yahoo's total revenues. In contrast, eBay's revenues came mostly from commissions from the items customers bought and sold on its site.

According to *BusinessWeek*, Koogle favored the merger, but Mallett, the president and COO who hoped eventually to take Koogle's place, didn't. His reason? Mallett wanted eBay CEO Meg Whitman to report to him, but she wanted to report to Koogle. Mallett persuaded both Yang and Filo to oppose the deal, and Filo even sent an e-mail to Koogle asking him to back away.

It was actually the second time that Yahoo and eBay had discussed a merger. Before eBay went public in late summer 1998, top executives from both sides had talked about pairing up. According to sources close to the talks, the two sides couldn't agree then, either. The sources say Yahoo was willing to offer $1 billion for eBay, but that didn't sway the online auction house. A smart decision: The day eBay went public, its market cap rose to nearly $1.9 billion. By late 2001, eBay's market cap was more than twice that of Yahoo, a sign of eBay's waxing and Yahoo's waning power.

Yahoo's failure to bag eBay very much dogs the portal today. While other companies were reporting miserable third-quarter 2001 earnings and facing the prospect of lackluster holiday sales, eBay announced that its third-quarter revenues had risen 71 percent while earnings had jumped 24 percent. Plus, analysts were forecasting that eBay would actually benefit from the economic slump as belt-tightening consumers sought out bargains on its site. It's no exaggeration to say that becoming YaBay largely could have shielded Yahoo from the troubles that lay ahead.

⌒

*F*orget the portal wars. By early 2000, the Internet industry was agog with buzz about online music. Tons of start-ups had innovated ways to digitize music, play it back via your computer, and even swap music files over the Internet—for free. All the portals, including Yahoo, began offering search engines that scouted out MP3 files: digitized, compressed songs.

MP3 was the most oft-searched term after sex on most search engines, and the portals all wanted to make their sites destinations for online-music seekers. In June 1999, AOL had snapped up Winamp, an MP3-player pioneer, for about $100 million, and Spinner, an online-radio network, for about $300 million. Lycos bought the Sonique player, a competitor to Winamp, in August 1999, beating out Yahoo. (Yahoo developed its own MP3-player software and released it the next year but, when it proved unpopular, stopped offering it.) The culprit that really turned up the volume, though, was Napster, the maker of file-sharing software that enabled millions of people to swap songs for free. Napster and dozens of Napster copycats were the talk of cyberspace.

In August 1999, Yahoo launched its Digital site, where people could find and download songs to their computers' hard drives, but its entry was considered late. Start-ups like MP3.com and ARTISTdirect's Ultimate Band List (UBL.com) were getting much more attention from music lovers. Yahoo tried to rectify that in early 2000 by meeting with several on-line-music start-ups to talk about partnerships and potential acquisitions.

But Yahoo's confusion over its music strategy got in its way, at least with one partnership. Ever since the music portal and search engine Ultimate Band List had launched in 1994, Mark Geiger, chairman and CEO of ARTISTdirect, had monitored Yahoo. He watched as it added more and more music content, and even chatted up David Filo about the possibility of buying Yahoo's music-search technology. Yahoo was a general site whose traffic was swelling, but in a vertical niche like music, Geiger wondered how Yahoo would stack up. In late 1999, after months of negotiation, ARTISTdirect entered into a multimillion-dollar deal with Yahoo to provide content as well as access to the commerce sites ARTISTdirect maintained for its well-known musician customers and partners like Beck, Aimee Mann, and Tom Petty.

Geiger wanted the deal to focus on ARTISTdirect's content, but Yahoo tried to make the deal strictly about commerce. "The deal went sour for us very quickly as they were not delivering on their promises and started to build up the content around us, in effect pushing us more into a corner," Geiger says. "We got moved to the side even though we were a multimillion-dollar partner."

Almost immediately, Geiger told Yahoo the deal wasn't working for ARTISTdirect and asked executives to renegotiate. Each time after three showdowns, Yahoo execs said they'd make changes, and didn't. Finally, Geiger took the matter up with Jeff Mallett and Anil Singh. "Instead of fixing the problem, they said they wanted to buy us," Geiger says. "We didn't understand why they still hadn't made up their mind on their overall strategy, so to put out a fire by buying someone didn't seem to make a lot of sense."

After a few weeks of due diligence, someone lower on the totem pole told Geiger the deal didn't work for Yahoo, either, and ARTISTdirect was able to get out of it. "Yahoo lost tens of millions of dollars," Geiger says, "because of their inability to resolve the conflict between the sales organization and the content organization."

And all that speaks to a fundamental problem: "They couldn't pick whether they were fish or fowl, whether they'd compete in vertical [markets] or not," Geiger says.

The ongoing music-related and other prospective-merger

meetings kept Yahoo busy. One day, Yahoo's deal team was meeting with executives from Launch.com, a Los Angeles–based start-up that offered music videos and free MP3s, plus tons of articles about bands and singers. The Yahoo people would excuse themselves for a while and come back: They had Meg Whitman and eBay execs in another conference room.

Yahoo had previously invested an undisclosed amount in Launch but decided a buyout would cost too much (though no price was ever mentioned), and passed.

In March, Yahoo got a call from Myplay, a start-up that gave users free online storage space (dubbed lockers) to stash songs they found on the Net. Myplay and Yahoo had met before, but now Myplay wanted Yahoo to know it was about to do a deal with another large portal. Myplay assumed such a deal—especially with AOL—might nix a future relationship with Yahoo and wanted Yahoo to know what was up. Yahoo gave Myplay its blessing.

Myplay inked a deal to be AOL's online music-storage provider. In exchange for building out the service for AOL, Myplay would get a flood of new customers—and would pay AOL $20 million over two years. Sounds like AOL was getting the better bargain, but Myplay thought it was a great deal: Instead of paying just for AOL's traffic, Myplay was paying for the precious e-mail addresses of users who signed up for the service. Such was the thinking in Internet land.

A couple of months later, Yahoo came calling and wanted to talk to Myplay about getting hitched. Jerry Yang, Jeff Mallett, and Ellen Siminoff went back and forth with Myplay, but finally settled on a deal worth $200 million.

But unbeknownst to Myplay and its lawyers, AOL had slipped something problematic into the earlier deal in one of its revisions to the contract, a process known as redlining. AOL would underline changes in red and send the amended contract to the prospective partner and its lawyers. But in the Myplay contract, a significant change somehow hadn't been redlined. The two-year deal was supposed to have been renewable upon the mutual agreement of the parties. Now the contract said it was renewable at AOL's discretion. "Yahoo said, 'We're not doing a deal with a company that has a sustained deal with AOL,'" says a person familiar with the discussions. "AOL later admitted they did that deal to prevent Myplay from being acquired by Microsoft or Yahoo or RealNetworks."

Myplay considered filing an antitrust suit against AOL but realized it would be too expensive and would take too long to settle in court. After losing out on Yahoo's rescinded $200 million offer, Myplay was acquired by Bertelsmann for about $30 million in May 2001, and Yahoo's music plans were derailed again.

$\backsim$

*B*y April, the mood in the dot-com world was turning dark. Investors were losing patience with the promise of future profits. Their speculative euphoria turned to pragmatic paranoia, and instead of start-ups maintaining their upward slant on stock charts, they started to fall. What caused investors to suddenly lose confidence? It could have been a *Barron's* story about once-cash-rich dot-coms running out of cash. It could have been the report that an influential analyst, Goldman Sachs' Abby Joseph Cohen, was adjusting her portfolio so it held fewer stocks.

While the stock market was collapsing, Jerry Yang continued his role as industry evangelist, giving a speech before the

National Press Club in Washington, preaching to his audience about the staggering number of people coming online. "At the end of last year, a hundred million people in the United States were on the Net. In 2003, the number will double in the United States to 200 million. Audience size and growth is what this is all about. You're seeing the transformation of changing people's lives and behavior. I always look at those numbers. If they're still going up, we have a tremendous opportunity.

"This is a great medium to try to reach consumers and change their behavior and influence their purchasing behavior," Yang said. "What's even more important is the growth of e-commerce. In 1999, there was $80 billion of Internet commerce. By 2003, that number will increase 900 percent to $726 billion. Statistics don't tell the whole story. What we're talking about is changing people's behavior."[4]

Ever the diplomat, Yang pointed out that while Yahoo had 625 million page views a day, "when the clock strikes midnight, we have zero and we have to earn those page views all over again."[5]

One way to keep on the good side of customers was to respect their privacy, Yang said. "Privacy is one of the most important issues we deal with. It's something I hold pretty dear to my heart. A lot of people assume businesses are in the business of ripping consumers off. In our business, people spend a lot of money to acquire customers. The best hope we have is to hold on to users forever. It's based on building a deep relationship with users. Very fundamental to that is our users' trust in us to safeguard their privacy."[6]

But privacy is a complicated issue, he said. "A user can choose to have information disclosed at certain times, or not at all, or anywhere in between. Privacy will differ depending on the application: Financial services will be different from health care, which will be different from doing transactions. But if you believe privacy will make a company like ours competitive in the end, then people will come up with different ways to protect privacy."[7]

To that end, in 1999, Yahoo and other top Net companies like AOL, Amazon, and eBay had formed NetCoalition.com, a lobbying group that represented their interests in Washington and raised public-policy issues. It was an extension of Yahoo's work with the Online Privacy Alliance, a group of businesses and associations Yahoo had joined in 1998 to spur awareness of the need to protect consumers' privacy.

∽

Even though Yahoo's fourth-quarter 1999 earnings had exceeded analysts' expectations, the stock bounced around aimlessly—but mostly fell. It was at $198 in mid-January when Yahoo introduced its online invitations, a service similar to that provided by the popular site Evite.com. The stock was down to $168.68 less than two weeks later, when Yahoo rolled out its tax center through a partnership with H&R Block, allowing Yahoo users to prepare and file their income taxes online. Thankfully, on March 13, after Yahoo announced its new original-content play, FinanceVision, the stock closed higher, at $175.81. But new Yahoo wireless services or a trendy business-to-business marketplace? They didn't boost the stock: It closed at $172.01 on March 20. There were plenty of other small announcements: a new look for Yahoo Sports, a Sundance channel on Yahoo Movies, an entertainment guide. But Yahoo seemed to have little control over the trajectory of its stock.

Whereas before investors had gone on buying sprees at the drop of an announcement, now they were holding back, cautiously. Gone were the 30-point jumps of the stock triggered by a morsel of news.

On the day Yahoo announced its excellent first-quarter earnings, the stock closed at $165. Net revenues were $228.4 million, up 120 percent after a restatement. Net income after assorted charges was $77.8 million, while two costly acquisitions had brought the amended figure for the period a year earlier down to $1.8 million.

By now, Yahoo had 22 international properties in 12 languages. Forty percent of the 145 million unique users who visited Yahoo every month were international, as were about 30 percent of Yahoo's advertisers. But only 14 percent of Yahoo's revenues came from abroad. The figure was up from 13 percent the quarter before but still lagged U.S. revenues substantially—despite the fact that Yahoo had made a big international push in 1999 and 2000, buying a Taiwanese portal called Kimo and expanding to India, Australia, China, Latin America, and throughout Europe.

Still, analysts saw Yahoo's international position as positive. Paul Noglows, whose firm now was called Chase Hambrecht & Quist, pointed out that Yahoo was No. 1 or 2 in several important international markets, even with little investment or marketing. "We believe international operations will continue to be a key driver of growth for Yahoo and uniquely position the company to exceed growth for U.S.-only or weaker international media companies," Noglows wrote. "A leading position in the Internet markets outside the U.S. is critical to sustain the growth rates expected by investors."[8] He predicted that in 2001 the Internet advertising market as a whole would grow 38 percent worldwide, with the U.S. market growing 28 percent and the international market growing 112 percent.

Along with its quarterly results, Yahoo announced that its

chief financial officer, Gary Valenzuela, was retiring. Analysts considered the loss of the hypercompetent Valenzuela negative news. Taking his place was Sue Decker, now 39, previously director of research at Donaldson, Lufkin & Jenrette, where as one of three underwriting sell-side analysts, she'd covered Yahoo for a year and a half after it went public.

Continuing an all-important rite, Yahoo held its second annual analyst powwow in May, at the company's headquarters. Seventeen Yahoo execs, including four from companies that Yahoo had acquired, regaled the assembled analysts with updates on the company.

In these briefings, Yahoo revealed a great deal about its business. Chief Technology Officer Farzad Nazem ("Zod") underscored how important wireless devices were to Yahoo's expansion plans. Already, Nazem said, 47 percent of households that used Yahoo owned at least one wireless device, and 15 million to 20 million Yahoo users were accessing Yahoo solely through wireless devices. Yahoo currently offered 16 applications—including Yahoo Mail, Calendar, Finance, and Sports—on various devices in 11 countries and planned to add four more countries by the end of the year. The company also planned to develop more wireless applications, like regional maps and directions, translation services, and shopping. The wireless platform was crucial to Yahoo's success in foreign markets, where wireless devices were more plentiful than PCs.

And while other companies were still planning their wireless strategies, Zod said, Yahoo was already executing.

Geoff Ralston, vice president and general manager of communications, presented Yahoo's plan to add voice capability to all its applications. Yahoo enabled 4 billion messages per month, and its chat service was the leading such site on the Web, Ralston said. By letting chat users communicate via voice, rather than simply typing messages to each other, Yahoo hoped to widen its lead. But, the analysts wanted to know, how would Yahoo make money from these services? Initially they'd be free, supported by advertising revenue, but eventually the company hoped to charge for so-called premium services that added value to the basic service.

The execs also touted Yahoo's shopping platform. Almost 250,000 people were selling products via Yahoo, either through classifieds or through auctions, according to Tim Brady, now senior vice president of network services. And the upcoming launch of Yahoo's new person-to-person payment services, using technology Yahoo had acquired along with the company Arthas.com, was expected to give shopping a bigger boost.

Since the acquisition of Broadcast.com the previous April, Yahoo hadn't leveraged its broadband strengths as much as observers had hoped it would, by getting its millions of users hooked on broadband content. Though 65 million Yahoo users had broadband access, it was mainly through their workplaces, according to Kevin Parke, vice president and general manager of broadcast services at Yahoo. Furthermore, Broadcast.com's NetRoadshow offering, which prepared virtual road shows, might have been a hot idea in 1999 but wasn't any longer, with the dearth of companies going public.

Still, Yahoo claimed it was a leader in live and on-demand video, with 11 million hours of streaming-media broadcasting viewed that March, 300 percent more than it had delivered the previous year. And Yahoo also talked up some of its newer broadband efforts, including FinanceVision, its Web-based financial program featuring live interviews with analysts and reporters. The brainchild of Eric Scholl, a former executive producer at CNNfn, FinanceVision aimed to tap the interactivity of the Web. In addition to a window showing the television-style broadcast, another window let viewers check stock quotes or ask questions.

A typical Yahoo bootstrap operation, the program was produced by all of about 10 employees in a makeshift studio, formerly a Yahoo conference room. To find anchors, Yahoo held a company-wide audition, choosing two of the faces of Finance-Vision from among employees with minimal reporting or on-air experience.

Beyond tapping broadband, FinanceVision was an attempt to build on the success of Yahoo Finance. Elizabeth Collet, who ran business development and strategic planning for the Finance team, says Yahoo perpetually added features to bolster its finance offerings, including the capability to call up account information from banks and brokerages on the My Yahoo page. "It was hard to do technically and yet a great value for the user, and also quite strategic for us to become more of a central dashboard for people," Collet says. "And of course, it meant much tighter relationships with the big financial players with deep pockets."

FinanceVision wasn't Yahoo's only stab at producing original content. At the end of the year, it launched ShoppingVision, a similar format that hawked products offered by Yahoo's 12,000-plus merchants. In May 2000, Yahoo had grand plans to roll out a broadband channel for each Yahoo section within 18 months, but it was derailed by the pressing need to generate revenues.[9]

Further whetting the appetites of the analysts at the May 18 meeting, John Willcutts, vice president of Yahoo Enterprise Services (YES), discussed the company's new Corporate Yahoo initiative to build portals for businesses, in partnership with Tibco and Hewlett-Packard. The corporate portals would merge Yahoo's basic services with the companies' information, creating a supercharged intranet. Yahoo could build a standard enterprise portal in a day, five days for a complicated one, Willcutts said, though he stressed that the new program was in a trial period and wasn't expected to generate revenue for at least six months. Still, YES jibed with Yahoo's growing priority to increase revenue from services and decrease dependence on advertising revenue.

Goldman Sachs analyst Michael Parekh gave YES a big thumbs-up, saying he believed Yahoo would be able to generate "significant revenues" by leveraging its powerful presence to the corporate desktop. "We expect announcements of large enterprise customers soon," he wrote.[10] Yahoo already had 650 corporate customers using services offered by Broadcast.com, like virtual conferences and online training, so analysts believed Yahoo would have no trouble convincing them to try the new corporate portal services. Yahoo officially launched Corporate Yahoo in June, but nine months later, it had signed up only 24 clients.

At the meeting, Heather Killen and Fabiola Arredondo shed some light on Yahoo's international strategy, which was nothing short of world domination: to be the top player in every major market; create as much local programming as possible; extend all of its services—including wireless, voice, and corporate—to each market; and establish a presence in second-tier markets.

At the time of its revealing analyst meeting, Yahoo's shares were down more than 50 percent from their January high. Parekh said Yahoo had sounder management than other companies in its sector and therefore deserved to be trading at a higher multiple than other companies. "We believe that the recent broad sell-off in Internet stocks was indiscriminate as investors sold shares without regard to fundamentals. In light of the continuing strong fundamentals of Yahoo, we view the decline in Yahoo's shares as a good opportunity for investors to build/add to their positions," he wrote.[11] Like many other analysts, he recommended that clients purchase the stock with a long-term mind-set.

But Yahoo's stock continued to fall, as did that of every other dot-com. Even bellwethers like Microsoft and Cisco were suffering from the widespread dumping of technology stocks. And soon after the market meltdown that hit in April, dot-coms started crashing. Toysmart closed in May. Value America filed for Chapter 11 protection in August. Boo.com shut down in May and sold its assets to Fashionmall.com in August. Though Pets.com had gone public as recently as February, it had laid off most of its staff and shuttered its retail operations by November. Living.com died in August, just over a year after it had signed its premier-merchant deal with Yahoo.

Suddenly, having done a massive portal deal didn't seem as smart as it once had.

"There was a lot of capital going to a lot of start-ups, and the best way for start-ups to get cachet was to ink one of these deals," says Aram Sinnreich of Jupiter Media Metrix. "Yahoo deals routinely could be worth in the tens of millions of dollars. But a Yahoo tenancy deal started making people look like idiots. These tenancy deals would cost companies up to half of their yearly marketing budgets." When you think that six months down the line you're going to have an initial public offering and raise tens or hundreds of millions of dollars, such deals make sense, Sinnreich says. "When chances of profits are three years down the line, it makes no sense whatsoever."

By the fall, analysts and industry watchers were cluing in that the rules of the game had changed and the online-advertising business model had faults, because the dot-coms that exemplified that business model were dying. Not only had they burned through all their cash, but the public-market route to raising capital was suddenly blocked. It had become clear that Yahoo couldn't rely on its advertising revenue—47 percent of which came from dot-coms—to perpetually buoy the company higher and higher.

‿

*I*n fact, even though Yahoo's results for its second fiscal quarter were astonishing, the stock reached new lows. Yahoo's revenues increased 110 percent, to $270.1 million from $128.6 million, after a restatement, for the same quarter a year earlier. Net income was $65.4 million. But the stock closed at $105.50 that day.

Softbank's sale of 3 million Yahoo shares in May hadn't helped investor confidence. After several previous sales, the Japanese company's stake now was down to about 22 percent.

Analysts had been excited when Yahoo reclaimed the No. 1 portal position in May, with a 64.5 percent home-work reach, according to Media Metrix (at the time, though, Media Metrix didn't measure MSN's reach). Yahoo also boasted the longest user time spent at a portal, an average of 95 minutes per month, according to Nielsen/NetRatings. But by the fall, Yahoo had slipped into the No. 2 position among users at home.

In the final analysis, Yahoo was still going strong, but growth in key areas—the number of new advertisers and therefore new contracts—was slowing. In the second quarter, Yahoo had added 110 advertisers, bringing its total to 3,675—a full 1,500 of which were international. Yahoo claimed it still had a 98 percent retention rate, and revenues per advertiser had increased to $67,000 from $58,000. The revenue garnered from international advertisers also had increased, but just a bit, to $26,500 from $23,500 the previous quarter. Analysts concluded that international customers were still testing the waters, but noted that the overseas advertisers Yahoo had signed up were larger, more stable companies than the venture-backed dot-coms that largely made up its domestic stable.

In July, in an ambitious bid to attract new users and bring its existing users greater value, Yahoo extended its earlier deal with Spinway, the free ISP, to offer cobranded Internet service in partnership with a range of companies, including Barnes & Noble and Costco. Free ISPs required their users to have a window on their computer screens constantly serving advertisements. But Spinway wasn't as intrusive as the free ISPs, like NetZero, that required users to click on the ads. Two and a half million people had already signed up for Spinway's free Internet access through BlueLight.com, the deal inked in late 1999. But by December, Spinway had spun itself out, with BlueLight scooping up its assets.

Yahoo also made a bold acquisition that summer. EGroups, a Web site that let people form groups based on common interests and communicate through e-mail lists, had more than 17 million members and 800,000 groups. In August, Yahoo anted up $432 million for the new users and the technology that helped people share ideas and collaborate.

Still, it seemed that nothing could stem the decline of its stock. By the time Yahoo released it once-again excellent results in October, the stock was down to $82.69. A week later, it had even dipped below $50.

Third-quarter revenues were $295.5 million, about 90 percent higher than the year before. Net income was a very respectable $47.7 million. Unique monthly users had increased by 30 million, to 185 million. Yahoo execs told analysts they were making progress shifting their advertising revenue from questionable dot-coms to more solid companies. Dot-com advertising now stood at 40 percent, down from 47 percent the previous quarter. Revenue per advertiser continued to climb, to $75,000 from $68,000 in the second quarter. And advertisers were buying multiple services: Just 18 percent of the top 200 advertisers had bought only banner ads, while 75 percent of all advertisers had contracted for two or more of Yahoo's marketing services.

Michael Parekh saw a rosy future for Yahoo's advertising-supported business, despite the current slump. "We continue to believe that the Internet is increasingly gaining acceptance among both online and offline marketers and, consequently, expect the Web advertising market to continue to experience robust growth," he wrote. "While we expect the next couple of quarters to represent a transitional period for Web advertising from Internet to mainstream advertisers and believe that the fall-off in spending from cash-constrained dot-coms will hurt the companies dependent on Web advertising, we continue to believe that Yahoo will be one of the primary beneficiaries of the growth of Web advertising over the long run."[12] Thirty of the Fortune 50 companies were advertising on Yahoo, plus 60 of *Advertising Age*'s top 100 companies, he pointed out.

But of course, since Goldman Sachs had taken Yahoo public and was one of its biggest institutional shareholders, it isn't a stretch to say Parekh had more to gain from propping Yahoo up than from tearing it down.

And there was clear evidence of tough times ahead for Yahoo. For the first time since the first quarter of 1999, the number of its advertisers had dropped, to 3,450 from 3,675. International advertisers also decreased, by 90. Yahoo execs said the decline was due to diminishing advertising by dot-coms. With many going out of business—well-known names like boo.com, Pets.com, and Living.com—how could Yahoo not be affected?

There was more bad news: Retention of advertisers had

fallen. While Yahoo usually reported advertiser retention in the high-90 percent range, now just 92 percent of its top 50 clients, 80 percent of its top 100 clients, and 85 percent of its top 200 clients had renewed.

Some analysts had begun questioning what Yahoo's future held. Lehman Brothers' Holly Becker, for one, predicted that the dot-com slump would have a decisively adverse effect on Yahoo's sales. Becker maintained that of Yahoo's top 200 advertisers, 61 percent were dot-coms and only 23 percent were traditional companies. "Our contacts suggest that the environment continues to worsen, and we believe it is only a matter of time before we see the impact on Yahoo's results," Becker wrote in a report for investors.[13] The day the report was issued, August 28, Yahoo's shares slid 9 percent.

Fall 2000 brought the project internally dubbed Yahoo 2.0, a crucial makeover of the company. Essentially, Yahoo planned to bring in new blood to head up important areas, reduce dependence on dot-com advertisers, and push ahead with diversification into fee-based services. Koogle and Yang hired Jana Rich, managing director for Korn/Ferry International, to spearhead the recruitment efforts. Rich, who has a Stanford M.B.A., also knew Mallett. "They said, 'Look, we have this concept idea Yahoo 2.0—we need to bring in talent for it,'" Rich says.

Hers was no small task: to hire an executive vice president for North American operations, a senior vice president for media and leisure, and vice president and general managers for Europe, Finance, Auctions, Small Business, and Direct Marketing.

The decision to charge users for services was difficult for Yahoo, since from the beginning, cofounders Yang and Filo had wanted to keep the site noncommercial. They even resisted advertising at first, because they didn't like it and didn't think their users would, either. But Yang and Filo ultimately went with advertising because they thought it would allow them to offer Yahoo's services for free. "We are probably the last people in the world that want to do this, but it will be tastefully done, and that will keep it free to the users, like TV," Yang said in 1995, when he was 25.[14]

But it turned out that even with advertising, Yahoo couldn't afford to stay completely free. Showing some foresight, Yahoo had begun quietly charging for some of its services toward the end of 1999. Bill Pay, introduced in September, let Yahoo users pay their bills online without writing checks. The first three months were free, after which Yahoo hoped users would be hooked and agree to pay a monthly fee of $2 to $7, depending on the number of bills.

Some analysts questioned Yahoo's—or anyone's—ability to get Internet surfers to pay for content or services, especially things they might be able get for free elsewhere on the Net, like the bill-paying services or real-time stock quotes, for which Yahoo wanted to charge $9.95 a month. In a report entitled "The Content Site Turnaround," Forrester Research reported that 26 percent of a sample of consumers had paid for content at some point, but fewer than half said they intended to pay again. And a report from the Consumer Electronics Association said that the vast majority of Net users—77 percent—were opposed to paying for content.

But faced with the deteriorating ad market, Yahoo continued its push to add features throughout the fall, some for free and others not. It introduced a $25 buyer-protection program for its auctions; film-development services through a partnership with PhotoWorks; and Yahoo by Phone, which let people access their e-mail or check stock quotes via the phone (originally for free and, starting in spring 2001, for $4.95 a month). There also were the free Yahoo Experts, an area on the site where people could research topics like archeology by asking experts questions, and the Yahoo Movies Online Shorts Directory, which listed short films on the Net. The new Buzz Index aimed to add value for advertisers by charting trends through Yahoo users' search queries.

In October, responding to longtime criticism from analysts that its small board was too insular, Yahoo added a new member, Edward Kozel, managing partner of the VC firm Open Range Ventures and also a board member of Cisco Systems (as was Jerry Yang). Kozel was the only new addition to the board since the first outsider, Arthur Kern, had joined back in 1996. The hope was that Yahoo could leverage Kozel's diverse experience to help jump-start new ideas for generating revenue and acquiring new technology.

Yahoo also was pushing ahead on the fronts it had outlined for analysts months earlier. In the international arena, it had signed up several partners that would offer its content and services on mobile devices to advance the Yahoo Everywhere strategy. Twenty-nine Yahoo applications were now available on mobile devices.

Yahoo began to add to its international sites some services that had been available only domestically, rolling out Yahoo Clubs in 10 countries, Yahoo Invites in 12 countries, and Yahoo Shopping in Asia and Spain. It also invested in some potential competitors abroad, like portal Mingpao.com in Hong Kong and PhoenixNet, a satellite broadband company in the Asia Pacific region.

A clear sign that times were changing: Yahoo had begun acting more solicitous toward potential and current advertisers.

Bill Bishop, cofounder and executive VP of CBS MarketWatch, which has partnered with Yahoo since 1998, says the portal had become "the king of performance deals," meaning the partner or advertiser doesn't pay unless a user clicks on its content or ad—or, in some cases, actually buys something. "Frankly, they are screwing up the market for the rest of us," Bishop adds.

To assuage agencies as well, Yahoo formed an alliance specifically to work with them. But agencies said the move was largely for show and that Yahoo still hadn't improved its attitude enough—not that AOL or MSN were any better. "Yahoo has become significantly better at servicing us," says Tim McHale, chief media officer of Tribal DDB Worldwide. "The biggest frustrations we've had with Yahoo are they try to be our friend, but they also try to screw us whenever they can. They have two different personalities, and they haven't resolved those personalities internally, so it gives us great hesitancy until they figure out who they want to be." McHale predicts that as the long-term contracts of many advertisers expire, few will be renewed.

Yahoo also was still trying to talk clients into buying packages of ads that bundled undesirable spots along with the desirable, a practice Mallett defended. "If I'm going to buy 'Survivor,' I have to buy s——," he said. "This has been going on forever. I don't know that I'm going to apologize for the industry doing what it's supposed to be doing."[15]

But there was no denying the phone lines weren't as busy.

Or that advertisers were demanding better results. When banner ads had first appeared and surfers weren't as savvy, 4 percent to 5 percent would click on them due to the novelty factor or sheer ignorance, but over time they learned to ignore them. Even the growing use of more visually interesting streaming banners and pop-up ads seemed to have little impact. In fact, the more in-your-face the ads, the more determined consumers seemed to shun them. By late 2000, only 0.3 percent to 0.5 percent were clicking on banner ads, making them less effective even than junk mail, which claimed up to a 2 percent result rate. The promise to deliver more effective online campaigns by targeting users' preferences simply wasn't living up to expectations—except perhaps in the case of prohibitively expensive direct e-mail.

Manish Shah, president of the investment-news site 123jump.com, says his experience advertising on Yahoo wasn't favorable. In 2000, Shah's company spent about $100,000 for Yahoo ads. "We got less than 500 people through Yahoo, so there's no way you can make money on it," Shah says. "When I called the marketing person to complain, I said, 'Look, your performance sucks.' I said, 'I just spent $100,000, and I got less than 500 people.' He said, 'That's all you lost? I don't have time to talk to you.' "

Shah's 1.4 percent return was worse than that of the typical direct-mail campaign. But the Yahoo ad salesman told Shah that unless he'd spent $2 million, he shouldn't complain. Presumably, the salesman had bigger unhappy clients. For Shah's part, he turned to vertical portals—those more focused niche sites— and found better results for his advertising dollars, he says.

"There was a gap between expectations and practical deliverables," Mallett admitted. "I think that gap is being questioned now."[16]

Plus, increasingly, Yahoo was competing against AOL Time Warner's network of properties for advertising. Yahoo could deliver a message to its millions of users on its site, but AOL Time Warner could offer bundles of advertising that stretched across its Internet offerings, movie studios, TV networks, and magazines. Mike Homer, the former Netscape/AOL exec as well as a board member of several Internet start-ups, including Kontiki, believes AOL's promises are more appealing. "I've actually see it happen, being involved with companies like Palm and TiVo, where I'm on the board, where they buy advertising in substantial amounts. AOL can make them a proposition that says, 'Hey, if you give us all your TV, we'll throw in another X million more online, and we'll do that all in a package,' " Homer says. "Yahoo can't compete for that kind of business."

That spring Yahoo had hired Murray Gaylord, a 30-year advertising veteran, to head up Fusion Marketing Online, a crucial program for the company as it tried to put more oomph in its marketing platform. In an interview with *Context* magazine, Jerry Yang pitched Yahoo's updated offerings: "I think that what started out as pure advertising has evolved to be much more comprehensive over the past four years," Yang said. "We have an audience from around the world that is now about 100 million to 120 million users a month. We have great information about the audience because they tell us their preferences. We have developed a unique ability to deliver different audiences to our advertisers or promotional partners."[17]

Yang pointed out how Yahoo's proposition had moved beyond traditional advertising. "While they used to just be able to advertise to our users, they can now do advertising, promotions, or direct marketing. They can sponsor or host events. They can do customer-satisfaction surveys and market research. Some, such as companies in financial services, can actually complete transactions online, because they never have to deliver anything physical. I think the ability to conduct an entire transaction on the Internet is a very big deal.

"Advertising is still a key component of what we do, but we now think of ourselves as helping our partners do 'fusion marketing.' "[18]

Regardless of Yang's high opinion of Yahoo's progress, analysts were weighing in with downgrades by the end of the year. On November 21, Net Queen Mary Meeker, the Morgan Stanley analyst, changed her recommendation on Yahoo's stock from "buy" to "outperform." The stock plunged 15 percent that day, to $41.68. On December 6, Henry Blodget, of Merrill Lynch, lowered his estimates on Yahoo for the first two quarters of 2001, though he remained bullish on the company's long-term prospects, saying he thought it would make up the difference in the two quarters after that. Blodget also cited reports predicting that online advertising would rebound and grow. Still, Yahoo's stock slid 15 percent that day, to $37.50. The next day, Derek Brown, of W. R. Hambrecht & Co., lowered his rating on Yahoo to "neutral." The stock fell 7 percent.

By December, 5.2 million people had signed up for free Internet access from Yahoo's partner BlueLight.com. But despite its high hopes of operating as a separate public company, BlueLight.com became part of Kmart in August 2001, and its former CEO, Mark Goldstein, pointed to advertising with Yahoo as a force in BlueLight's undoing. When asked what his biggest mistake was, Goldstein said, "Spending as much money as we did on advertising with Yahoo too early on. We weren't ready for the traffic—we were only selling 1,200 items on the site back then. We were very quick to sign the deal."[19]

The deal also ended up being a disappointment to Yahoo and the users who had signed up for free, unlimited Net access after BlueLight imposed a fee for the service in early 2001.

At the end of 2000, Yahoo was calling its e-commerce operation a bright spot. Yahoo Shopping had enabled $1 billion in sales for each of the first three quarters of the year, or $3 billion. But in context, AOL had enabled $5 billion in transactions in its third quarter alone. After the holiday season, Yahoo reported that its order volume had "nearly doubled" from the previous year. And according to Nielsen/NetRatings, Yahoo Shopping was the No. 1 e-commerce destination among all the portals.

But it certainly wasn't enough to buoy the stock price. On the last day of trading for 2000, Yahoo's shares closed at $30.06, down more than 87 percent from January's high.

The Turmoil, 2001

Key Events

- January: AltaVista scraps its second planned IPO.
- January: Disney changes Go.com from a mainstream portal to a Disney site.
- January: The Federal Reserve cuts interest rates twice.
- February: Fed Chairman Alan Greenspan tells the House of Representatives: "The risks continue skewed toward the economy's remaining on a path inconsistent with satisfactory economic performance."
- March: The Conference Board's index of consumer confidence records the biggest two-month drop since the 1991 recession.
- March: The Nasdaq is off 56 percent from its March 2000 peak.
- March: More than $3 trillion of investment wealth has been wiped out since that peak.

Comparatively, the first year of the new millennium had been good to Yahoo. For one thing, the company was still there. While other big brands, like Pets.com and boo.com, proved to be overnight sensations, Yahoo's measured approach and emphasis on the long haul had kept it going strong and earned it respect on Wall Street. For another thing, it had bagged a striking $1.1 billion in revenues, amounting to an 88 percent jump over the previous year, and $70.8 million in net income.

In fact, in some ways, the bad times for the other dot-coms had even been good to Yahoo, which scooped up ad dollars that might otherwise have gone to now-defunct companies. Analysts and investors for the most part were still backing the portal, now ranked No. 2 by Nielsen/NetRatings with 68 million registered users, trailing only the behemoth AOL.

But inside Yahoo, management knew the good times wouldn't last. Ad sales were slowing dramatically: Online-ad spending for the third quarter of 2000 had dipped to $2 billion, down 6.5 percent from the second quarter, according to the Internet Advertising Bureau (IAB). It was the first time the IAB had reported a drop in spending from a previous quarter since it began measuring such expenditures in 1996. CFO Sue Decker and her team drew up new financial outlooks for the year. But management and Yahoo observers would still be caught off guard by just how dramatically things had changed for the worse.

The first big sign of this change fell on January 10 during Yahoo's fourth-quarter earnings conference call. "Yahoo continued to outperform the industry and took market share despite a challenging environment," Koogle began.[1] The company reported a pro-forma profit of $80.2 million on sales of $310.9 million, falling a hairbreadth above analysts' estimates. But after various charges, including a $163.2 million write-off for its money-losing investments in other companies, largely tech, Yahoo recorded a whopping net loss of $97.8 million. Analysts were especially startled when the company sharply lowered its revenue forecast by 25 percent, to a range of $220 million to $240 million. Koogle blamed the slowdown in online advertising and characterized the new numbers as a "short-term" problem, insisting that business and corporate services would double and that more premium services planned for the year would eventually ease the company's reliance on advertising for 90 percent of its revenues. In fact, the execs spun, it could be a good thing.

"The great companies use challenging times to their advantage," Koogle said.[2] Mallett emphasized Yahoo's push into broadband areas and called FinanceVision, the company's Web-based CNBC knockoff, a "bright spot" in Yahoo's cloudy picture—a view not shared by everyone. In a story in the *Industry Standard* the following month, writer Gary Rivlin described FinanceVision's production values as "barely a cut above *Wayne's World.*"[3]

The stock plunged 19 percent in after-hours trading, to $24.42 from $30.50.

Jeffries & Co. analyst Fred Moran was "shockingly disappointed" by the results.[4] Though Lehman Brothers' Becker had expected Yahoo to lower its estimates, the bearish analyst sounded an alarm on learning the news. "The outlook is much worse than anyone anticipated," she said. "They're not just being cautious. They've got to get away from the dotcom business."[5]

Certainly, they were trying to. The Yahoo 2.0 drive to decrease dependence on dot-com advertising and increase nonadvertising revenue streams had been given top priority. In early

January, Yahoo took another step in that direction, imposing a fee on auction listings for the first time. Now auction sellers were charged between 20 cents and $2.25, depending on the price of the item. Merrill Lynch's Blodget anticipated the fees would generate between $30 million and $80 million in revenues per year for the company.[6]

The Corporate Yahoo initiative launched in 2000 had drawn some big clients like McDonald's and Quaker Oats, but the total numbered just a paltry 24. Murray Gaylord's fusion-marketing department was developing several campaigns for traditional advertisers, including one for Pepsi that asked consumers to choose their favorite Pepsi Super Bowl commercial at pepsi.yahoo.com. Yahoo gained 76,000 new members for its database and deepened its relationship with Pepsi.

In an earlier promotion, in fall 2000, Yahoo had first proved its worth to Pepsi. The portal had created a campaign for Pepsi in which consumers could get points and win prizes at a Yahoo-created site after they registered personal information and input a code from Pepsi bottles. The campaign was a hit with consumers and Pepsi executives, who received data like name, age, and gender from 3 million registrants, plus a 5 percent increase in sales of Pepsi bottles spurred by the campaign.

Yahoo was trying to nab more traditional advertisers by changing its reputation at the bargaining table, where ad agencies were all too familiar with the swagger best exemplified by Mallett: "If they didn't get it, we moved on."[7]

In contrast, at the end of January, Yahoo hosted a splashy bash at the exclusive Silverado Resort in Napa Valley for execs from agencies like Foote, Cone & Belding and Young & Rubicam. To underscore their earnestness, Yahoo's entire senior management team was on hand, including goodwill ambassador Jerry Yang, who typically saved himself for the higher-level schmoozing that accompanied an acquisition. It was a routine networking event for ad execs but a rare display for a dot-com.

And that fact certainly didn't escape the notice of the ad community. "They're playing nice," says David Smith, president and CEO of San Francisco interactive-media agency Mediasmith. They had to. Advertisers were actually increasing their online spending, but more companies were opting to develop Web sites for that purpose, as BMW had done for its BMWfilms.com campaign. The carmaker had hired several marquee movie directors, including Ang Lee (*Crouching Tiger, Hidden Dragon*), to make short online films featuring BMWs. The campaign carried little benefit for online media, though, since BMW chose to alert consumers to the films mainly through ads in offline media.

The closing of AOL's acquisition of Time Warner at the end of January—and the advertising opportunities that the merged company represented—also helped explain Yahoo's newfound respect for the agencies. Rather than taking a hard line on deals or trying to go direct to clients, Yahoo was nurturing the agencies to land not only ad contracts but also a more meaningful relationship that extended to Corporate Yahoo services and to content and commerce deals.

New hires were helping to wash away some of the hubris associated with the old hands at Yahoo. Jana Rich, the Korn/Ferry International headhunter brought on board in October, had helped Yahoo fill some of the many vacancies in its various divisions. Showing their simpatico natures—and the new order taking shape at Yahoo—Koogle, Mallett, and Yang each met individually with Rich and told her they supported shaking up the company's stagnant culture. "They realized they needed to bring in new people to do it," Rich says. Their plan rankled some former employees: Through Yahoo's many acquisitions, management had had the chance to integrate new players into its upper ranks but, time and again, had stuck with the status quo.

These changes were happening too slowly for Wall Street, though. Enamored of AOL Time Warner's sprawling empire of content and distribution channels, investors roundly criticized Yahoo for failing to do a similar deal of its own. Yahoo went on the defensive. "We really believe it becomes more difficult to carry a broad range of content if you take the step of vertically integrating," Koogle told Fox News Channel anchor Neil Cavuto on his business-news show in January.[8]

Not helping matters, Yahoo had a public relations fiasco on its hands. In November, a French court responding to a lawsuit had ordered the company to block all users in France from its auction area, where Nazi items like daggers and concentration camp uniforms were listed, as well as chat rooms and other sections of the site that contested Nazi war crimes. The French government threatened to fine Yahoo $14,500 a day if it didn't comply. Instead, Yahoo filed its own suit in a San Jose, California, court, citing a violation by the French of the United States' First Amendment and stating that the French court had no jurisdiction over Yahoo. The two French groups that had brought the suit, the United Jewish Students and the International League against Racism and Anti-Semitism, filed a motion to dismiss and were turned down. On November 7, the U.S. court sided with Yahoo, ruling that the French court's judgment was invalid; U.S. companies, it said, are subject to U.S. laws, not French laws.

But now a group of Holocaust survivors in France were filing suit against the company. And this time the charges were criminal—and they named Koogle, since French law requires that accusations of justifying war crimes be brought against an individual rather than a company. The suit filed on January 22 by the Association of Deportees of Auschwitz and Upper Silesia asked for symbolic damages of one French franc—about 15 cents—but also demanded that Yahoo cover the cost of publicizing the earlier judgment against the company. The timing was odd, since earlier that month, Yahoo had changed its commerce guidelines to include a ban on the sale of items that "are associated with groups deemed to promote or glorify hatred and violence"[9]—and had cited Nazi and Ku Klux Klan memorabilia as examples. The suit apparently was later dropped. But Yahoo had learned its lesson and, in the future, would move preemptively to stop the sale of controversial items on its site or the posting of hate-related speech. It was one more blow to a free and open Web, but one that Yahoo considered necessary to preserve its public image.

Yahoo's stock reflected its troubles. Since hitting $42.87 on January 24, the shares had veered downward and were trading for around $24 on March 1 when long-swirling merger rumors gathered the steam of a tornado. In mid-January, investors anxious for a pairing with a major media company had caused the company's stock to spike 24 percent in two days on buzz of a Viacom deal. The drama further depleted confidence in the portal. "Yahoo has sailed downwind extraordinarily well for five years," said Merrill Lynch's Henry Blodget. "They are now sailing upwind into a hurricane."[10]

Analysts were clamoring for a marriage. Vivendi Universal, Disney, and Viacom all seemed poised for pairings and had held discussions with Yahoo involving a range of scenarios: designating Yahoo the primary Internet partner for their content, for example, or handing over some of their Internet operations to Yahoo to reduce overhead. To the media conglomerates, Yahoo's distribution platform with 180 million unique monthly visitors looked like a tasty dish. Meanwhile, Yahoo was hungrily eyeing their hoards of content.

An outright takeover was unlikely, because Yahoo was still way too expensive. Even with a $13 billion market cap, about one-tenth of what it had once been worth, Yahoo was valued at about 200 times its trailing earnings, a much higher multiple than the typical media company enjoyed. And no one expected the tight-knit board and management, which owned 46 percent of the stock, to vote in favor of a merger. As always, they saw Yahoo's glory as inseparable from its independence. Plus, Yahoo was hardly desperate: It could still claim a war chest of $1.7 billion in cash and a leading brand.

But things soon took a turn for the worse. Within two weeks, the heads of three of Yahoo's foreign outposts quit. First to go, on February 15, was Fabiola Arredondo, reportedly after Santa Clara pulled the planned IPO of Yahoo Europe against her wishes. The next day, her counterpart in Asia, Savio Chow, also resigned. Last to quit, on March 1, was the managing director of Yahoo Canada, Mark Rubinstein. The executives were reportedly frustrated by heavy-handed edicts coming down from Yahoo headquarters.

These high-level departures were symbolic, but they also had serious business implications. While Yahoo was struggling to increase its international ad revenues to more than about 14 percent of the total, its competitors were gaining heft. Lycos' merger with the Spain-based Terra Networks had given it a boost in growing markets like Europe and Latin America. AOL now had the benefit of Time Warner's international reach, Microsoft had expanded to 30 countries, and European conglomerates like Bertelsmann and Vivendi had grown Net savvier in the past year.

Strains in Yahoo's once-happy family were becoming more

and more evident, and the world was beginning to realize the "three amigos"—as the Netnoscenti called Koogle, Mallett, and Yang—were now hurting the company as much as they had once helped it. "Their culture helped them build a superb site and a really edgy brand, but it also held them back from making forward-looking business decisions," Lehman's Becker said.[11]

Mallett, ensconced as overseer of Yahoo 2.0, expected to take over when Koogle stepped down, which he apparently thought would be sooner rather than later. In January, he had told a sales-job candidate he would "move up"[12] soon. Others seemed to buy his rap. A gushing February 19 *BusinessWeek* piece dubbed him "General"[13] and credited him with making things happen at Yahoo: He negotiated the deals, motivated the troops, hustled projects to completion—in fact, the story made it seem like Mallett was the only one doing any work at Yahoo.

But an emergency board meeting called for February 27 to discuss the company's options put an end to Mallett's hopes. On the agenda: the stock price, trading at $23.44 per share that day, and the office of the CEO.

With the stock liable to keep slipping, the primary concern was preventing a hostile takeover. Accordingly, on March 1, Yahoo adopted a poison-pill provision, allowing company stockholders to buy shares at a deep discount to keep them out of the hands of predatory companies. A two-year 500 million stock-buyback plan would serve as extra insurance. "That had a positive impact. Employees were feeling, 'Great, so we will stay independent,' " says a recruiter close to the company.

Ever since November and that particularly humiliating downgrade by one of the Net's biggest boosters, Mary Meeker—who had advised Yahoo to rethink its management—the board had been kicking around the idea of a change at the top. Koogle had even offered to resign. But with Yahoo expecting to top $1 billion in sales for 2000, almost twice its 1999 take, the idea didn't take hold. Now, with the pressure building, the board, led by Jerry Yang and Mike Moritz, finally reached a decision: Koogle had to go. Deemed unready for the job, Mallett wasn't dubbed successor. "He is not a candidate," Koogle told a colleague at the time. The board, he said, had "had that tough discussion, but he is not a candidate."

A recruiter close to the company observes that there was "always some hope from T.K. and Jeff that Jeff would grow into the position. But the thought was that it was further out so he could grow more."

Koogle resigned with grace. He "was well aware of his shortcomings,"[14] said a close Yahoo associate. And that night, it was Koogle who inaugurated the next phase of Yahoo's life with a call to Spencer Stuart headhunter Jim Citrin with the assignment. A Harvard M.B.A. and former McKinsey & Company exec whose books include *Lessons from the Top* (Currency Doubleday, 1999), Citrin had made a name for himself in Internet circles as the recruiter behind the CEO searches at music site Tonos.com and greeting-cards site Blue Mountain Arts. But finding a CEO for the flailing portal would stretch even his talents.

It would be a full eight days before the rest of the world learned the news: Yahoo was just like all the other dot-coms that had to fire their first CEO in order to stay viable.

⌇

As soon as the market opened on the morning of March 7, Yahoo's stock nosedived. Merrill Lynch's Blodget had circulated a note speculating that a management shakeup might be brewing because Sue Decker had canceled her plans to appear at his firm's Internet conference that week. Word also had leaked out that Jerry Yang had nixed a planned speaking engagement in Utah the same week. The twin cancellations smacked of more than mere coincidence, and investors began swapping shares at a furious pace. Nasdaq officials watched with alarm. Only weeks earlier, Nasdaq had played host to another bout of irrational trading after a bad purchase order for a company called Axcelis had caused its stock to skyrocket 830 percent in just minutes. Fearing a wild swing the other way, Nasdaq placed calls to Yahoo management to try to confirm the rumors.

But due to the early hour on the West Coast, Yahoo's offices were deserted. Playing it safe, Nasdaq halted trading of the stock at 9:37 A.M. EST. In the seven minutes it was available that day, Yahoo's stock had lost 6 percent, or $1.44, of its value, falling to $20.94. The stock didn't trade for the rest of the day, while Nasdaq and the industry awaited word from Yahoo's leaders, who were wrangling over the script for a conference call they'd scheduled for that afternoon.

Meanwhile, the press, analysts, and regular people were having a field day. Some 8,000 new messages were posted on Yahoo's finance message board that day. Blodget fueled the rumors by suggesting in his note that the news would be a merger—and naming just about every major media and telecom company as a likely suspect. Regarding the possibility of a management shift, he wrote, "Yahoo's management has had an amazing six years. It would be understandable if one or more members of the core senior team decided to call it a day."[15]

Finally Yahoo broke its silence. At 5 P.M., after the market had closed, a press release went out announcing that Yahoo

214

once again was lowering its expectations on performance for the first quarter, to a range of $170 million to $180 million. Yahoo said its outlook for the ad market had been too optimistic and that its customer-base transition to traditional companies from dot-coms was taking longer than expected.

In the conference call, Koogle, Mallett, Yang, and Decker clued investors in to part two of the double whammy: Koogle was stepping down and would move into the chairman role once a successor was found.

Analysts generally applauded the news of Koogle's departure—a move that had been rumored for weeks ("When a company is going through this much change, the CEO is usually in trouble," says U.S. Bancorp's Safa Rashtchy). Lehman's Becker wrote in a note that day, "We applaud Yahoo's decision to bring in fresh blood given recent management turmoil."[16] The main distraction for analysts was the second lowering of guidance. "It was a shock," Rashtchy said. "The revenue guidelines were below even our worst-case estimates."[17]

And the company lost still more value. In after-hours trading, the share price dropped 11 percent to $18.69 and then to $17.68 the next day.

In the company's press release revising its first-quarter guidance, Yahoo blamed the effects of a "weakening macroeconomic global climate" on ad budgets, but that did nothing to mute reaction to the announcement, which arrived like an exclamation point on a year of bad news for the dot-com sector. Now even the once-mightiest of pure plays was vulnerable.

While the media and analysts cranked out devastating near-death notices for the portal, Yahoo moved ahead with its campaign to bring in new blood. Just 13 days after Koogle announced his departure, the company named its first heavyweight outside hire: Gregory Coleman, a 25-year media veteran who had headed the magazine division of Reader's Digest Association. Coleman would be Yahoo's executive vice president of North American operations, overseeing sales and marketing and reporting to Mallett. He, meanwhile, was preoccupied with international affairs. Three major international posts remained vacant, MSN and AOL were gaining ground abroad, and ad spending continued to fall out from under the drastically weakening foreign markets.

But amid all the instability, the pace of Yahoo's deal making never slackened. Yahoo viewed partnerships, particularly those in the wireless arena, as key to its future. On the day of Coleman's appointment, the company also announced that Yahoo would send content and services—like Yahoo Messenger, Mail, and Finance—over Verizon Wireless systems in keeping with its Yahoo Everywhere strategy.

By now, media and entertainment executives were obsessed with the free music-file sharing service Napster, which had been ordered in various court battles to cease and desist from distributing music without a copyright and then legitimized in a strategic alliance with Bertelsmann. But Napster's cult following (at its height, 20 million users were swapping files on the service) had convinced the music labels and media companies that digital music was the next big moneymaker.

That spring two groups took shape that aimed to pry loose the grip of Napster and its various copycats on the public imagination. In March and April, the five major music labels split into separate camps to harness the music and video files being traded for free on the Net. Warner Music, BMG, and EMI, along with RealNetworks, teamed up to create music-subscription venture MusicNet. Yahoo fell in with Duet, later renamed Pressplay, formed by Sony Music and

Universal Music Group. Duet reportedly would pay Yahoo for distribution and promotion to Yahoo's audience, once again proving the value of that audience to partners.

∽

*Y*ahoo was going through another major change, too, this one physical. Construction was nearly complete on its new $300 million 800,000-square-foot, four-building headquarters on First Avenue in Sunnyvale. After several years of separation, everyone would be together again. Instead of driving down the street to meetings, soon Yahoos need merely stroll the walkways that crisscrossed a bright green lawn. A company store off the main lobby would hawk Yahoo paraphernalia, while a purple cow kiosk, a refugee from CowParade New York 2000, stood sentinel near the reception area. The furnishings featured Yahoo's trademark purple and yellow, right down to the purple sprinkler heads. And Yahoo employees would get a lot more perks than the proverbial cappuccino machine when they stepped inside, where they would behold the fruits of the dotcom boom: a central cafeteria, a gym, and basketball, volleyball, and bocce ball courts (where regular tournaments would be held, naturally).

During the first week of April, hard hats were handed out for a party at the site of the new headquarters. Employees downed diet Coke and tried not to think about their underwater stock options or the fact that the company seemingly had little to celebrate. Plus, word had leaked out that the quarterly results to be announced the following week would include layoffs, despite Mallett's insistence in January that there would be none.

There was one smidgen of good news. As Yahoo's stock

continued to slide, along with the rest of the market, Lehman's Becker had finally decided it was worth buying. "It is now widely understood that Yahoo's business model needs to change and management appears more open-minded and ready to move," she wrote in a research note on April 5. "A new CEO will have myriad options to monetize Yahoo's valuable platform and re-accelerate growth."[18]

From below $13, the stock shot up 23 percent, regaining a minuscule portion of the 90 percent it had lost since the previous August, when Becker had voiced serious doubts about the company. If nothing else, the impact of Becker's words demonstrated her pull on Wall Street. For Yahoo, which had been fighting the fallout of her earlier words, there was at least a shred of relief.

On April 11, in his last earnings conference call with analysts, Koogle reported that the company had exceeded the revised targets it had announced on March 7, but just barely. Revenues for the first quarter were $180.2 million—Yahoo's lowest since the third quarter of 1999—and net loss totaled $11.5 million, compared to a profit of $77.8 million in the first quarter of 2000.

After the mind-blowing climb of the stock to a split-adjusted $237.50 in January 2000, it had sunk lower than its original offering price because the market, and the company along with it, had contracted faster than anyone would ever have imagined. Again, Koogle revised estimates for the rest of the year and, most alarming to observers, said his "visibility" into the future was limited, a degree of uncertainty that implied he couldn't even be sure what direction business would, or should, take.

Rumors of the layoffs weren't exaggerated: 420 of the company's 3,500 employees were being jettisoned to save $7 million to $9 million per quarter. The same day, pouring salt on Yahoo's wounds, Heather Killen, head of the entire international division, handed in her resignation, leaving the foreign properties rudderless.

A report by the influential Blodget the day after the conference call summed up the situation neatly. "Yahoo is clearly at a crossroads, and we believe it is critical that the company hire a strong CEO in the next month or two. We continue to believe the company will either turn its business around (with considerable long-term upside possible) or sell to a major media or technology company at $10–$15 within a year."[19] Blodget maintained his near-term "neutral" and long-term "buy" ratings on the stock, but 24 of the 33 analysts who covered Yahoo lowered their recommendations. Becker and Meeker remained proponents.

Reporters quizzed Koogle about the CEO search the day of his earnings announcement, but they also had something else on their minds: porn. An April 11 *Los Angeles Times* piece noting Yahoo's extensive selection of racy DVDs and tapes had caught the attention of several antiporn groups. By the end of that week, Mallett said, the company had received more than 100,000 e-mailed complaints from users, many at the behest of just one group, the American Family Association. As a result, the portal would discontinue sales of pornographic material, refuse ads by porn sites, and limit the number of porn links pulled up by its search engine.

Though Yahoo claimed that less than 10 percent of its revenues were porn-related, not everyone bought that story. "I don't think anyone on the outside knows how much was really generated by porn, but some of us, including me, believe they did in fact generate a significant portion of revenue from porn sales," Lise Buyer says. Yang and Filo also came under attack for not standing by their ideals of an open, uncensored Web. And it was yet another very public embarrassment for Yahoo.

The search for a new leader was in full swing. Yahoo's board wanted a replacement fast: The company's identity was at stake. As long as Koogle remained at the helm, Yahoo still would be perceived as a dot-com rather than the media company it claimed to be. Since February 28, Citrin and his team of recruiters had been researching the backgrounds of 200 top executives, had talked to 100 of them, met in person with 35, and chosen 5 to present to Yahoo's board. Three had entertainment backgrounds, while the other two came from the advertising and software industries.

The media was primed for an announcement. The *Wall Street Journal*'s Kara Swisher went into speculative high gear after a CNET article on March 28 reported that former BMG Entertainment CEO Strauss Zelnick had been offered the job and turned it down. "We had one meeting with him but didn't feel he was appropriate," maintains a member of Yahoo's recruiting team.

But the publication of this rumor, along with a longer report by Swisher detailing other potential candidates, threw the search off course. The real candidates grew leery of looking like runners-up. It fell to the recruiting team, along with Yahoo's board, to soothe the ruffled feathers.

Even while Citrin and his team scoured the landscape, one candidate had taken an early lead: Terry Semel, former cochairman of the entertainment behemoth Warner Brothers.

It was Yang who had asked the board to consider Semel, whom he'd met in 1999 at the infamous Sun Valley, Idaho, mogul retreat hosted by Herb Allen, head of Allen & Co., the media deal broker behind the mergers of AOL and Time Warner in 2000 and ABC/Capital Cities and Disney in 1995. And it was Yang who broke the news of Semel's candidacy to him at a lunch meeting on March 9. "My immediate reaction was, 'Wow, what a great challenge for someone,' " Semel said. "I thought, 'My goodness, what they're really talking about—the experience, the background—is fundamentally my own.' "[20] In the following weeks, Semel spent 50 hours in meetings with Yahoo executives and board members.

Along with his cochair, Bob Daly, Semel had built Warner Brothers from a one-trick pony into a diversified media company with booming TV and music divisions, revenues of $11 billion, and a presence in 50 countries. Since Semel and Daly, now manager of the Los Angeles Dodgers, had left Warner— some say, been forced out—in 1999, Semel had dabbled in the Net, starting his own new-media venture firm, Windsor Media, and investing in a few L.A.-area dot-coms, among them, the filmmaking site Nibblebox and the now-defunct Digital Entertainment Network.

Several of Yahoo's board members were concerned that in the fine Hollywood tradition, Semel might be too hands-off and too accustomed to big budgets. But Semel, said an observer at the meetings, "persuaded them that the big-spending, big-glitz era in Hollywood had come to a close. He said, 'I'd never try to build a big cost structure. I'd build lean cost structure.' "[21] The board bought it, voting unanimously to hire him. Koogle said the offer was the only one extended by the company.

At just five weeks long, the search had been a record setter, compared to the typical CEO hunt of at least six months. And it came during a time that CEOs were running scared from dot-coms. At least two other major Internet companies, search engine AltaVista and online bookseller Barnes&Noble.com, had gone begging for a boss for months. While dot-coms had never offered very compelling salaries (only in the $300,000 range for a CEO), they were looking even less appealing now, with their stocks and business models in tatters. There had been 75,000 layoffs at dotcoms in the past 16 months, according to the outplacement firm Challenger, Gray and Christmas, and 260 out of 351 Net stocks were trading below $5. Nor could the lesson of George Shaheen easily be forgotten. Shaheen, who had left the top post at Andersen Consulting, now called Accenture, to head up the groceries site Webvan, reportedly had seen his stock and options package shrink from $280 million to $150,000 by the time he quit in April.

⮌

*O*n April 17, Yahoo announced that the 58-year-old Semel—soon to be the most senior person on the staff in both age and title—would assume the role of CEO and chairman on May 1. To seal the deal, Koogle had had to surrender his chairman title, too—Semel's idea, according to *BusinessWeek*—in favor of a vice-chairman role. In August, Koogle would have to give up that title also, but would remain on Yahoo's board of directors. Semel didn't think he could muster the support he needed to transform Yahoo with such a popular former leader still so closely tied to the company. It was both a compliment to Koogle and a decisive stab by Semel at distancing himself from his predecessor.

On top of a salary of $310,000, matching Koogle's, Semel received options to buy 10 million Yahoo shares—about 2 percent of the company—vesting periodically until 2005 and priced between $17.62 and $75.

Many found the choice of Semel perplexing. While he clearly represented a break from Yahoo's pure-play past, he lacked both advertising and technology experience. He might have been behind megahits like *Batman* and *Driving Miss Daisy*, but he was no turnaround specialist. And his knowledge of the

Internet was, at best, limited. Warner Brothers' own digital arm, Entertaindom, had been perceived as a failure after its launch was repeatedly delayed by pressures to include content from other Time Warner divisions. The site was put on hold after Time Warner announced its planned merger with AOL (after Semel and Daly's time).

One of the few satisfied with Yahoo's choice, Paul Noglows, now of J. P. Morgan Chase, commented that the company "doesn't need a visionary. They have plenty of good ideas. They need a manager who can build the business to scale."[22] Scott Reamer, an analyst with SG Cowen, differed, calling Semel a "fish out of water."[23] And Lanny Baker of Salomon Smith Barney offered a skeptical sound bite: "The media business is all about selling ads. The movie business is all about spending money."[24]

In her Boom Town column in the *Wall Street Journal*, Kara Swisher gave Semel a taste of the culture gap he'd be confronting: "Terry, sweetheart," she cooed in an open memo to him, "let me be the first to congratulate you on getting the green light on one of Silicon Valley's most boffo projects. Or as we say here, on deploying a major multi-platform operating system with a simplified user interface and innovative support services using a world-wide network that focuses on standards-based security, manageability, and reliability."[25]

Semel gave himself a $17.6 million vote of confidence by buying 1 million shares of Yahoo with his own money the day his appointment was announced.

Investors were less confident. Yahoo's stock barely budged that day, opening at $17.32 and closing at $17.31. The consensus of the market seemed to be that Semel represented a superficial attempt by Yahoo to look more like a diversified media company. Some observers even speculated that Semel's hiring was the work of another major media company looking to pounce on the portal and predicted that Yahoo would be forced into a merger with the likes of Vivendi or Sony within a year.

The market at large continued to deteriorate. No longer the world's most valuable company, Cisco Systems warned the day before Semel's appointment that its sales likely would be off by 30 percent for the quarter and it would lay off 8,500. The day of Semel's appointment, Intel reported a dramatic drop in its earnings—82 percent over the year-ago period. The slowdown had taken hold of the tech sector at large.

And in the midst of all this upheaval, Yahoo 2.0 needed to find a market.

Chapter

10

The Semel Era

Key Events

- September: Terrorist attacks on New York and Washington, D.C., add to economic woes.
- October: U.S. and British forces begin military strikes in Afghanistan.
- November: Microsoft and the U.S. government settle their antitrust suit.
- November: For the 10th time this year, the Federal Reserve cuts interest rates, to their lowest levels since 1961, as a recession begins.

With the naming of Terry Semel as its CEO, Yahoo could finally move into the grown-up phase of its evolution. While the adolescent Yahoo had coasted along on its popularity, many of its fellow start-ups had become elderly in Net years. Some were already sputtering and even dying.

Lycos, which had briefly surpassed Yahoo in traffic in 1999, had faded to a clear fifth among search engines and portals. It boasted an impressive 98 million registered users worldwide, but the company's merger with Terra Networks wasn't doing much for the bottom line. First-quarter revenues of $164 million fell short of Wall Street's expected $177.3 million. The company lost its longtime CEO, Bob Davis, in February and in May announced it would trim its staff by 15 percent.

Excite@Home, that once much-lauded merger of a portal and a cable-modem company, was in more dire straits. It had burned through too many millions too quickly and was forced into bankruptcy by fall. By the end of the year, after dropping its portal strategy in favor of its legacy cable business in the first quarter, it would all but cease to exist. And Infoseek *had* ceased to exist in 1999, after its ill-fated merger with Disney and transformation into the Go.com portal. The merger essentially eliminated the brand, reducing Infoseek to the technology that ran Go.com's search engine. In retrospect, however, the deal, valued at more than $1.5 billion, gave Infoseek a profitable exit strategy compared to Excite@Home's bleak outcome.

Measured against these former competitors, Yahoo was well positioned. "Most start-ups make the transition into grown-up companies sooner. Yahoo didn't have to," says a senior-level Yahoo executive who joined the company through one of its recent acquisitions.

Through the years, Yahoo had remained in many ways like

its original start-up self, full of gold-rush swagger and go-it-alone mentality. "People advanced at Yahoo either by building products and applications that generated traffic, or because people [at Yahoo] liked them. There was a don't-upset-the-apple-cart mentality. People were so focused on traffic and the Yahoo brand—things that were so 1998," the Yahoo executive says.

Yahoo had known for years that the advertising model couldn't be relied on as a sole source of income and yet hadn't taken decisive enough action—a failing observers could perhaps forgive on a human level, but not investors and Wall Street. And not the executives to whom Yahoo had continued to pay below-market salaries while letting them dream of earning millions with their now-worthless stock options. Wall Street was partly to blame for this, since it had stroked management for too long in its love affair with the stock. Of course, some execs did escape with millions, including head of ad sales Anil Singh, who cashed in at least $14 million worth of options before retiring in May, and former international-operations chief Heather Killen, who reported a gain of about $30 million. But when Yahoo's stock dipped into the teens and below, the promise of such riches faded like a quaint memory.

The limitations of being an independent Internet pure play were clearer than ever. While AOL owned the content to put on its service and pitch to advertisers, Yahoo had to find partners and sometimes share revenue with them. Microsoft could snag partners for MSN by entering into multitiered relationships with them, especially through its popular Internet Explorer browser and Windows Media Player software. But Yahoo was still drawing on the power of its brand, its wide-ranging distribution deals, and its huge audience to sway partners—just as it had several years ago.

Worse, the company hadn't revamped its centralized management structure to accommodate a changed competitive landscape. Yahoo had accumulated 44 operating units, each headed by a general manager, few of whom had budget responsibilities and the authority to make sweeping changes. Major deals and shifts in strategy were still dictated by upper management, slowing the pace of progress and leaving the real power concentrated at the top.

Yahoo needed a seasoned executive to run a business with 3,000 employees and about 200 million monthly users that had no real prototype.

True, Terry Semel was a grown-up. Gray-haired and staid, the Brooklyn native had earned his reputation as a nice guy by deciding early in his 20-year stint at Warner Brothers that actors were the most important element in making movies. He coddled them and paid them well. In one example of Semel's penchant for excess, he rewarded Range Rovers to stars like Mel Gibson and Danny Glover for helping make the Warner movie *Lethal Weapon* a hit.

Semel was a star in his own right. His handprints are etched in the Hollywood sidewalk in front of the famous Mann's Chinese Theater, along with those of Steven Spielberg, George Lucas, and Cecil B. De Mille. He mingled with actors like Clint Eastwood and Jack Nicholson and was a regular at Herb Allen's annual Sun Valley mogul fest.

Semel had proved he could grow a business. When he was appointed Warner's chief operating officer in 1978, the company was a simple studio with a single source of income: the box office. Over the course of his tenure, as he moved up to cochair with Daly in 1994, Warner Brothers developed diverse revenue streams, including television (with hits like *ER* and *Friends*, and a network, The WB), music, videos, retail stores, and eventually the Internet. In the process, Warner grew from a $750 million company into the $11 billion multimedia entertainment conglomerate it is today.

But critics called the choice of Semel shortsighted. As CEO, he would have to be intimately involved with the business of advertising. At Warner Brothers, he'd focused on the movie business while Daly handled the TV units. With TV, you build a viewing audience that you can use to court advertisers—similar to Yahoo's model. But in the movie business, you create a stand-alone product and sell it to consumers, not advertisers.

Semel did have some impressive advertising experience, though. In 1981, he'd spearheaded the formation of an in-house advertising agency at Warner to create campaigns and buy media time to promote movies. And it was under Semel that Warner, along with Disney, forever changed movie marketing with innovations like in-store promotions and merchandising tie-ins. Semel also oversaw the development of franchises like the *Batman* movies, a gold mine for promos.

Clearly, Semel could run a media company, the identity Yahoo had chosen. He also had experience being inside a public company. But at Time Warner, he was a division head, while the job of painting the big picture to the public fell to Levin and others at the top of the Time Warner food chain. This missing piece of the puzzle would prove to be Semel's Achilles' heel.

Semel and Daly left Warner Brothers together in 1999 after faltering under their newly added responsibility for the Warner Music Group, which had lost artists and executives under previous Warner Music CEO Michael Fuchs. Semel and Daly weren't replacing them quickly enough, fueling long-standing tension between them and Time Warner CEO Gerald Levin.

Since leaving Warner, Semel had busied himself with Windsor Media, which had a shoddy record in the new-media sector.

The company had taken a stake in Nibblebox, an entertainment hobbyist site aimed at college kids. Nibblebox was eventually acquired for an undisclosed sum by Vivendi Universal, likely returning some minor dividends for Windsor. But Semel himself had a black mark in new media, having sunk $2 million of his own money into the Digital Entertainment Network (DEN), a company that produced high-bandwidth, TV-quality video for its Web site. The site featured 30 shows and required viewers to download special software to see them. Even then, without high-speed connections (just 5 million households—or 5 percent, well under earlier predictions of 20 percent—were suitably wired), viewers were unlikely to receive anything but choppy images reminiscent of satellite feeds from undeveloped countries. DEN ultimately collapsed in June 2000 under economic pressures and a management shakeup triggered by a sexual-abuse lawsuit against one of the company's cofounders. Windsor Media continued despite the departures of Semel and two key managers he brought with him to Yahoo, though the pace of investment slowed.

Semel did better when he stuck to traditional media. In 2000, he helped his friend Edgar Bronfman Jr., the former CEO of Seagram's, owner of Universal Studios, find a buyer for the company. Semel knew executives at the French entertainment company Canal Plus from an earlier deal between Canal and Warner Brothers. Now Canal Plus was under the ownership of a newly formed company called Vivendi, an odd conglomeration of media companies and public-utility companies that was looking to raise its media-business profile. Semel brokered the sale of Seagram's Universal to Vivendi in a deal valued at $34 billion.

Even though he remained a player among the corporate elite, Semel had learned to live life without the kid-glove treatment he'd received at Warner Brothers, a skill he'd definitely need to survive in the dressed-down dot-com culture. "He knew how to operate outside of a big, $10 billion structure," one associate says. "He handled his own e-mail and returned his own phone calls," rare traits among Hollywood executives.

Still, he was Koogle's opposite in almost every respect—and Koogle was well loved by Wall Street and Yahoos alike. Whereas T.K. had a casual, entrepreneurial style and used the sweeping language of a visionary, Semel was formal and pragmatic, preferring to talk operations. "Terry Semel is a very, very cautious guy," says U.S. Bancorp Piper Jaffray analyst Safa Rashtchy. "He moves smoothly. He's a clever businessman. He's not what you'd consider an entrepreneurial, visionary Silicon Valley type." But as Paul Noglows had said, maybe Yahoo didn't need a visionary. What it clearly did need was someone to help it develop new revenue streams, including forging alliances with players in the entertainment industry.

When Semel spoke, he sounded like a politician—and who better than a politician to forge alliances? "I think of our challenge as an evolution rather than a revolution," he told investors in his first earnings conference call on July 11. He'd already announced his plan to spend his first 60 days on the job taking a crash course in Yahoo's business. One by one, all 44 of the divisions had delivered an elaborate presentation. "That is so unmanageable," Semel had said at the end. "Too many people and no focus."[1]

Semel dedicated himself to streamlining operations, reducing overhead, and honing the staff's focus. Immediately, he started bringing in new managers to establish Yahoo in Hollywood.

Toby Coppel was Semel's highest-profile hire. The former Allen & Co. executive had recently worked for Semel at Windsor, managing investments. At Yahoo, Coppel took over mergers and acquisitions—which had been Senior Vice President Ellen Siminoff's bailiwick after Healy's departure—and, along with former Entertaindom COO and Windsor investment partner Jeff Weiner, adopted the title Corporate Development Yahoo. The two were charged with making acquisitions that would take Yahoo deeper into its existing categories—instead of spreading its content offerings wider, as it had done in the past, to attract users. Better to figure out how to monetize the existing businesses than rush headlong into new ones. Lynda Keeler, vice president of interactive services at Sony, with whom Yahoo would enter into a partnership, says Coppel "is a very important player" in the new order because he has the ear and the confidence of Semel.

Coppel and Weiner had an instant impact on Yahoo's top ranks. By taking over corporate development, they essentially displaced Siminoff, who'd previously held that title. Just outside the circle of the three amigos, Siminoff had been one of the primary decision makers at Yahoo. But she also had long been contentious for her abrasive manner, which alienated partners and Yahoos alike, and for her failure to close any significant acquisitions. Now she was given the duties of managing Small Business and Entertainment, which she shared with Vice President and General Manager David Mandelbrot, who had moved from his position as senior corporate counsel, in which he oversaw the acquisitions of GeoCities, Broadcast.com, and Online Anywhere.

Not surprisingly, Siminoff announced her resignation about six months later, "I woke up one morning and just lost the desire to come into work," she wrote in an e-mail to colleagues.[2] Her announcement followed that of marketing head Karen Edwards, who in August had said she was leaving the company, and added to an exodus of old-timers that by then included Tim Koogle, Anil Singh, Heather Killen, and Gary Valenzuela.

Jeff Mallett also found himself in a new role, focusing on the company's international business, since day-to-day operations for domestic business now fell to Greg Coleman, the media-industry heavyweight hired away from Reader's Digest in the spring. Some observers interpreted Mallett's unofficial demotion as payback for his arrogance. The only question on their minds was when he'd admit defeat and announce his resignation.

Then there was Jerry Yang. Now that Semel was the head of Yahoo, his relationship with Yang developed some strains. The senior Yahoo executive, who asked not to be identified, points to a holdover from the early days of Yahoo, when Yang was very involved in directing the business. "He inserts himself into areas that interest him—even areas he doesn't know anything about. Terry has to sort of manage Jerry. It's a strange dynamic—you have this founder floating around with no operational role."

⌐

*T*he new regime started pushing deals through, particularly in Hollywood.

Semel had inherited a pending deal to buy Launch Media, the eight-year-old digital-music company Yahoo had vetted for a possible acquisition a year earlier. Launch had its roots in creating CD-ROM magazines featuring editorial content and music. The company had eventually branched out into Web-based streaming music and videos, and gone public in April 1999.

By spring 2001, Launch's stock was languishing under $1

per share. Its board had decided to find a buyer for the company and approached Yahoo, since it had earlier shown interest. This time Launch had an ally. Launch execs had met Semel before, through Coppel, their banker when he was at Allen & Co., which had partially underwritten Launch's IPO. Once Semel was settled into his position, Coppel, at the behest of the Launch board, approached Semel about a deal.

Near the end of May—when Yahoo finally moved into its gleaming new headquarters—all parties had agreed to terms. But the day before the Memorial Day weekend, the deal screeched to a halt. The Recording Industry Association of America (RIAA) chose that day to slap a lawsuit on Launch, claiming its LAUNCHcast radio service violated the streaming rights the company had obtained from four major record labels. Since LAUNCHcast allowed users to choose the music they wanted to hear instead of the prepackaged format presented to them, the RIAA claimed it was making the service too interactive and must obtain additional licenses for "interactivity"—or else suspend service.

Yahoo's board balked. It was interested in Launch because Yahoo needed to bulk up its music offerings and become a heftier entertainment player in Los Angeles, but it wasn't interested in acquiring an expensive lawsuit to do that. The deal was off unless Launch settled with one or two of the labels.

The next development showed Semel's clout. While Launch executives scrambled to reach an agreement with any of the increasingly hostile record labels, Semel stepped in to make reparations and hasten the close of the deal. On June 28, when Yahoo announced it planned to acquire Launch in a deal valued at $12 million, Launch also announced it had settled its dispute with Universal Music Group, a division of Vivendi Universal, the company Semel had helped form.

Besides the lawsuit angle, the Launch merger was unique in another way: Yahoo's decision to leave Launch's business all but untouched. Unlike previous acquisitions, Launch wouldn't be transplanted to Sunnyvale, its executives wouldn't be phased out, and the name of the company, now a unit of Yahoo, wouldn't be changed. Even more surprising, Yahoo's own office in Southern California, a sales outpost in Manhattan Beach, would be closed and staffers moved to Launch's Santa Monica office, partly to learn from the Launch staff, which had snagged more traditional advertisers than Yahoo, and partly to increase back-office efficiencies. Finally, a few Yahoo staffers would be let go instead of Launch staffers when it came time to relaunch the three-year-old Yahoo Music as LAUNCH. Could a new, less controlling Yahoo be emerging?

Possibly. Yet there were still very few hands at the wheel of this new Yahoo. Semel not only closed the Launch deal but also hastened along a wide-ranging marketing partnership with Sony that had been lingering for months. When the deal was finally announced on July 31, Yahoo and Sony had agreed to create a site for Sony products and services called Sony on My Yahoo, which would be the default start page for Sony Style Connect, Sony's own Internet-access service. Yahoo also would offer Sony content on Yahoo Messenger, and Sony would get premier placement on Yahoo Shopping. But the deal was more than just a swapping of promotions: It helped Yahoo gain entrée to Hollywood. Yahoo would consult on the development of the Sony U.S. Group Portal, a gateway for consumers to Sony movies, music, video games, electronics, entertainment site Screenblast, and games site ImageStation. And the two companies would jointly promote Sony's films.

Yahoo aspired to be Hollywood's online marketing partner, with Yahoo Broadcast the hub for movie trailers and the rest of its site used for less dynamic promotions. Besides its deal with Sony, Yahoo also had struck a movie-marketing deal with Disney and was rumored to be close to a similar deal with Vivendi Universal.

With Semel the catalyst behind these deals, even less responsibility was being delegated to the lower levels. But, despite those widespread charges of insular management, could this actually be a good thing? Some companies that dealt with Yahoo executives didn't think they had much polish.

Take Yahoo Broadcast. The long-awaited result of the company's $5.7 billion acquisition of Broadcast.com in 1999 featured a directory of entertainment and news video and audio programming. But Yahoo wanted to add content. In the first few months of 2001, Yahoos kicked the project into high gear, signing rapid-fire deals with more than 20 companies. But Yahoo offered little incentive for the takers: a simple 40 percent ad-revenue split. "We've been offered that before, and I'm not exactly in Hawaii relaxing because of it," says Robert Moskovits, director of business development for MovieFlix.com, a broadband movie site that signed on as a content provider.

Moskovits says the deal was hastily put together. Yahoo Entertainment General Manager David Mandelbrot handled it almost entirely by phone rather than setting up the in-person meetings companies typically arrange when trying to wheedle goods or services. And according to Moskovits, Mandelbrot first demanded that MovieFlix provide all of its content, some 1,500 titles—and that it cover the cost and maintenance of the back-end technology. MovieFlix declined. "The days of doing all-or-nothing deals with Yahoo are over," Moskovits says. Mandelbrot countered with a much more modest request—10 clips chosen by MovieFlix—that proved palatable to the tiny Los Angeles start-up. "We liked the deal, because we got to be included in the press release," Moskovits says. The inclusion was the primary payoff: "It sparked calls and other articles."

Yahoo might have had lots of deals in the hopper, but many of them were small-time. While Yahoo was carrying sweepstakes and banners for Disney's *Pearl Harbor*, AOL was offering its members exclusive access to its lineup of artists and entertainment. Fans of Warner Brothers Television's "The Drew Carey Show" could enter a contest on AOL to name a character's baby. AOL members could get sneak listening previews of Madonna's and Rod Stewart's latest Warner Music Group albums.

Of course, AOL had only to make an internal call to make these things happen. Yahoo had to court a Hollywood that had soured on the Net thanks to flops like Semel's DEN and an experiment from DreamWorks SKG that never got far enough along to launch the Web-based short films and series it had planned. The priority of the studios had shifted from producing new content to distributing their existing content over the Web, but they were looking for partners that controlled the Internet connection, like the broadband delivery company Intertainer.

So, despite Semel's best efforts—and Yahoo's plans to start selling audio and video subscriptions by the end of the year—for now the company would have to rely on its ever-shrinking ad revenue. CPMs had long since been going for a paltry $3, down from $9 at the beginning of 2000 and as much as $150 at the height of the boom. The day before Yahoo released the results of its second-quarter earnings, the CEO of online-advertising powerhouse DoubleClick had told investors, "We don't see any indication that ad revenue is going to pick up in the third quarter."[3]

Anyone who called in for the company's second-quarter earnings results on July 10 heard similarly downbeat news. Yahoo had bested the Street's revenue estimate of $175.1 million with $182.2 million, but that was down a dismal $90.8 million (after an amended filing) from the second quarter the year before. And after restructuring and acquisition-related charges, the company's net loss totaled $48.5 million.

But in the weird world that is Wall Street, analysts responded positively. "The company's transformation has begun—it will be no one single event, but rather a series of events, including joint ventures, acquisitions, and internal innovations," Becker wrote in a research note. "Overall we are optimistic that the worst is behind us and that the risk/reward on the stock is favorable."[4] Two analysts, Merrill Lynch's Henry Blodget and U.S. Bancorp Piper Jaffray's Safa Rashtchy, upgraded their ratings, to "accumulate" and "buy," respectively.

But data coming from Blodget's office a couple of months later indicated that, in fact, things might not improve. On September 4, Merrill Lynch released its latest figures on the online-ad market. The overall market had slipped 6 percent from the year before, to $1.6 billion for the second quarter. Forecasts for the entire year ranged from $4.7 billion to $7.3 billion, down from revenues of $8.2 billion the year before.

In the face of a global economic slump, the advertising industry was retrenching. First to go in a downturn is a company's marketing budget, sacrificed along with other nonessentials. Old-line as well as online media companies were feeling the heat, meaning Yahoo couldn't look to traditional advertisers to solve its problems. In fact, even though Yahoo said it had reduced its dot-com advertisers to 26 percent from 30 percent of the total in the second quarter, the number of its largest, established clients was falling. From the second to the third quarter, Yahoo's Fortune 50 advertisers dropped to 25 from 31, and its Fortune 100 advertisers to 48 from 54.

Meanwhile, media giant Viacom had to trim its workforce and reported significant financial losses. Long-standing magazines—

like *Individual Investor*, *Working Woman*, and *Mademoiselle*—were crumpling. Even AOL Time Warner Chairman Steve Case admitted that the advertising promise of the merger wasn't panning out as hoped in the current economic climate.

Not just in overall dollars but also in comparison to its closest peers, Yahoo's share of the ad market had slipped. With 9 percent of total online-ad revenues, down from 15 percent in the second quarter of 2000, by Merrill's estimate, Yahoo lagged MSN's 10 percent take. And AOL boasted 44 percent of all dollars spent on online advertising.

"Yahoo continues to be one of the most important drivers of Internet usage on a global basis," Paul Noglows wrote in April.[5] After all, of the 513 million people online around the world, 40 percent—210 million—used Yahoo. Globally, the company was No. 1 in traffic, but how could it monetize that traffic in the face of shrinking ad budgets?

Even Yahoo's overseas crown jewel, Yahoo Japan, had taken a big hit. "Things are bad and getting worse," wrote Nikko Salomon Smith Barney analyst Thomas Rodes in a September 4 report in which he lowered his forecast for the online-ad market by 30 percent and his rating on Yahoo Japan from "buy" to "underperform." "Yahoo Japan was the quintessential equity story of the Internet bubble. It was growing, had great margins, and was forecastable. From Q1 FY01, however, the story has gone from bad to worse. Advertising revenue is slowing and declining sales have been substituted with murky intra-Softbank group transactions. We believe that while there is still room for future growth, the shares need to be discounted heavily."[6]

Several international-division vacancies had been filled in July, by Mark Opzoomer as managing director of Yahoo Europe, replacing Fabiola Arredondo; Allan Kwan as managing director of Yahoo's North Asia operations; and S. I. Lee as chief executive of Yahoo Korea. But these units were unlikely to pick up the slack, since the new managers also faced withering economies. In the first quarter of the year, Yahoo's non-U.S. revenues had fallen 34 percent to $34 million. By the third quarter, that figure had fallen to $27 million. While nearly 50 percent of U.S. households had an Internet connection, just 25 percent of European homes were similarly wired, meaning the predictions of wild growth had failed to materialize.

Analysts were disappointed but not completely disillusioned. "On a longer-term basis, all the growth down the road will be international," says John Corcoran, an Internet analyst for CIBC World Markets. "It is absolutely critical to Yahoo. But generally speaking, Yahoo has done a good job expanding internationally. The challenge is monetizing it."

Monetize. The m-word again. How much, after all, is a "good job" worth to investors?

Yahoo's ad problem at home was at least partly attributable to its lack of an ad-sales chief. Since Anil Singh had resigned in May, Yahoo had had no one to spearhead the effort. It would go five months with this vacancy while recruiters ferreted out someone experienced enough and willing to tackle the beastly market. Finally, on October 9, Wenda Harris Millard, a Ziff Davis Media and DoubleClick veteran, was hired as executive vice president of advertising.

❧

*B*y the third quarter, Yahoo's more aggressive push into new revenue streams had brought nonadvertising sales to 20 percent of the total. But Yahoo needed to make much more progress to counter the evaporating ad business, and its efforts were meeting with mixed success. There was the auction-listings fee fiasco. Instead of being the revenue generator Blodget had predicted, the fees had caused listings to drop off by 90 percent. In the fall, the company tried a different tack: charging sellers a small commission on each item while cutting its listing fee by about half. Yahoo also started charging from $24.95 to $59.95 for real estate listings and $14.95 for auto listings, and added a section to its shopping area featuring used and discounted merchandise. Classified were integrated into Shopping. Corcoran praised these changes. "But the challenge is to come up with offerings that are mass-appeal and not niche-market appeal," he adds. And it would take much more sweeping change to narrow the huge lead of competitors like Amazon and eBay.

Wall Street was looking for more definitive results, and tolerance for Semel was running low. During earnings calls, his understated manner and monotone delivery did little to inspire anxious investors or help forge a personal connection with them. His live performances weren't any better. In July, Semel had made his first, much-anticipated public appearance at the *Industry Standard* magazine's annual Internet Summit conference. A highly touted affair, it featured boldfaced names of the new economy like AOL Time Warner's Gerald Levin, Microsoft's Steve Ballmer, and eBay's Meg Whitman. On day two of the Carlsbad, California, event, Semel stepped to the podium with Jerry Yang for an interview by Morgan Stanley analyst Mary Meeker.

Semel failed to cut a colorful figure, either in looks or in personality. He wore gray flannel pants, loafers, and a sweater, and he spoke in platitudes. When Meeker asked him why he'd joined Yahoo, he replied, "Because I think it can be larger and better and more financially successful than maybe ever before."[7] Despite his tepid remark, the room was perfectly silent, as attendees waited for him to reveal the secret to restoring Yahoo to its former greatness. But all Semel said was that the company would develop more "premium services"[8] and "rely very heavily on the areas that have been a great success to us: news, sports, finance, entertainment."[9] Yahoo wouldn't shy away from advertising, he said. And when asked about his own advertising experience, he grew defensive, saying that Warner Brothers had bought a lot of advertising, so he ought to know how the ad business works. After his brief appearance, Semel beat a hasty retreat from the event.

In the charisma department—something Tim Koogle had in spades—Semel was sorely lacking, and intangibles like that can help make or break a company.

By fall, 13 analysts from major brokerage houses still had a "hold" on Yahoo, not an auspicious sign. "One sort of big criticism I have of the quote-unquote new regime is that what they seem to have announced so far has been more of the same, only better," said Derek Brown of W. R. Hambrecht. "And quite frankly, that doesn't seem to be good enough."[10] Corcoran was similarly unimpressed: "Yahoo will be a survivor, but it needs to remake itself. The glory days are behind."

Indeed, Yahoo's stock had fallen so far and so fast that by September, it was a new Wall Street favorite—but only because it was so cheap. Again, Yahoo's nemesis, Lehman Brothers' Holly Becker, drew attention to that fact. The 40 percent slide in the past month had created a "compelling buying opportunity," Becker wrote in a research note on September 6. "We recognize that Yahoo's challenges are formidable and a re-acceleration in growth may be a few quarters off. However, we believe that estimates are low enough and that the valuation has become much more reasonable."[11] Yahoo's stock closed at $11.10 that day—a small boost from the previous day's new 52-week low of $10.64.

On September 26, the stock hit an all-time low of $8.11, sinking

Yahoo's market cap to $5 billion, where it had last been in 1998. But the company was still valued at about seven times its expected 2001 revenues.

And of course, Yahoo wasn't the only one getting hammered. On September 24, AOL Time Warner lowered its own expectations. And in its earnings announcement on October 17, it reported a decline in ad revenues to 21 percent of the total from 25 percent in the same period a year earlier. AOL's ad revenues fell short of the $2.3 billion expected by the Street, with $2.2 billion. Analysts were concerned about AOL's subscriber growth, which seemed to be reaching the end of its rapid expansion. In its third quarter, AOL added just 1.3 million new members, down from 1.4 million in the previous year's third quarter.

A raft of other companies, both old- and new-line, weighed in with weak third-quarter reports of their own and announcements of layoffs. Plus, the terrorist attacks on September 11 seemed to have sapped any remaining confidence that consumers had in the economy.

But Jeff Mallett, speaking during Yahoo's October 10 earnings conference call, actually noted an upside to that day's events. "There is no question the Internet came of age last month," he said. For Yahoo, the day had brought 40 times more page views of news and 60 times more streams of FinanceVision. With airports shut, corporate clients upped their use of the company's Web-based videoconferencing service. And Yahoo moved quickly to remove hateful speech against Arabs and Muslims from its message boards and, along with eBay, to ban the sale of items related to the World Trade Center attack from its auction site. Hopefully, there would be no lawsuits this time.

Yahoo continued to roll out one new service after another, many of them fee-based. There were packages for GeoCities members with advanced page-building tools and personal domain names, available for $11.95 and $8.95, respectively. A deal with LendingTree let consumers sign up for mortgages and home loans through Yahoo, and small businesses could now purchase a corporate version of its e-mail for $9.95 a month. The box on Yahoo's home page, under the main search form, was swapped out to feature shopping content during the day and to lure users to the personals section at night.

In September, further embracing a trend that had been picked up by just about every portal and search engine, Yahoo raised the ceiling on its commercial-listings fees to $299 from $199, the first increase since it had started charging for the listings in 1999. Even the avowedly noncommercial Google now featured paid listings, which appeared above or to the side of the regular search results and were flagged with a "sponsored link" label. (In June 2000, Yahoo had licensed Google's technology to enhance its search capability and had bought an undisclosed stake in the company.) But Yahoo sold listings only in its yellow pages and shopping areas, not in its general search area. That, as Elizabeth Collet had said, was still considered sacrosanct.

Yahoo's 5 percent stake in Net2Phone had brought the service's free PC-to-phone calling feature to Yahoo Messenger in fall 2000. Since spring 2001, Yahoo had been trying to wring revenue from Net2Phone by charging users to access their e-mail and other Yahoo content over the phone for $4.95 per month. Corcoran doesn't expect Internet telephony to bring any immediate returns for Yahoo. "It's a smart place to be if you can monetize it," he says. "But right now, the phone works 99.9 percent of the time. [Net2Phone] is a bet on the future," when improved quality makes voice-over-Internet calls more commonplace.

On the Corporate Yahoo front, the company introduced a version of its intranet software that was easier to use and offered more personalization. Though Yahoo had signed up more heavyweights like Honeywell, Merck, and Enron (before its fall), its corporate clients still numbered only 32 by November. But the Web conferences, online training, and virtual corporate meetings Yahoo offered were showing promise at a time when people were leery of air travel.

And Yahoo clearly still had its popularity going for it. Rashtchy notes that Yahoo's 80 million registered users surpassed the 79 million subscribers to cable network MTV. And those users were still drawn to some of Yahoo's earliest, simplest (and of course, free) features, like the Site of the Day, chosen for its redeeming qualities by Yahoo's surfers.

The Site of the Day actually turned into a business proposition for Chris Barrett and Luke McCabe, two New Jersey high school seniors looking for a sponsor to cover their college-tuition costs. Yahoo selected their site as Site of the Day in the spring. It featured the pair holding surfboards with the words "Your logo here!" and outlined their scheme to promote a sponsor's products and services in return for having their tuition paid to colleges in southern California. Credit card issuer First USA saw the site listed on Yahoo and became Barrett and McCabe's sponsor.

Cute, but not the sort of thing to move investors. Semel was still underwhelming them. In the company's third-quarter earnings call on October 10, he broke the bad news: Yahoo was once again lowering revenue estimates. Thanks to the rapidly deteriorating ad market and global economy, the company was revising its original goal of $700 million to $775 million downward to a range of $688 million to $708 million for the year. Revenues had also dropped—a drastic 44 percent from the same quarter in 2000—to $166.1 million from $295.5 million.

Nor could Yahoo wriggle out of its tight spot by emphasizing pro-forma earnings. Wall Street was beginning to crack down on the fuzzy pro-forma numbers that strike one-time charges and expenses—reportedly a total of more than $200 billion of them in 2001 alone—thus painting a much rosier portrait of a company's financial health. Standard & Poor's, for one, had begun treating those charges as part of a company's operating earnings—bad news for Yahoo and all the other tech companies that had risen to such heights partly by riding their pumped-up results. Under pro-forma accounting methods, Yahoo had earned one cent per share, or $8.4 million, in the third quarter, but factoring in the assorted charges that Yahoo would like people to ignore, it had lost four cents per share, or $24.1 million. Using the same Generally Accepted Accounting Principles (GAAP), Yahoo had had only two profitable years, 1999 and 2000, in its history and, in the first nine months of 2001, had lost $84 million.

Go one step further and account for stock-based compensation—which GAAP rules permit companies to exclude—and the picture gets even worse: Yahoo lost $1.3 billion in 2000, $269 million in 1999, and $64 million in 1998. Even if the company hit its lowered financial targets in 2001, revenues would be down more than 35 percent. But Semel tried to find the silver lining, saying he expected improvement with new ad-sales chief Millard on board.

On November 15, Semel finally gave investors what they'd been waiting for since his arrival six months earlier: his vision for Yahoo's future.

Before a crowd of analysts invited to Yahoo headquarters, Semel stressed the company's need to become a "much more diversified company."[12] Ad revenues would be cut to 50 percent of the total by 2004, down from 2001's expected 76 percent. Semel would accomplish this by adding more paid content and reducing the company's 44 units to six: listings, access, commerce, communications, media and information, and enterprise solutions. Classifieds for Careers, Real Estate, Autos, and Personals would be expanded, along with yellow pages and white pages directories. Peripheral areas like Yahoo Everywhere and the B2B marketplace would be scaled back.

Layoffs hinted at in the company's third-quarter earnings call would total 400 employees, or 13 percent of the staff, but 100 new employees would be added to the new areas of focus. "They're doing something smart, which is bringing in some gray hairs," says Corcoran, who attended the analyst day. Acquisitions would continue, aimed at giving Yahoo a direct billing relationship with the consumer. And there would be a double dose of new blood for the company's board: Ronald Burkle, founder of the Yucaipa Companies investment and M&A firm, and Gary Wilson, chairman of Northwest Airlines and a director of the Walt Disney Company.

Two new deals also signaled Yahoo's commitment to change. One with telecom SBC Communications would create a digital subscriber line (DSL) service featuring Yahoo's brand and content. Semel said the service would ultimately produce 10 million paying customers for Yahoo.

The other deal represented perhaps the biggest change for Yahoo: No longer would it place user experience above monetizing its assets when it came to search. Yahoo had decided to tap the for-fee search service Overture to provide paid search listings while it developed its own. Soon even sites listed in Yahoo's directory would have to pay an annual fee for the privilege, marking a breathtaking departure from Yang and Filo's original vision.

Yahoo would still use the popular Google search engine, but now the first five listings users saw would be links to companies that had bid top dollar for that placement, followed by editorial and Google results. Still, this switch merely placed Yahoo on a level playing field with the rest of the portals, which by now were all using paid search results. Along with directory listings, it was an area Yahoo had "left on the table for years," Semel told the analysts.[13] Yahoo execs also said the company would make better use of its consumer data in the future by selling it to other companies.

The bid for monetization had sidelined Yahoo Everywhere, the wireless strategy Yahoo had been touting for three years and which had resulted in countless partnerships. "It'll be years before it makes money" through advertising and premium services, Rashtchy says. Fewer people than expected were accessing the Internet through wireless devices, and those who were complained of unreliable service and small, user-unfriendly screens and keypads. In the wireless arena, just like broadband, Yahoo was ahead of its time.

Analysts said the changes were hardly dramatic but called them a decent start. "The company is heading in the right direction," Corcoran says. But he suggested that the price of diversification might be loss of cohesion: "Can I say in one sentence what Yahoo does? No."

Investors weren't wowed, either. Yahoo's stock actually lost 38 cents that day, closing at $14.83. But by the next day, once the news had had some time to settle, the shares had climbed back up to $15.47. And the shares continued to climb gradually, hitting $19.14 on December 12 before finishing out the year at $17.74.

Yahoo's acquisition of recruitment site HotJobs about a month later was in line with Semel's goal of pushing services. In addition to generating classified-advertising revenue—$22 million in the third quarter of 2001—HotJobs produces enterprise-recruitment software that could give Corporate Yahoo a boost. Plus, jobs sites like HotJobs and Monster.com are up there with porn in terms of relative protection from the advertising downturn. But the price Yahoo paid—$436 million—was steep considering that HotJobs has yet to turn a profit and probably wouldn't start contributing to Yahoo's cash flow for six months to a year.

In the end, would analysts and investors discover that Semel's grand design was to smarten Yahoo up for a sale to another media company? It's unlikely that another company would be interested in Yahoo until online advertising rebounds—and no one really knows when that will be, or expects the market to grow by more than 10 percent to 15 percent in 2002. "What company would want to diversify into the ugliest business out there—online advertising?" Corcoran asks.

If Yahoo does merge with another company, some observers say it should choose EarthLink, which offers the advantage of being an Internet service provider and having subscribers, just like AOL. But Yahoo's corporate psychology might prevent it from hooking up with an unglamorous yet practical partner like EarthLink. "I was out there and spoke with people in the organization," Corcoran says. "Taking a quick pulse, I'd say they are still thinking they are the prettiest partner at the prom. They are still thinking upstream, A-plus, blue-chip—like eBay."

∽

*B*y the end of 2001, Yahoo was a high-profile Internet company and a tool used every day by consumers and companies looking for information, news, entertainment, merchandise, and the ability to communicate. But it was no longer the darling of Wall Street or the vibrant start-up that inspired employees to brainstorm together into the wee hours, spinning out new software and services.

Not that it had shed *all* its start-up qualities. In a global in-house e-mail sent to Yahoos on October 3, an executive asked them to "help Yahoo generate revenue" by signing up for Yahoo's souped-up personals, ClubConnect, at a cost of $19.95 per month, $42.95 for three months, or $89.95 for a year. They could also help out by purchasing a $4.95 Yahoo Personals Enhanced Ad featuring five photos and a "cool customized background." The e-mail reassured that the need for warm bodies was just short-term, to make the service look popular and well trafficked to potential outside customers. Still, some staffers found the pitch cheesy.

That fall, there was a stale odor wafting through Yahoo's new Sunnyvale digs. In late September, employees had first noticed the sulfurous smell, which seemed to heighten in the mornings and evenings, filling the halls and cubicle pods. An e-mail from Becky McCloskey, Yahoo safety manager, went out with the subject heading, "What is that weird smell?" to soothe employees' jangled nasal membranes. It appeared the culprit was either low tide in the San Francisco Bay, the Sunnyvale water treatment plant, or nearby salt ponds. "We have investigated the source of the odor, and unfortunately there is nothing that can be done to lessen or eliminate it," the e-mail read. "Rest assured, however unpleasant, the odor does not present any danger to Yahoos."

But perhaps the strange smell was fitting. Few investors expected the stock to perform any miracles; most observers saw the company as still mired in the past, when cocky dot-coms didn't have to explain themselves to anyone. And if Wall Street fund managers—who along with other institutions now held 34 percent of Yahoo—were savvy enough to peel back their positions before the real trouble started or to start shorting the stock, many individual investors weren't so fortunate.

"I think the tragedy of the story is how much the American public bought into the concept of Yahoo and ultimately how much money was lost," says hedge-fund manager David Ganek. "If you think about it, going from $130 billion to $5 billion, that's $125 billion of market cap that just vanished, and all these people who got attracted to the Internet ended up taking a bath. To me, that's the story of Yahoo—it was really more about the company as a symbol for the Internet bubble and the hopes and dreams the Internet represented."

Notes

Preface

1. *Yahoo! Unplugged*, by David Filo and Jerry Yang (Foster City, CA: IDG Books, 1995), p. 7.
2. Ibid., p. 11.
3. Credit Suisse First Boston, Equity Research, Lise Buyer and Tracey Ford, October 7, 1998, p. 1.
4. "Do You Believe? How Yahoo! Became a Blue Chip; A Tale of How Wall Street and the Rest of Us Learned to Stop Worrying and Love an Insanely Valued Internet Stock," by Joseph Nocera, *Fortune*, June 7, 1999, p. 76.
5. "To Move Past Turmoil, Yahoo! Must Reform from the Inside," by Kara Swisher, *Wall Street Journal*, March 9, 2001.
6. "Yahoo!: The Company, the Strategy, the Stock," by Linda Himselstein, with Heather Green, Richard Siklos, and Catherine Yang, *BusinessWeek*, September 7, 1998, p. 66.
7. "Inside Yahoo!: The Untold Story of How Arrogance, Infighting, and Management Missteps Derailed One of the Hottest Companies on the Web," by Ben Elgin, *BusinessWeek*, May 21, 2001, pp. 115–123.

Chapter 1   Stanford, 1994

1. *Yahoo! Unplugged*, by David Filo and Jerry Yang (Foster City, CA: IDG Books, 1995), p. 11.

2. "Found You on Yahoo!," by *Red Herring*, *Red Herring*, October 1, 1995, www.redherring.com/story_redirect.asp?layout=story_generic&doc_id=RH1520015952&channel=70000007.
3. "Yahoo.com," BusinessWeek Online, July 18, 1995.
4. "How a Virtuoso Plays the Web," by Brent Schlender, *Fortune*, March 6, 2000, p. F-79.
5. "The Wired Diaries," *Wired* Archive, 7.01—January 1999, www.wired.com/wired/archive/7.01/diaries.html.
6. *The Silicon Boys and Their Valley of Dreams*, by David A. Kaplan (New York: William Morrow, 1999), p. 313.
7. "Big Thinkers," TechTV, June 1999.
8. Ibid.
9. *Champions of Silicon Valley*, by Charles S. Sigismund (New York: John Wiley & Sons, 2000), p. 119.
10. Ibid., p. 120.
11. "Found You on Yahoo!"
12. Ibid.
13. "How a Virtuoso Plays the Web."
14. "Found You on Yahoo!"
15. Ibid.
16. Ibid.
17. Ibid.
18. Ibid.
19. "How a Virtuoso Plays the Web."
20. Ibid.
21. *The Silicon Boys and Their Valley of Dreams*, p. 312.

Chapter 2   Pioneer Way, 1995

1. "Found You on Yahoo!," by *Red Herring*, *Red Herring*, October 1, 1995, www.redherring.com/story_redirect.asp?layout

=story_generic&doc_id=RH1520015952&channel
=70000007.

2. Ibid.

3. Ibid.

4. "Yahoo.com," BusinessWeek Online, July 18, 1995.

5. *Yahoo! Unplugged*, by David Filo and Jerry Yang (Foster City, CA: IDG Books, 1995), p. 13.

6. *Architects of the Web*, by Robert H. Reid (New York: John Wiley & Sons, 1997), p. 258.

7. Ibid., p. 254.

8. "Yahoo.com."

9. "How a Virtuoso Plays the Web," by Brent Schlender, *Fortune*, March 6, 2000, p. F-79.

10. *Architects of the Web*, p. 257.

11. "Meet the Grown-Up Voice of Reason at Yahoo!," by Linda Himselstein, *BusinessWeek*, September 7, 1998, p. 74.

12. Ibid.

13. Ibid.

14. Ibid.

15. "Found You on Yahoo!"

16. *Champions of Silicon Valley*, by Charles S. Sigismund (New York: John Wiley & Sons, 2000), p. 121.

Chapter 3 Sunnyvale, 1996

1. *The Internet Bubble*, by Anthony B. Perkins and Michael C. Perkins (New York: HarperBusiness, 1999), p. xvii.

2. *Architects of the Web*, by Robert H. Reid (New York: John Wiley & Sons, 1997), p. 263.

3. *The Internet Bubble*, p. xvii.

4. *Yahoo! Unplugged*, by David Filo and Jerry Yang (Foster City, CA: IDG Books, 1995), p. 13.

5. *Do You? Business the Yahoo! Way*, by Anthony Vlamis and Bob Smith (Dover, NH: Capstone, 2001), p. 147.
6. Ibid., p. 162.
7. *The Internet Bubble*, p. xviii.
8. *Do You? Business the Yahoo! Way*, p. 164.
9. "How Yahoo! Won the Search Wars," by Randall E. Stross, *Fortune*, March 2, 1998, p. 148.
10. Ibid.
11. Ibid.
12. *Champions of Silicon Valley*, by Charles S. Sigismund (New York: John Wiley & Sons, 2000), p. 123.
13. "Found You on Yahoo!," by *Red Herring, Red Herring*, October 1, 1995, www.redherring.com/story_redirect.asp?layout =story_generic&doc_id=RH1520015952&channel =70000007.
14. Ibid.
15. Ibid.
16. Ibid.
17. Ibid.
18. *Champions of Silicon Valley*, p. 122.
19. "Found You on Yahoo!"
20. Hambrecht & Quist, Paul Noglows and Christina Ku, January 14, 1997, p. 2.

Chapter 4   Santa Clara, 1997

1. Hambrecht & Quist, Paul Noglows and Christina Ku, October 9, 1997, p. 2.
2. "Big Thinkers," TechTV, June 1999.
3. "How to Build a Continental Yahoo!," BusinessWeek Online, January 27, 2000, www.businessweek.com/technology/ content/0001/0127arredondo.htm.

4. Hambrecht & Quist, Paul Noglows and Christina Ku, October 9, 1997, p. 2.

Chapter 5 Staying Put and Scaling Up, 1998

1. "Do You Believe? How Yahoo! Became a Blue Chip: A Tale of How Wall Street and the Rest of Us Learned to Stop Worrying and Love an Insanely Valued Internet Stock," by Joseph Nocera, *Fortune*, June 7, 1999, p. 76.
2. "How Did They Value Stocks? Count the Absurd Ways— Those Lofty 'New Economy' Measures Fizzle," by Gretchen Morgenson, *New York Times*, March 18, 2001.
3. Credit Suisse First Boston, Equity Research, Lise Buyer and Tracey Ford, July 28, 1998, p. 4.
4. "Yahoo!: The Company, the Strategy, the Stock," by Linda Himselstein, with Heather Green, Richard Siklos, and Catherine Yang, *BusinessWeek*, September 7, 1998, p. 66.
5. National Press Club speech, Jerry Yang, April 11, 2000.
6. Credit Suisse First Boston, Equity Research, Lise Buyer and Tracey Ford, July 28, 1998, p. 4.

Chapter 6 The Portal Wars, 1996 to 1998

1. "What Hath Yahoo! Wrought?" by John W. Verity, *BusinessWeek*, February 12, 1996.
2. "Yet Again, Wall Street Is Charmed by the Internet," by Peter H. Lewis, *New York Times*, April 3, 1996.
3. "Do You Believe? How Yahoo! Became a Blue Chip; A Tale of How Wall Street and the Rest of Us Learned to Stop Worrying and Love an Insanely Valued Internet Stock," by Joseph Nocera, *Fortune*, June 7, 1999, p. 76.
4. Ibid.
5. "The Next Big Thing: Yahoo! Co-founder Jerry Yang Lays

Out His Vision of the Internet's Future. He Thinks the Revolution Is Just Getting Started," by Paul Carroll, *Context*, April/May 2000, www.contextmagazine.com/set FrameRedirect.asp?src=/archives/200004/Feature0the NextBigThing.asp.

6. "The Parting of the Portal Seas," by Charlene Li, Forrester Research, December 1999.
7. *The Internet Bubble*, by Anthony B. Perkins and Michael C. Perkins (New York: HarperBusiness, 1999), p. 167.
8. "Found You on Yahoo!," by *Red Herring*, *Red Herring*, October 1, 1995, www.redherring.com/story_redirect.asp?layout=story_generic&doc_id=RH1520015952&channel=70000007.

Chapter 7   The Euphoria, 1999

1. "At Least There Was Lobster," by Eric Savitz, TheStandard.com, June 30, 2001, www.thestandard.com/article/0,1902,28289,00.html.
2. *The Internet Bubble*, by Anthony B. Perkins and Michael C. Perkins (New York: HarperBusiness, 1999), p. 25.
3. "Yahoo Link Sends *Individual Investor* Soaring," by Bloomberg News, February 12, 1999, news.cnet.com/news/0-1005-200-338691.html.
4. "Short Take: Lycos Says It's Passed Yahoo," by CNET News.com staff, April 20, 1999, news.cnet.com/news/0-1005-200-341475.html.
5. "Yahoo Stays Away from Major Media Outlets," by Bloomberg News, March 1, 1999, news.cnet.com/news/0-1005-200-339368.html.
6. Credit Suisse First Boston, Lise Buyer, January 13, 1999, p. 1.
7. Ibid.

8. "Big Thinkers," TechTV, June 1999.

9. Ibid.

10. Ibid.

11. "Watch This Space: Yahoo's Grand Vision for Web Advertising Takes Some Hard Hits—Clients and Agencies Balk at High Rates, Question Medium's Effectiveness—Vowing to 'Crack the Code,' " by Suein Hwang and Mylene Mangalindan, *Wall Street Journal*, September 1, 2000.

12. Goldman Sachs, Michael Parekh, November 9, 1999, p. 1.

13. Credit Suisse First Boston, Lise Buyer, July 8, 1999, p. 2.

Chapter 8   The Unraveling, 2000

1. "AOL Buys Time Warner in Historic Merger," by Sandeep Junnarkar and Jim Hu, CNET News.com, January 10, 2000, news.cnet.com/news/0-1005-200-1518888.html.

2. "Do You Believe? How Yahoo! Became a Blue Chip; A Tale of How Wall Street and the Rest of Us Learned to Stop Worrying and Love an Insanely Valued Internet Stock," by Joseph Nocera, *Fortune*, June 7, 1999, p. 76.

3. *Speed Is Life*, by Bob Davis (New York: Currency Doubleday, 2001), p. 181.

4. National Press Club speech, Jerry Yang, April 11, 2000.

5. Ibid.

6. Ibid.

7. Ibid.

8. Chase Hambrecht & Quist Media Research Note, Paul Noglows, October 11, 2000, p. 5.

9. "Surprise! Yahoo Goes Broadband," by Daniel Roth, *Fortune*, May 29, 2000, p. 186.

10. Goldman Sachs, Michael Parekh, May 18, 2000, p. 4.

11. Ibid., p. 22.

12. Goldman Sachs, Michael Parekh, October 27, 2000, p. 3.
13. "Investors Brace for Possible Yahoo Revenue Slump," by Jim Hu and Evan Hansen, CNET News.com, August 28, 2000, news.cnet.com/news/0-1005-200-2632600.html.
14. "Yahoo!, the Homespun Web Map/For Creators, It's Becoming a Career," by Leslie Miller, *USA Today*, April 13, 1995.
15. "Watch This Space: Yahoo's Grand Vision for Web Advertising Takes Some Hard Hits—Clients and Agencies Balk at High Rates, Question Medium's Effectiveness—Vowing to 'Crack the Code,' " by Suein Hwang and Mylene Mangalindan, *Wall Street Journal*, September 1, 2000.
16. Ibid.
17. "The Next Big Thing: Yahoo! Co-founder Jerry Yang Lays Out His Vision of the Internet's Future. He Thinks the Revolution Is Just Getting Started," by Paul Carroll, *Context*, April/May 2000, www.contextmagazine.com/setFrame Redirect.asp?src=/archives/200004/Feature0theNextBig Thing.asp.
18. Ibid.
19. "If I Knew Then What I Know Now: Mark Goldstein; What Went Wrong with Bluelight.com," by Owen Thomas, *Business 2.0*, August 2000, www.business2.com/articles/mag/ 0,1640,16693,FF.html.

Chapter 9 The Turmoil, 2001

1. "Yahoo Lowers Earnings Outlook for 2001," by Ari Weinberg, TheStandard.com, January 10, 2001, www. thestandard.com/article/0,1902,21394,00.html.
2. "Sickly Net Companies Shudder as Yahoo!'s Cold Worsens," by George Mannes, TheStreet.com, January 10, 2001, www.thestreet.com/tech/internet/1251119.html.

Notes

3. "Under Repair," by Gary Rivlin, *Industry Standard*, February 2, 2001.
4. "Yahoo Issues Warning on 2001 Revenue—Fourth Quarter Earnings Meet Analysts' Estimates; Stock Falls After Hours," by Mylene Mangalindan, *Wall Street Journal*, January 11, 2001.
5. "Yahoo Lives Down to Its Name," by Brian Hale, *Sydney Morning Herald*, January 12, 2001, www.smh.com.au/news/0101/12/bizcom/bizcom1.html.
6. "Yahoo! Enhances Commerce Sites for Higher Quality Online Experience," company press release, January 2, 2001.
7. "Inside Yahoo!: The Untold Story of How Arrogance, Infighting, and Management Missteps Derailed One of the Hottest Companies on the Web," by Ben Elgin, *BusinessWeek*, May 21, 2001, p. 112.
8. "Your World with Neil Cavuto," Fox News Channel, January 11, 2001.
9. "Yahoo! Enhances Commerce Sites for Higher Quality Online Experience."
10. "Sagging Stock Boosts Yahoo Appeal," by Charles Piller and Sallie Hoffmeister, *Los Angeles Times*, March 1, 2001.
11. "Gang of Six: Coterie of Early Hires Made Yahoo! a Hit but an Insular Place," by Mylene Mangalindan and Suein L. Hwang, *Wall Street Journal*, March 9, 2001.
12. "Inside Yahoo!: The Untold Story," p. 112.
13. "The General Says 'Charge!' " by Ben Elgin, *BusinessWeek*, February 19, 2001, p. 34.
14. "Inside Yahoo!: The Untold Story," p. 112.
15. "Koogle Bowing Out as Yahoo's CEO," by Ari Weinberg, TheStandard.com, March 7, 2001, www.thestandard.com/article/0,1902,22693,00.html.
16. "Skittish Analysts Slash Yahoo! and Express Concerns for

Other Internet Plays," by Eric Gillin, TheStreet.com, March 8, 2001, www.thestreet.com/markets/market features/1334725.html.

17. "Yahoo! CEO Stepping Aside, Earnings Guidance Lowered," by David Streitfeld, WashingtonPost.com, March 7, 2001, www.washtech.com/news/media/8145-1.html.

18. "Yahoo Investors Shout 'Yahoo!,' " by Eric J. Savitz, TheStandard.com, April 5, 2001, www.thestandard.com/article/0,1902,23396,00.html.

19. Merrill Lynch, Henry Blodget, April 12, 2001, p. 1.

20. "Yahoo! Taps Hollywood's Semel as CEO," by Mylene Mangalindan and John Lippman, *Wall Street Journal*, April 18, 2001, p. B1.

21. "CEO Selection Signals Yahoo's Media Hopes," by Alan Goldstein, *Dallas Morning News*, April 18, 2001.

22. "Yahoo Turns to Hollywood for a Chief," by Saul Hansell and Geraldine Fabrikant, *New York Times*, April 18, 2001.

23. "Yahoo! Taps Hollywood's Semel as CEO," p. B1.

24. "Terry Semel's Stress Test at Yahoo!," by Ben Elgin, BusinessWeek Online, April 19, 2001, www.businessweek.com/bwdaily/dnflash/apr2001/nf20010419_632.htm.

25. "Terry, Kiss-Kiss, You Gotta Direct a Big Comeback," by Kara Swisher, *Wall Street Journal*, April 18, 2001.

Chapter 10   The Semel Era

1. "Time Runs Short for Terry Semel to Show Signs of Gains at Yahoo," by Kara Swisher, *Wall Street Journal*, October 15, 2001.

2. "Yahoo Loses Key Senior Exec," by Jim Hu, CNET News.com, November 16, 2001, news.cnet.com/news/0-1005-200-7901008.html.

3. "AOL Asks: What Ad Bust?" by Jane Black, BusinessWeek Online, July 12, 2001, www.businessweek.com/technology/content/jul2001/tc20010712_491.htm.
4. "Yahoo Shares Up After It Meets Profit Expectations," Reuters, July 15, 2001.
5. J. P. Morgan Securities, Equity Research, Paul W. Noglows, April 9, 2001, p. 4.
6. Nikko Salomon Smith Barney, Equity Research, Thomas Rodes, September 4, 2001, p. 1, 3.
7. "Terry Semel Unwraps Some of the Mystery," by Cory Johnson, TheStandard.com, July 24, 2001, www.thestandard.com/article/0,1902,28191,00.html.
8. Ibid.
9. Ibid.
10. "Yahoo Needs a Salesman," by Ryan Tate, *Upside Today*, September 5, 2001.
11. "Time to Buy Yahoo?," by Eric J. Savitz, TheStandard.com, September 6, 2001, www.thestandard.com/article/0,1902,28905,00.html.
12. "Yahoo Restructuring to Slash 400 Jobs, Help Cut Its Dependence on Ad Revenue," by Nick Wingfield, *Wall Street Journal*, November 16, 2001.
13. "Do You Recognize This Yahoo!?" by George Mannes, TheStreet.com, November 15, 2001, ww.thestreet.com/tech/georgemannes/10004071.html.

Index

INDEX

America Online (AOL) *(continued)*
 Instant Messenger, 138
 membership in, 78, 244
 Myplay, 181–182
 NetCoalition.com, 184
 Netscape acquisition, 102, 137, 140, 174
 1-800-flowers.com, relationship with, 167–168
 online music, 179, 181–182
 position-placement deals, 79, 141
 services provided by, 49–50, 141, 144, 250
 Time Warner merger, 32, 174
Analyst(s):
 meetings, 184–191, 247–250
 recommendations, 75, 105, 200, 218–219, 239, 243
 upgrades/downgrades, 105–106, 154, 200
Andreessen, Marc, 2, 6, 13–14, 18, 158
AOL Time Warner, 159, 172, 174, 176, 198–199, 208–209, 223
AppSoft, 17
Architects of the Web (Reid), 37
Architecture, 27–28
Arredondo, Fabiola, 95–96, 98, 189, 211, 240
Arthas.com, 187
ARTISTdirect's Ultimate Band List (UBL.com), 179–180
Asia, 196, 211
At Home, 118, 140, 148, 151, 159
AT&T, 111–112
AT&T WorldNet, 112, 151
Auctions, 113, 130, 195, 207, 242. *See also* eBay; Yahoo Auctions
Augustin, Larry, 13
Australia, 97, 185
Avenue A, 90
Axcelis, 214

Ballmer, Steve, 242
Banner advertising, 66–67, 193, 197, 238
Bargaining/negotiation reputation, 110–111, 196–198, 207–208

Barnes&Noble.com, 221
Barrett, Chris, 246
Barron's, 182
Batkin, Andy, 30–31
Baum, Seth, 165
Becker, Holly, 194, 212, 215, 218–219, 243
Bell, George, 117–118
BellSouth, 73
Beninato, Joe, 131
Bertelsmann, 211
Beta test, 37
Billing relationships, 141, 248, 250
Bill Pay, 195
Bishop, Bill, 197
Black Rocket, 53
Blackwell, Trevor, 116–117
Blodget, Henry, 154, 200, 207, 210, 213–214, 219, 239, 242
BlueLight.com, 169–170, 192, 200
Blue Mountain Arts, 135
BMG, 216
Board of directors, 42, 56, 196, 221, 248
Bogometer, 116–117
Bonforte, Jeffrey, 162–163
Boo.com, 190, 193, 205
Bookmarks, 64
Bots, 11
Boyer, Maggie, 90–91
Brady, Tim, 14, 16, 18, 26, 29–30, 35, 37, 68, 95, 115, 126, 128, 187
Brainstorming, 39, 83, 250
Brand equity, 16
Brand loyalty, 125
Brand name, significance of, 89, 108–109, 228
Briggs, John, 109
British Telecommunications, 112
Broadband, 187–188
Broadcast.com, 155–161, 163, 187, 189, 233, 237
Bronfman, Edgar, Jr., 231
Brown, Derek, 87–88, 200, 243
Budlong, Pete, 132–134
Bullington, Brett, 117
Burke, Katie, 94–95, 128–129
Burkle, Ronald, 248

Index

Index

Index

INDEX

272

Index

INDEX

Index